The Pag

SHAKESPEARE
TO
GOLDSMITH

Reverend Joseph T. Browne, S.J.
St. Peter's Preparatory School
Jersey City, New Jersey

CATHOLIC **EDUCATION DIVISION**
CED

New York   THE MACMILLAN COMPANY

The Macmillan Company, New York
Brett-Macmillan, Ltd., Galt, Ontario
Printed in the United States of America

4D

Contents

SHAKESPEARE
TO
GOLDSMITH

THE RISE OF THE THEATER

The Medieval Theater

The English had always found delight in dramatic entertainment. Long before the development of the Elizabethan drama, processions and pageants had been a part of every Englishman's life. Wandering entertainers, jugglers, acrobats, fortune tellers, and clowns roamed the countryside and performed at local bazaars and feasts.

The Church, in her liturgy, provided the basis for dramatic entertainment. The solemn ceremonies of the liturgy, the singing and rubrics, all appealed to the dramatic sense in man. Little plays were performed in the Church on feastdays to teach the people their catechism. Stories from the Old and New Testaments were dramatized and the "Word of God" came to life. Eventually, because the casts became unmanageably large and the comic elements became more and more boisterous, the plays were moved out of the Churches and into the market square before the Cathedral.

On certain feastdays, like *Corpus Christi*, the town would hold a carnival after Mass. Part of the day's attractions would be a *miracle play* produced by local guilds, or associations of tradesmen. These plays were usually in cycles, based on the Bible, beginning with the creation of man and ending with the Last Judgment. Often the guilds presented a play suited to their professions. At York, for example, the shipbuilders' guild presented a play about Noah's Ark.

At times, these plays were performed on floats and would be put on at specified locations in the town until the whole cycle had been seen in sequence. We know that the town of York had a play cycle of 50 plays—all of which were performed in one day, starting after early Mass and continuing to nightfall. Given in the language of the people, these plays were very popular and continued to be performed in some places until Shakespeare's time. At Coventry, only a few miles from Stratford, these plays were performed until 1580.

As might be expected, non-Biblical material crept into the scripts, particularly in roles that offered opportunities for comedy. Noah, for example, often had great difficulty getting his wife into the ark, and had to beat her "black and blue." The devils in the Last Judgment received great laughs as they snatched little boys and girls from the street and carried them off into Hell.

Another type of religious drama flourished in the fifteenth century. This was the *morality play*, an allegory in which characters represented abstractions such as Pride, Mercy, Gluttony, and Friendship. These dramas always centered around the conflict between good and evil for the soul of Man. These plays were very popular and continued down to Elizabethan times.

In the sixteenth century, a new form of play developed during the reign of Henry VIII, called *interludes*. They were short plays and were performed in halls of the great manor houses, often during a dinner for some visiting dignitary. Most of the interludes were written for sheer entertainment, unlike the earlier plays whose purpose it was to teach a lesson or moral. As the sixteenth century wore on, the interlude players took to the highways, and their plays were presented all over England. Under the patronage of some noble, they wandered from town to town entertaining the people. Such players were often suspected of being vagabonds and thieves, and only the patronage of their noble protected them from the local authorities.

The Elizabethan Theater

The popular interest and demand for plays created the need for professional playhouses. In 1576 James Burbage erected the first building in London designed exclusively for the use of the players. Called "The Theater," it was built just north of the city to avoid the jurisdiction of the city fathers of London. The next year saw the opening of "The Curtain," a second professional theater. This playhouse was also located outside the city limits to avoid the hostility of the Aldermen of London. The civil officials had declared open war on actors because, as they claimed, they caused disturbances, gathered crowds that spread the plague, enticed people from their work, and were, in general, an evil lot.

The architecture of the Elizabethan theater was influenced by the inns. For, long before the erection of regular theaters, inn yards had been used. Under the open sky, stages had been set up at one end of the yard and the spectators stood in the yard or watched from the balconies. The professional theaters retained this court-yard effect. For a penny, "groundlings" stood in the pit and watched the wonders performed on the stage. The better classes could pay a higher fee and watch from the covered galleries. There being no way of lighting these early theaters, plays were performed in the afternoon. In bad weather and in winter, the playhouses were not open.

The best known of these theaters was "The Globe." Erected in 1599, it became Shakespeare's own playhouse. He was one of its stockholders, one of its dramatists, and a member of its acting company.

"The Globe" was octagonal in shape. Its stage was a bare plat-form without a front curtain. There was no painted, movable scen-ery, but stage props were used. An inner stage was curtained off and used for more intimate scenes. A balcony above the back part of the stage was used for castle ramparts and scenes like the balcony scene in *Romeo and Juliet*. Above the balcony, on a third level, was the "tiring room" used for dressing and storage. From a trap door in the balcony, called the "heavens," gods and angels could descend when the action required. Often the nobles and wealthy people sat on the stage as well as in the galleries, while the working people stood in "the pit," or standing section.

During Shakespeare's time, companies of actors occupied the principal theaters. Shakespeare was a member of the Lord Chamber-lain's Company. Since women were never employed as players, young boys were recruited from the choir schools of St. Paul's and Windsor Chapel to play the female roles. The boys seemed to suc-ceed in their roles and held the attention of a restless and unruly audience.

The audiences of Shakespeare's day did not expect realistic stage sets or colorful scenery. Often a boy would carry a placard announc-ing the location of the scene. The actors, too, would clearly indicate the place, time, and their own identity in their speeches. The Eliza-bethan plays were written primarily for the ear rather than for the eye. Shakespeare's vividness of description and characterization were partly the result of the limitations of the theaters of his time. He had to present in words what a carpenter, scene painter, or costume designer achieves in our modern-day theater.

William Shakespeare

In 1564 on the feast of St. George, Patron of England, William Shakespeare was born in the village of Stratford-on-Avon. His father was a prosperous merchant and a prominent figure in the small community; his mother was the daughter of a wealthy landowner. As a boy, Shakespeare probably attended the local grammar school. This seems to have been the sum of his formal education.

He married Anne Hathaway in 1582, and in the following year their first child, Susanna, was born. In 1585, Shakespeare seems to have left Stratford in search of opportunities for supporting his family and restoring its lost social status. The year 1593 found him in London as an actor-apprentice. He began to write plays of his own and prosperity seemed to smile once again on his family fortunes back in Stratford.

For almost twenty years, he wrote an average of two plays a year. This was the period of his highest genius during which he produced the greatest plays in English. He retired to his new home in Stratford in 1612 and died there in 1616. He was buried in the Stratford church in which he had been baptized.

The normality of Shakespeare's life gives no clue to his genius. As a dramatist, he towers above every other playwright. He has provided the world with characters and plays that have moved and entertained every generation since his own time and will continue to do so in the generations to come.

Macbeth

Macbeth, written in 1606, is a play about Scotland. When James IV of Scotland was crowned James I of England in 1603, great interest was manifested in his homeland and its history. Shakespeare took his plot from Ralph Holinshed's *Chronicles*, an old history of the British Isles. Since Shakespeare was writing a play and not a history, he took certain liberties with his material. He changed his plot a great deal; he "created" the character of Macbeth; he added new characters; and gave a unity to *Macbeth* that makes it one of his great tragedies.

Shakespeare, as a dramatist, had to build up the character of Macbeth as someone in whom we can believe. He had to tell us who Macbeth and the other characters are so that we have a sufficient knowledge of the background required for understanding the play. In other forms of literature, such as the novel, this can be done with a few paragraphs of exposition or description. But a playwright must do it all through dialogue and action. The characters speak and act for themselves. The playwright does not speak for them; they do everything for themselves. Dramas are written to be performed, and in reading them, we must try to imagine how the actors would interpret the lines, what gestures they would make, what the set looks like, and what props are used.

What do we mean when we say that *Macbeth* is a tragedy? A tragedy is a drama in which the fortunes of the main character end in defeat. Like any play, a tragedy contains a conflict. The chief character, or *protagonist*, fights against some opposing force and fights so well that for a while the outcome is in doubt. But eventually he is overcome.

The chief character in every tragedy originally wins our sympathy. But when he violates some basic principle on which society stands, we lose sympathy for him. There must be a certain nobility in the protagonist for him to win our sympathy. He cannot be spineless or a mere victim of circumstances. He will possess a grave defect in his character, which eventually leads to his ruin. His downfall will not be caused by some accident, but rather by some fault in himself.

In the character of Macbeth, Shakespeare has fulfilled all of these requirements. He has presented a powerful portrait of a man torn between good and evil, spurred on by a fierce ambition, driven to murder, and yet, because of the depth of his struggle and the magnificent verse with which it is expressed, Macbeth emerges as a character we care about even as we condemn his villainy.

Since Shakespeare had to appeal to the ear and imagination of his audiences, *Macbeth* presents a challenge. Imagine that you are at "The Globe" on a warm summer afternoon. The bare stage is surrounded by a noisy audience. Suddenly there is a crashing sound of thunder. Silence falls on the crowd. The first act of *Macbeth* has begun!

WILLIAM SHAKESPEARE

(1564–1616)

Macbeth

Characters

DUNCAN, *king of Scotland*

MALCOLM,
DONALBAIN, } *his sons*

MACBETH, } *generals of the*
BANQUO, } *King's army*

MACDUFF,
LENNOX,
ROSS,   *noblemen of*
MENTEITH,   *Scotland*
ANGUS,
CAITHNESS,

FLEANCE, *son to* BANQUO

SIWARD, *earl of Northumberland,*
general of the English forces

YOUNG SIWARD, *his son*

SEYTON, *an officer attending on*
MACBETH

BOY, *son to* MACDUFF

An English Doctor

A Scotch Doctor

A Sergeant

A Porter

An Old Man

LADY MACBETH

LADY MACDUFF

Gentlewoman attending on LADY
MACBETH

HECATE

Three Witches

Apparitions

Lords, Gentlemen, Officers, Soldiers, Murderers, Attendants,
and Messengers

SCENE: Scotland and England.

6

ACT I

SCENE 1—*A deserted place.*

(*Thunder and lightning. Enter three* WITCHES.)

FIRST WITCH. When shall we three meet again
In thunder, lightning, or in rain?
SECOND WITCH. When the hurlyburly's [1] done,
When the battle's lost and won.
THIRD WITCH. That will be ere the set of sun.   5
FIRST WITCH. Where the place?
SECOND WITCH.   Upon the heath.
THIRD WITCH. There to meet with Macbeth.
FIRST WITCH. I come, Graymalkin.[2]
ALL. Paddock [3] calls:—anon! [4]
Fair is foul, and foul is fair.   10
Hover through the fog and filthy air.   (*Exeunt.*)

SCENE 2—*A camp near* FORRES.[1]

(*Alarum* [2] *within. Enter* DUNCAN, MALCOLM, DONALBAIN, LEN-
NOX *with* ATTENDANTS, *meeting a bleeding* SERGEANT.)

DUNCAN. What bloody man is that? He can report,
As seemeth by his plight, of the revolt
The newest state.
MALCOLM.   This is the sergeant
Who like a good and hardy soldier fought
'Gainst my captivity.[3] Hail, brave friend!   5
Say to the king the knowledge of the broil [4]
As thou didst leave it.

Scene 1:
1 hurlyburly: uproar
[2] Graymalkin: gray cat
[3] Paddock: a spirit in the form of a frog
[4] anon: I'm coming now

Scene 2:
[1] Forres: town in Northern Scotland
[2] alarum: call to arms
[3] captivity: to prevent my capture
[4] broil: battle

SERGEANT.   Doubtful it stood;
    As two spent swimmers, that do cling together
    And choke their art. The merciless Macdonwald—[5]
    Worthy to be a rebel, for to that   10
    The multiplying villainies of nature
    Do swarm upon him—from the western isles [6]
    Of kerns [7] and gallowglasses [8] is supplied;
    And fortune, on his damned quarrel smiling,
    Show'd like a rebel's whore: but all's too weak: 15
    For brave Macbeth—well he deserves that name—
    Disdaining fortune, with his brandish'd steel,
    Which smoked with bloody execution,
    Like valor's minion [9] carved out his passage
    Till he faced the slave;   20
    Which [10] ne'er shook hands, nor bade farewell to him,
    Till he unseam'd him from the nave to the chaps,[11]
    And fix'd his head upon our battlements.
DUNCAN. O valiant cousin! [12] worthy gentleman!
SERGEANT. As whence the sun 'gins his reflection   25
    Shipwrecking storms and direful thunders break,
    So from that spring whence comfort seem'd to come
    Discomfort swells. Mark, king of Scotland, mark:
    No sooner justice had, with valor arm'd,
    Compell'd these skipping kerns to trust their heels,   30
    But the Norweyan lord,[13] surveying vantage,
    With furbish'd arms and new supplies of men,
    Began a fresh assault.
DUNCAN.   Dismay'd not this
    Our captains, Macbeth and Banquo?
SERGEANT.   Yes;
    As sparrows eagles, or the hare the lion.   35
    If I say sooth, I must report they were

---

[5] **Macdonwald**: Irish rebel
[6] **western isles**: Ireland and the Hebrides
[7] **kerns**: Irish soldiers
[8] **gallowglasses**: heavily-armed Irish soldiers
[9] **minion**: pet, favorite
[10] **which**: Macbeth
[11] **nave to the chaps**: navel to the jaws
[12] **cousin**: Macbeth is Duncan's cousin
[13] **Norweyan lord**: Sweno, King of Norway

As cannons overcharged with double cracks;[14] so they
Doubly redoubled strokes upon the foe:
Except they meant to bathe in reeking wounds,
Or memorize another Golgotha,[15]   40
I cannot tell—
But I am faint; my gashes cry for help.

DUNCAN. So well thy words become thee as thy wounds;
They smack of honor both. Go get him surgeons.

                             (*Exit* SERGEANT, *attended.*)

Who comes here?
  (*Enter* ROSS.)

MALCOLM.   The worthy thane [16] of Ross.   45

LENNOX. What a haste looks through his eyes! So should he look
That seems to speak things strange.

ROSS.   God save the king!

DUNCAN. Whence camest thou, worthy thane?

ROSS.   From Fife,[17] great king;
Where the Norweyan banners flout the sky
And fan our people cold.[18] Norway himself   50
With terrible numbers,
Assisted by that most disloyal traitor
The thane of Cawdor,[19] began a dismal conflict;
Till that Bellona's [20] bridegroom, lapp'd in proof,[21]
Confronted him with self-comparisons,   55
Point against point rebellious, arm 'gainst arm,
Curbing his lavish spirit: and, to conclude,
The victory fell on us.

DUNCAN.   Great happiness!

ROSS. That now
Sweno, the Norway's king, craves composition;[22]   60
Nor would we deign him burial of his men

[14] cracks: charges
[15] another Golgotha: another Calvary
[16] thane: a noble, earl
[17] Fife: on the east coast of Scotland
[18] flout . . . cold: the banners now insult the sky but fan our soldiers ,at the same time
[19] Cawdor: a traitor
[20] Bellona: goddess of war
[21] lapped in proof: clad in armor
[22] craves composition: begs peace

Till he disbursed, at Saint Colme's inch,[23]
Ten thousand dollars [24] to our general use.

DUNCAN. No more that thane of Cawdor shall deceive
Our bosom interest: go pronounce his present death,   65
And with his former title greet Macbeth.

ROSS. I'll see it done.

DUNCAN. What he hath lost, noble Macbeth hath won.   (*Exeunt.*)

SCENE 3—A *heath.*

(*Thunder. Enter the three* WITCHES.)

FIRST WITCH. Where hast thou been, sister?

SECOND WITCH. Killing swine.[1]

THIRD WITCH. Sister, where thou?

FIRST WITCH. A sailor's wife had chestnuts in her lap,
And mounch'd,[2] and mounch'd, and mounch'd.   5
'Give me,' quoth I:
'Aroint thee,[3] witch!' the rump-fed [4] ronyon [5] cries.
Her husband's to Aleppo gone, master o' the Tiger;
But in a sieve I'll thither sail,
And, like a rat [7] without a tail,   10
I'll do, I'll do, and I'll do.

SECOND WITCH. I'll give thee a wind.

FIRST WITCH. Thou'rt kind.

THIRD WITCH. And I another.

FIRST WITCH. I myself have all the other;   15
And the very ports they blow,
All the quarters that they know
I' the shipman's card.[8]
I will drain him dry as hay: [9]

---

[23] inch: St. Columba's Island
[24] dollars: Spanish dollars

Scene 3:
[1] swine: witches were thought to kill animals out of malice
[2] mounched: munched
[3] aroint thee: be gone
[4] rump-fed: fat-rumped
[5] ronyon: scabby creature
[6] sieve: witches supposedly used sieves as boats
[7] like a rat: in the shape of a rat
[8] card: the compass
[9] drain . . . hay: keep him at sea until all the water is gone

Sleep shall neither night nor day   20
Hang upon his pent-house lid; [10]
He shall live a man forbid:
Weary se'nnights [11] nine times nine
Shall he dwindle, peak, and pine: [12]
Though his bark cannot be lost,   25
Yet it shall be tempest-tost.
Look what I have.

SECOND WITCH. Show me, show me.

FIRST WITCH. Here I have a pilot's thumb,
  Wreck'd as homeward he did come.   (*Drum within.*) 30

THIRD WITCH. A drum, a drum!
  Macbeth doth come.

ALL. The weird [13] sisters, hand in hand,
  Posters [14] of the sea and land,
  Thus do go about, about: 35
  Thrice to thine, and thrice to mine,
  And thrice again, to make up nine.
  Peace! the charm's wound up.
    (*Enter* MACBETH *and* BANQUO.)

MACBETH. So foul and fair a day I have not seen.

BANQUO. How far is't call'd to Forres? What are these   40
  So wither'd, and so wild in their attire,
  That look not like the inhabitants o' the earth,
  And yet are on't? Live you? or are you aught
  That man may question? You seem to understand me,
  By each at once her choppy [15] finger laying   45
  Upon her skinny lips: you should be women,
  And yet your beards forbid me to interpret
  That you are so.

MACBETH.   Speak, if you can: what are you?

FIRST WITCH. All hail, Macbeth! hail to thee, thane of Glamis!

SECOND WITCH. All hail, Macbeth! hail to thee, thane of Cawdor! 50

THIRD WITCH. All hail, Macbeth, thou shalt be king hereafter!

[10] **pent-house lid:** eyelid
[11] **se'nnights:** weeks
[12] **pine:** waste away
[13] **weird:** fatal
[14] **posters:** travelers
[15] **choppy:** chappy

BANQUO. Good sir, why do you start, and seem to fear
   Things that do sound so fair? I' the name of truth,
   Are ye fantastical, or that indeed
   Which outwardly ye show? My noble partner   55
   You greet with present grace and great prediction
   Of noble having and of royal hope,
   That he seems rapt withal: to me you speak not:
   If you can look into the seeds of time,
   And say which grain will grow and which will not,   60
   Speak then to me, who neither beg nor fear
   Your favors nor your hate.
FIRST WITCH. Hail!
SECOND WITCH. Hail!
THIRD WITCH. Hail!   65
FIRST WITCH. Lesser than Macbeth, and greater.
SECOND WITCH. Not so happy, yet much happier.
THIRD WITCH. Thou shalt get [16] kings, though thou be none:
   So all hail, Macbeth and Banquo!
FIRST WITCH. Banquo and Macbeth, all hail!   70
MACBETH. Stay, you imperfect speakers, tell me more:
   By Sinel's [17] death I know I am thane of Glamis;
   But how of Cawdor? the thane of Cawdor lives,
   A prosperous gentleman; and to be king
   Stands not within the prospect of belief,   75
   No more than to be Cawdor. Say from whence
   You owe this strange intelligence? or why
   Upon this blasted heath you stop our way
   With such prophetic greeting? Speak, I charge you.
              (WITCHES *vanish.*)

BANQUO. The earth hath bubbles as the water has,   80
   And these are of them: whither are they vanish'd?
MACBETH. Into the air, and what seem'd corporal [18] melted
   As breath into the wind. Would they had stay'd!
BANQUO. Were such things here as we do speak about?
   Or have we eaten on the insane root [19]   85

[16] get: beget
[17] Sinel: Macbeth's father
[18] corporal: corporeal, having a body
[19] insane root: probably hemlock root

That takes the reason prisoner?
MACBETH. Your children shall be kings.
BANQUO.   You shall be king.
MACBETH. And thane of Cawdor too: were it not so?
BANQUO. To the selfsame tune and words. Who's here?
    (*Enter* ROSS *and* ANGUS.)
ROSS. The king hath happily received, Macbeth,   90
    The news of thy success: and when he reads
    Thy personal venture in the rebels' fight,
    His wonders and his praises do contend
    Which should be thine or his: silenced with that,
    In viewing o'er the rest o' the selfsame day,   95
    He finds thee in the stout Norweyan ranks,
    Nothing afeard of what thyself did'st make,
    Strange images of death. As thick as hail
    Came post with post,[20] and every one did bear
    Thy praises in his kingdom's great defense,   100
    And pour'd them down before him.
ANGUS.   We are sent
    To give thee, from our royal master, thanks;
    Only to herald thee into his sight,
    Not pay thee.
ROSS. And for an earnest [21] of a greater honor,   105
    He bade me, from him, call thee thane of Cawdor:
    In which addition, hail, most worthy thane!
    For it is thine.
BANQUO.   What, can the devil speak true?
MACBETH. The thane of Cawdor lives: why do you dress me
    In borrow'd robes?
ANGUS.   Who was the thane lives yet,   110
    But under heavy judgment bears that life
    Which he deserves to lose. Whether he was combined
    With those of Norway, or did line the rebel [22]
    With hidden help and vantage, or that with both
    He labor'd in his country's wreck, I know not;   115
    But treasons capital, confess'd and proved,

[20] post with post: one messenger after another
[21] earnest: an advance payment to seal a bargain
[22] line the rebel: support Macdonwald

Have overthrown him.

MACBETH. (*Aside*)   Glamis, and thane of Cawdor:
The greatest is behind.[23]—Thanks for your pains.—
Do you not hope your children shall be kings,
When those that gave the thane of Cawdor to me   120
Promised no less to them?

BANQUO.   That, trusted home,[24]
Might yet enkindle you unto the crown,
Besides the thane of Cawdor. But 'tis strange:
And oftentimes, to win us to our harm,
The instruments of darkness tell us truths,   125
Win us with honest trifles, to betray 's
In deepest consequence.
Cousins,[25] a word, I pray you.

MACBETH. (*Aside*)   Two truths are told,
As happy prologues to the swelling act
Of the imperial theme.—I thank you, gentlemen.—   130
(*Aside*) This supernatural soliciting
Cannot be ill; cannot be good: if ill,
Why hath it given me earnest of success,
Commencing in a truth? I am thane of Cawdor:
If good, why do I yield to that suggestion   135
Whose horrid image doth unfix my hair
And make my seated [26] heart knock at my ribs,
Against the use of nature? Present fears
Are less than horrible imaginings:
My thought, whose murder yet is but fantastical,[27]   140
Shakes so my single state of man that function
Is smother'd in surmise, and nothing is
But what is not.

BANQUO.   Look, how our partner's rapt.

MACBETH. (*Aside*) If chance will have me king, why, chance may
     crown me,   145
Without my stir.

BANQUO.   New honors come upon him,

---

[23] behind: is yet to come
[24] home: to its logical conclusion
[25] cousins: a common greeting among nobles
[26] seated: not easily upset
[27] fantastical: imaginary

Like our strange garments, cleave not to their mold
But with the aid of use.
MACBETH. (*Aside*)   Come what come may,
  Time and the hour runs through the roughest day.
BANQUO. Worthy Macbeth, we stay upon your leisure.   150
MACBETH. Give me your favor: my dull brain was wrought
  With things forgotten. Kind gentlemen, your pains
  Are register'd where every day I turn
  The leaf to read them. Let us toward the king.
  Think upon what hath chanced, and at more time,   155
  The interim having weigh'd it, let us speak
  Our free hearts each to other.
BANQUO.   Very gladly.
MACBETH. Till then, enough. Come, friends.   (*Exeunt.*)

SCENE 4—FORRES. *The palace.*

(*Flourish. Enter* DUNCAN, MALCOLM, DONALBAIN, LENNOX, *and*
  ATTENDANTS.)
DUNCAN. Is execution done on Cawdor? Are not
  Those in commission yet return'd?
MALCOLM.   My liege,
  They are not yet come back. But I have spoke
  With one that saw him die, who did report
  That very frankly he confess'd his treasons,   5
  Implored your highness' pardon and set forth
  A deep repentance: nothing in his life
  Became him like the leaving it; he died
  As one that had been studied in his death,
  To throw away the dearest thing he owed [1]   10
  As 'twere a careless trifle.
DUNCAN.   There's no art
  To find the mind's construction in the face:
  He was a gentleman on whom I built
  An absolute trust.
    (*Enter* MACBETH, BANQUO, ROSS, *and* ANGUS.)
        O worthiest cousin!

Scene 4:
[1] owed: owned

The sin of my ingratitude even now   15
Was heavy on me: thou art so far before,
That swiftest wing of recompense is slow
To overtake thee. Would thou hadst less deserved,
That the proportion both of thanks and payment
Might have been mine! only I have left to say,   20
More is thy due than more than all can pay.

MACBETH. The service and the loyalty I owe,
In doing it, pays itself. Your highness' part
Is to receive our duties; and our duties
Are to your throne and state children and servants; 25
Which do but what they should, by doing every thing
Safe toward your love and honor.

DUNCAN.   Welcome hither:
I have begun to plant thee, and will labor
To make thee full of growing. Noble Banquo,
That has no less deserved, nor must be known   30
No less to have done so: let me infold thee
And hold thee to my heart.

BANQUO.   There if I grow,
The harvest is your own.

DUNCAN.   My plenteous joys,
Wanton ² in fullness, seek to hide themselves
In drops of sorrow. Sons, kinsmen, thanes,   35
And you whose places are the nearest, know,
We will establish our estate upon
Our eldest, Malcolm, whom we name hereafter
The Prince of Cumberland: ³ which honor must
Not unaccompanied invest him only,   40
But signs of nobleness, like stars, shall shine
On all deservers. From hence to Inverness,⁴
And bind us further to you.

MACBETH. The rest is labor, which is not used for you:
I'll be myself the harbinger,⁵ and make joyful   45
The hearing of my wife with your approach;

² wanton: contrary, perverse
³ Prince of Cumberland: Duncan here makes his son successor to the crown of
Scotland
⁴ Inverness: Macbeth's castle
⁵ harbinger: messenger

So humbly take my leave.

DUNCAN.   My worthy Cawdor!

MACBETH. (*Aside*) The Prince of Cumberland! that is a step
  On which I must fall down, or else o'erleap,
  For in my way it lies. Stars, hide your fires;   50
  Let not light see my black and deep desires:
  The eye wink at the hand; [6] yet let that be
  Which the eye fears, when it is done, to see.   (*Exit.*)

DUNCAN. True, worthy Banquo; he is full so valiant,
  And in his commendations I am fed;   55
  It is a banquet to me. Let's after him,
  Whose care is gone before to bid us welcome:
  It is a peerless kinsman.   (*Flourish. Exeunt.*)

SCENE 5—INVERNESS. MACBETH's *castle.*

(*Enter* LADY MACBETH, *reading a letter.*)

LADY MACBETH. 'They met me in the day of success; and I have learned
by the perfectest report, they have more in them than mortal
knowledge. When I burned in desire to question them further,
they made themselves air, into which they vanished. Whiles I stood
rapt in the wonder of it, came missives from the king, who all-hailed
me "Thane of Cowdor;" by which title, before, these weird sisters
saluted me, and referred me to the coming on of time, with "Hail,
king that shalt be!" This have I thought good to deliver thee, my
dearest partner of greatness, that thou mightst not lose the dues
of rejoicing, by being ignorant of what greatness is promised thee.
Lay it to thy heart, and farewell.'

Glamis thou art, and Cawdor, and shalt be
What thou art promised: yet do I fear thy nature;
It is too full o' the milk of human kindness
To catch the nearest way thou wouldst be great;
Are not without ambition, but without   5
The illness [1] should attend it: what thou wouldst highly,
That wouldst thou holily; wouldst not play false,
And yet wouldst wrongly win; thou 'ldst have, great Glamis,

[6] **eye . . . hand:** let my eyes not see the deed my hand commits

Scene 5:
[1] **illness:** wickedness

That which cries 'Thus thou must do, if thou have it;
And that which rather thou dost fear to do   10
Than wishest should be undone.' Hie thee hither,
That I may pour my spirits in thine ear,
And chastise with the valor of my tongue
All that impedes thee from the golden round,[2]
Which fate and metaphysical [3] aid doth seem   15
To have thee crown'd withal.[4]
   (*Enter a* MESSENGER.)
                            What is your tidings?
MESSENGER. The king comes here to-night.
LADY MACBETH.   Thou 'rt mad to say it:
  Is not thy master with him? who, were 't so,
  Would have inform'd for preparation.
MESSENGER. So please you, it is true: our thane is coming: 20
  One of my fellows had the speed of him,
  Who, almost dead for breath, had scarcely more
  Than would make up his message.
LADY MACBETH.   Give him tending;
  He brings great news.   (*Exit* MESSENGER.)
                   The raven himself is hoarse
That croaks the fatal [5] entrance of Duncan   25
Under my battlements. Come, you spirits
That tend on mortal [6] thoughts, unsex me here,
And fill me, from the crown to the toe, top-full
Of direst cruelty! make thick my blood,
Stop up the access and passage to remorse,   30
That no compunctious visitings of nature
Shake my fell [7] purpose, nor keep peace between
The effect and it! Come to my woman's breasts,
And take my milk for gall, you murdering ministers,
Wherever in your sightless substances   35
You wait on nature's mischief! Come, thick night,

[2] golden round: crown
[3] metaphysical: supernatural
[4] withal: with
[5] fatal: directed by fate, and fatal to Duncan
[6] mortal: deadly
[7] fell: cruel, savage

And pall thee in the dunnest [8] smoke of hell,
That my keen knife see not the wound it makes,
Nor heaven peep through the blanket of the dark,
To cry 'Hold, hold!'
  (*Enter* MACBETH.)

                      Great Glamis! worthy Cawdor!   **40**
Greater than both, by the all-hail hereafter!
Thy letters have transported me beyond
This ignorant present, and I feel now
The future in the instant.
MACBETH.   My dearest love,
Duncan comes here to-night.
LADY MACBETH.   And when goes hence?   **45**
MACBETH. To-morrow, as he purposes.
LADY MACBETH.   O, never
Shall sun that morrow see!
Your face, my thane, is as a book where men
May read strange matters. To beguile the time,
Look like the time; bear welcome in your eye,   **50**
Your hand, your tongue: look like the innocent flower,
But be the serpent under 't. He that's coming
Must be provided for: and you shall put
This night's great business into my dispatch;
Which shall to all our nights and days to come   **55**
Give solely sovereign sway and masterdom.
MACBETH. We will speak further.
LADY MACBETH.   Only look up clear;
To alter favor ever is to fear:
Leave all the rest to me.   (*Exeunt.*)

SCENE 6—*Before* MACBETH's *castle.*

(*Hautboys and torches. Enter* DUNCAN, MALCOLM, DONALBAIN,
    BANQUO, LENNOX, MACDUFF, ROSS, ANGUS *and* ATTENDANTS.)
DUNCAN. This castle hath a pleasant seat; [1] the air

---

[8] **dunnest:** blackest

Scene 6:
[1] **seat:** site

Nimbly and sweetly recommends itself
Unto our gentle senses.

BANQUO.   This guest of summer,
The temple-haunting martlet,[2] does approve,
By this loved mansionry that the heaven's breath   5
Smells wooingly here: no jutty, frieze,
Buttress, nor coign of vantage,[3] but this bird
Hath made his pendant bed and procreant cradle:
Where they most breed and haunt, I have observed
The air is delicate.

   (*Enter* LADY MACBETH.)

DUNCAN.   See, see, our honor'd hostess!   10
The love that follows us sometime is our trouble,
Which still we thank as love. Herein I teach you
How you shall bid God 'ild us for your pains,
And thank us for your trouble.

LADY MACBETH.   All our service
In every point twice done, and then done double,   15
Were poor and single business to contend
Against those honors deep and broad wherewith
Your majesty loads our house: for those of old,
And the late dignities heap'd up to them,
We rest your hermits.[4]

DUNCAN.   Where's the thane of Cawdor?   20
We coursed him at the heels, and had a purpose
To be his purveyor:[5] but he rides well,
And his great love, sharp as his spur, hath holp him
To his home before us. Fair and noble hostess,
We are your guest to-night.

LADY MACBETH.   Your servants ever   25
Have theirs, themselves, and what is theirs, in compt,
To make their audit[6] at your highness' pleasure,
Still to return your own.

---

[2] martlet: the martin, called "temple-haunting" because it often builds its nest in the nooks of churches
[3] coign of vantage: convenient corner
[4] hermits: beadsmen who received alms and were bound to pray for their benefactors
[5] purveyor: one who arranges for supplies
[6] audit: account

DUNCAN.   Give me your hand;
   Conduct me to mine host: we love him highly,
   And shall continue our graces towards him.   30
   By your leave, hostess.   (*Exeunt.*)

SCENE 7—MACBETH's *castle.*

(*Hautboys and torches. Enter a* SEWER,[1] *and divers* SERVANTS *with
   dishes and service, and pass over the stage. Then enter* MAC-
   BETH.)

MACBETH. If it were done when 'tis done, then 'twere well
   It were done quickly: if the assassination
   Could trammel up [2] the consequence, and catch,
   With his surcease,[3] success; that but this blow
   Might be the be-all and the end-all here,   5
   But here, upon this bank and shoal of time,
   We 'ld jump the life to come. But in these cases
   We still have judgment here; that we but teach
   Bloody instructions, which being taught return
   To plague the inventor: this even-handed justice   10
   Commends the ingredients of our poison'd chalice
   To our own lips. He's here in double trust:
   First, as I am his kinsman and his subject,
   Strong both against the deed; then, as his host,
   Who should against his murderer shut the door,   15
   Not bear the knife myself. Besides, this Duncan
   Hath borne his faculties so meek, hath been
   So clear in his great office, that his virtues
   Will plead like angels trumpet-tongued against
   The deep damnation of his taking-off: 20
   And pity, like a naked new-born babe,
   Striding the blast,[4] or heaven's cherubim horsed
   Upon the sightless couriers [5] of the air,
   Shall blow the horrid deed in every eye,

Scene 7:
[1] **Sewer:** head server
[2] **trammel up:** tangle up
[3] **surcease:** Duncan's death
[4] **striding the blast:** riding the wind
[5] **sightless couriers:** invisible steeds

That tears shall drown the wind. I have no spur   25
To prick the sides of my intent, but only
Vaulting ambition, which o'erleaps itself.[6]
And falls on the other.
   (*Enter* LADY MACBETH.)
                      How now! what news?

LADY MACBETH. He has almost supp'd: why have you left the
   chamber?   30

MACBETH. Hath he ask'd for me?

LADY MACBETH.   Know you not he has?

MACBETH. We will proceed no further in this business:
   He hath honor'd me of late; and I have bought
   Golden opinions from all sorts of people,
   Which would be worn now in their newest gloss,   35
   Not cast aside so soon.

LADY MACBETH.   Was the hope drunk
   Wherein you dress'd yourself? Hath it slept since?
   And wakes it now, to look so green and pale
   At what it did so freely? From this time
   Such I account thy love. Art thou afeard   40
   To be the same in thine own act and valor
   As thou art in desire? Would'st thou have that
   Which thou esteem'st the ornament of life,
   And live a coward in thine own esteem,
   Letting 'I dare not' wait upon 'I would,'   45
   Like the poor cat i' the adage?[7]

MACBETH.   Prithee, peace:
   I dare do all that may become a man;
   Who dares do more is none.

LADY MACBETH.   What beast was 't then
   That made you break this enterprise to me?
   When you durst do it, then you were a man;   50
   And, to be more than what you were, you would
   Be so much more the man. Nor time nor place
   Did then adhere, and yet you would make both:
   They have made themselves, and that their fitness now

[6] o'erleaps itself: leaps too high and falls disgracefully on the other side
[7] adage: a proverb which says: "The cat would eat fish, and would not wet her
feet."

Does unmake you. I have given suck, and know   55
How tender 'tis to love the babe that milks me:
I would, while it was smiling in my face,
Have pluck'd my nipple from his boneless gums,
And dash'd the brains out, had I so sworn as you
Have done to this.

MACBETH.   If we should fail?

LADY MACBETH.   We fail!   60
But screw your courage to the sticking-place,[8]
And we'll not fail. When Duncan is asleep—
Whereto the rather shall his day's hard journey
Soundly invite him—his two chamberlains
Will I with wine and wassail [9] so convince,   65
That memory, the warder of the brain,
Shall be a fume, and the receipt of reason
A limbec [10] only: when in swinish sleep
Their drenched natures lie as in a death,
What cannot you and I perform upon   70
The unguarded Duncan? what not put upon
His spongy [11] officers, who shall bear the guilt
Of our great quell?

MACBETH.   Bring forth men-children only;
For thy undaunted mettle should compose
Nothing but males. Will it not be received,   75
When we have mark'd with blood those sleepy two
Of his own chamber, and used their very daggers,
That they have done 't?

LADY MACBETH.   Who dares receive it other,
As we shall make our griefs and clamor roar
Upon his death?

MACBETH.   I am settled, and bend up   80
Each corporal agent to this terrible feat.
Away, and mock the time with fairest show:
False face must hide what the false heart doth know.   (*Exeunt.*)

---

[8] **sticking-place:** the cross-bow was worked by a screw until the string would catch in a notch (sticking-place) and was ready to discharge
[9] **wassail:** carousal
[10] **limbec:** the cap of the still into which the fumes would rise during the process of distillation
[11] **spongy:** drunken

ACT II

SCENE 1—INVERNESS. *Court of* MACBETH's *castle*.

(*Enter* BANQUO, *and* FLEANCE *bearing a torch before him*.)

BANQUO. How goes the night, boy?

FLEANCE. The moon is down; I have not heard the clock.

BANQUO. And she goes down at twelve.

FLEANCE.   I take 't, 'tis later, sir.

BANQUO. Hold, take my sword. There's husbandry [1] in heaven,
   Their candles are all out. Take thee that too.[2]   5
   A heavy summons lies like lead upon me,
   And yet I would not sleep. Merciful powers,
   Restrain in me the cursed thoughts [3] that nature
   Gives way to in repose!
       (*Enter* MACBETH, *and a* SERVANT *with a torch*.)
                              Give me my sword.
   Who's there?   10

MACBETH. A friend.

BANQUO. What, sir, not yet at rest? The king's a-bed:
   He hath been in unusual pleasure, and
   Sent forth great largess to your offices:
   This diamond he greets your wife withal,   15
   By the name of most kind hostess; and shut up
   In measureless content.

MACBETH.   Being unprepared,
   Our will became the servant to defect,
   Which else should free have wrought.

BANQUO.   All's well.
   I dreamt last night of the three weird sisters: 20
   To you they have show'd some truth.

MACBETH.   I think not of them:
   Yet, when we can entreat an hour to serve,
   We would spend it in some words upon that business,

Scene 1:

[1] husbandry: thrift

[2] that too: his dagger

[3] cursed thought: temptation to hasten the witches' prophecies by murdering Duncan

If you would grant the time.

BANQUO.   At your kind'st leisure.

MACBETH. If you shall cleave to my consent, when 'tis,   25
It shall make honor for you.

BANQUO.   So I lose none
In seeking to augment it, but still keep
My bosom franchised and allegiance clear,
I shall be counsel'd.

MACBETH.   Good repose the while!

BANQUO. Thanks, sir: the like to you!   30

                        (*Exeunt* BANQUO *and* FLEANCE.)

MACBETH. Go bid thy mistress, when my drink is ready,
She strike upon the bell. Get thee to bed.   (*Exit* SERVANT.)
Is this a dagger which I see before me,
The handle toward my hand? Come, let me clutch thee.
I have thee not, and yet I see thee still.   35
Art thou not, fatal vision, sensible [4]
To feeling as to sight? or art thou but
A dagger of the mind, a false creation,
Proceeding from the heat-oppressed brain?
I see thee yet, in form as palpable   40
As this which now I draw.
Thou marshal'st [5] me the way that I was going;
And such an instrument I was to use.
Mine eyes are made the fools o' the other senses,
Or else worth all the rest: I see thee still;   45
And on thy blade and dudgeon [6] gouts of blood,
Which was not so before. There's no such thing:
It is the bloody business which informs
Thus to mine eyes. Now o'er the one half-world
Nature seems dead, and wicked dreams abuse   50
The curtain'd sleep; witchcraft celebrates
Pale Hecate's offerings; [7] and wither'd murder,
Alarm'd by his sentinel, the wolf,
Whose howl's his watch, thus with his stealthy pace,

[4] sensible: perceptible
[5] marshal'st: urges
[6] dudgeon: hilt
[7] Hecate's offerings: Hecate was Queen of the underworld

With Tarquin's [8] ravishing strides, towards his design   55
Moves like a ghost. Thou sure and firm-set earth,
Hear not my steps, which way they walk, for fear
Thy very stones prate of my whereabout,
And take the present horror from the time,
Which now suits with it. Whiles I threat, he lives: 60
Words to the heat of deeds too cold breath gives.   (A *bell rings*.)
I go, and it is done: the bell invites me.
Hear it not, Duncan, for it is a knell
That summons thee to heaven, or to hell.   (*Exit*.)

SCENE 2—*The same*.

(*Enter* LADY MACBETH.)

LADY MACBETH. That which hath made them drunk hath made me
    bold;
  What hath quench'd them hath given me fire. Hark! Peace!
  It was the owl that shriek'd, the fatal bellman,
  Which gives the stern'st good-night. He is about it: 5
  The doors are open, and the surfeited grooms
  Do mock their charge with snores. I have drugg'd their possets,[1]
  That death and nature do contend about them,
  Whether they live or die.
MACBETH. (*Within*)   Who's there? what, ho!   10
LADY MACBETH. Alack, I am afraid they have awaked
  And 'tis not done: the attempt and not the deed
  Confounds [2] us. Hark! I laid their daggers ready;
  He could not miss 'em. Had he not resembled
  My father as he slept, I had done 't.
    (*Enter* MACBETH.)
                              My husband!   15
MACBETH. I have done the deed. Didst thou not hear a noise?
LADY MACBETH. I heard the owl scream and the crickets cry.
  Did not you speak?

[8] **Tarquin:** wicked ruler of Rome who so infuriated the Romans that they over-
threw him and set up a Republic

Scene 2:
[1] **possets:** drink of curdled wine
[2] **confounds:** ruins

MACBETH.   When?
LADY MACBETH.   Now.
MACBETH.   As I descended?
LADY MACBETH. Aye.
MACBETH. Hark!   20
  Who lies i' the second chamber?
LADY MACBETH.   Donalbain.
MACBETH. This is a sorry sight.   (*Looking on his hands.*)
LADY MACBETH. A foolish thought, to say a sorry sight.
MACBETH. There's one did laugh in 's sleep, and one cried 'Murder!' 25
  That they did wake each other: I stood and heard them:
  But they did say their prayers, and address'd them
  Again to sleep.
LADY MACBETH. There are two lodged together.³
MACBETH. One cried 'God bless us!' and 'Amen' the other,   30
  As they had seen me with these hangman's hands:
  Listening their fear, I could not say 'Amen,'
  When they did say 'God bless us!'
LADY MACBETH. Consider it not so deeply.
MACBETH. But wherefore could not I pronounce 'Amen'?   35
  I had most need of blessing, and 'Amen'
  Stuck in my throat.
LADY MACBETH.   These deeds must not be thought
  After these ways; so, it will make us mad.
MACBETH. Methought I heard a voice cry 'Sleep no more!
  Macbeth does murder sleep'—the innocent sleep,   40
  Sleep that knits up the ravel'd sleave ⁴ of care,
  The death of each day's life, sore labor's bath,
  Balm of hurt minds, great nature's second course,⁵
  Chief nourisher in life's feast,—
LADY MACBETH.   What do you mean?
MACBETH. Still it cried 'Sleep no more!' to all the house: 45
  'Glamis hath murder'd sleep, and therefore Cawdor
  Shall sleep no more: Macbeth shall sleep no more.'
LADY MACBETH. Who was it that thus cried? Why, worthy thane,
  You do unbend ⁶ your noble strength, to think   50

³ **two lodged together:** Donalbain and Malcolm
⁴ **sleave:** a skein of thread
⁵ **second course:** the main course
⁶ **unbend:** relax

So brainsickly of things. Go get some water,
And wash this filthy witness from your hand.
Why did you bring these daggers from the place?
They must lie there: go carry them, and smear
The sleepy grooms with blood.

MACBETH.   I'll go no more: 55
I am afraid to think what I have done;
Look on 't again I dare not.

LADY MACBETH.   Infirm of purpose!
Give me the daggers: the sleeping and the dead
Are but as pictures: 'tis the eye of childhood
That fears a painted devil. If he do bleed,   60
I'll gild [7] the faces of the grooms withal,
For it must seem their guilt.   (*Exit. Knocking within.*)

MACBETH.   Whence is that knocking?
How is 't with me, when every noise appals me?
What hands are here? ha! they pluck out mine eyes!
Will all great Neptune's [8] ocean wash this blood   65
Clean from my hand? No; this my hand will rather
The multitudinous seas incarnadine, [9]
Making the green one red.
        (*Re-enter* LADY MACBETH.)

LADY MACBETH. My hands are of your color, but I shame
To wear a heart so white. (*Knocking within.*) I hear a knocking   70
At the south entry: retire we to our chamber:
A little water clears us of this deed:
How easy is it then! Your constancy
Hath left you unattended.[10] (*Knocking within.*) Hark! more knock-
        ing: 75
Get on your nightgown, lest occasion call us
And show us to be watchers: be not lost
So poorly in your thoughts.

MACBETH. To know my deed, 'twere best not know myself.   80
                        (*Knocking within.*)
    Wake Duncan with thy knocking! I would thou could'st! (*Exeunt.*)

---

[7] gild: smear
[8] Neptune: god of the sea
[9] incarnadine: turn blood-red
[10] your constancy . . . unattended: your firmness has abandoned you

SCENE 3—*The same.*

(*Enter a* PORTER. *Knocking within.*)

PORTER. Here's a knocking indeed! If a man were porter of hell-gate, he should have old turning the key. (*Knocking within.*) Knock, knock, knock! Who's there, i' the name of Beelzebub? [1] Here's a farmer, that hanged himself on th' expectation of plenty: come in time; have napkins enow [2] about you; here you'll sweat for 't. (*Knocking within.*) Knock, knock! Who's there, in th' other devil's name? Faith, here's an equivocator, [3] that could swear in both the scales against either scale; who committed treason enough for God's sake, yet could not equivocate to heaven: O, come in, equivocator. (*Knocking within.*) Knock, knock, knock! Who's there? Faith, here's an English tailor come hither, for stealing out of a French hose: [4] come in, tailor; here you may roast your goose. [5] (*Knocking within.*) Knock, knock; never at quiet! What are you? But this place is too cold for hell. I'll devil-porter it no further: I had thought to have let in some of all professions, that go the primrose way to the everlasting bonfire. (*Knocking within.*) Anon, anon! I pray you, remember the porter.   (*Opens the gate.*)

(*Enter* MACDUFF *and* LENNOX.)

MACDUFF. Was it so late, friend, ere you went to bed,
    That you do lie so late?

PORTER. Faith, sir, we were carousing till the second cock. [6]

MACDUFF. I believe drink gave thee the lie last night.

PORTER. That it did, sir, i' the very throat on me: but I requited him for his lie, and, I think, being too strong for him, though he took up my leg sometime, yet I made a shift to cast him.

MACDUFF. Is thy master stirring?

(*Enter* MACBETH.)

    Our knocking has awaked him; here he comes.

Scene 3:
[1] **Beelzebub:** Prince of devils
[2] **enow:** enough
[3] **equivocator:** a sarcastic reference to the Jesuits who were supposed to justify doubleness of meaning in speech
[4] **French hose:** tight-fitting breeches from which only a clever thief could steal cloth
[5] **goose:** a tailor's pressing iron
[6] **second cock:** 3 A.M.

LENNOX. Good morrow, noble sir.

MACBETH.   Good morrow, both.

MACDUFF. Is the king stirring, worthy thane?

MACBETH.   Not yet.

MACDUFF. He did command me to call timely on him: I had   5
  almost slipp'd the hour.

MACBETH.   I'll bring you to him.

MACDUFF. I know this is a joyful trouble to you;
  But yet 'tis one.

MACBETH. The labor we delight in physics pain.
  This is the door.

MACDUFF.   I'll make so bold to call,   10
  For 'tis my limited service.   (*Exit.*)

LENNOX. Goes the king hence to-day?

MACBETH.   He does; he did appoint so.

LENNOX. The night has been unruly: where we lay,
  Our chimneys were blown down, and, as they say,
  Lamentings heard i' the air, strange screams of death,   15
  And prophesying with accents terrible
  Of dire combustion and confused events
  New hatch'd to the woeful time: the obscure bird [7]
  Clamor'd the livelong night: some say, the earth
  Was feverous and did shake.

MACBETH.   'Twas a rough night.   20

LENNOX. My young remembrance cannot parallel
  A fellow to it.
    (*Re-enter* MACDUFF.)

MACDUFF. O horror, horror, horror! Tongue nor heart
  Cannot conceive nor name thee.

MACBETH.⎱   What's the matter?
LENNOX. ⎰

MACDUFF. Confusion now hath made his masterpiece.   25
  Most sacrilegious murder hath broke ope
  The Lord's anointed temple,[8] and stole thence
  The life o' the building.

MACBETH.   What is 't you say? the life?

LENNOX. Mean you his majesty?

---

[7] **obscure bird:** owl
[8] **temple:** the body of the king, anointed as one chosen by God to rule

MACDUFF. Approach the chamber, and destroy your sight   30
  With a new Gorgon: [9] do not bid me speak;
  See, and then speak yourselves.   (*Exeunt* MACBETH *and* LENNOX.)
                       Awake, awake!
  Ring the alarum-bell. Murder and treason!
  Banquo and Donalbain! Malcolm! awake!
  Shake off this downy sleep, death's counterfeit,[10]   35
  And look on death itself! up, up, and see
  The great doom's image! [11] Malcolm! Banquo!
  As from your graves rise up, and walk like sprites,
  To countenance this horror. Ring the bell.   (*Bell rings.*)
    (*Enter* LADY MACBETH.)
LADY MACBETH. What's the business,   40
  That such a hideous trumpet calls to parley
  The sleepers of the house? speak, speak!
MACDUFF.   O gentle lady,
  'Tis not for you to hear what I can speak:
  The repetition, in a woman's ear,
  Would murder as it fell.
    (*Enter* BANQUO.)
               O Banquo, Banquo!   45
  Our royal master's murder'd.
LADY MACBETH.   Woe, alas!
  What, in our house?
BANQUO.   Too cruel any where.
  Dear Duff, I prithee, contradict thyself,
  And say it is not so.
    (*Re-enter* MACBETH *and* LENNOX, *with* ROSS.)
MACBETH. Had I but died an hour before this chance,   50
  I had lived a blessed time; for from this instant
  There's nothing serious in mortality:
  All is but toys: renown and grace is dead;
  The wine of life is drawn, and the mere lees [12]
  Is left this vault to brag of.   55
    (*Enter* MALCOLM *and* DONALBAIN.)

[9] Gorgon: Medusa, woman in mythology, the sight of whom turned men to stone
[10] counterfeit: imitation
[11] great doom's image: sight as terrible as that on Doom's Day
[12] lees: dregs

DONALBAIN. What is amiss?

MACBETH.   You are, and do not know 't:
The spring, the head, the fountain of your blood
Is stopp'd; the very source of it is stopp'd.

MACDUFF. Your royal father's murder'd.

MALCOLM.   O, by whom?

LENNOX. Those of his chamber, as it seem'd, had done 't: 60
Their hands and faces were all badged with blood;
So were their daggers, which unwiped we found
Upon their pillows:
They stared, and were distracted; no man's life
Was to be trusted with them.   65

MACBETH. O, yet I do repent me of my fury,
That I did kill them.

MACDUFF.   Wherefore did you so?

MACBETH. Who can be wise, amazed, temperate and furious,
Loyal and neutral, in a moment? No man:
The expedition [13] of my violent love   70
Outrun the pauser reason. Here lay Duncan,
His silver skin laced with his golden blood,
And his gash'd stabs look'd like a breach in nature
For ruin's wasteful entrance; there, the murderers,
Steep'd in the colors of their trade, their daggers   75
Unmannerly breech'd [14] with gore: who could refrain,
That had a heart to love, and in that heart
Courage to make 's love known?

LADY MACBETH.   Help me hence, ho!

MACDUFF. Look to the lady.

MALCOLM. (Aside to DONALBAIN) Why do we hold our tongues,   80
That most may claim this argument [15] for ours?

DONALBAIN. (Aside to MALCOLM) What should be spoken here, where
our fate,
Hid in an auger-hole, may rush, and seize us?   85
Let 's away;
Our tears are not yet brew'd.

MALCOLM. (Aside to DONALBAIN) Nor our strong sorrow

---

[13] expedition: haste
[14] breech'd: covered in an immodest fashion
[15] argument: subject matter

Upon the foot of motion.[16]

BANQUO.   Look to the lady: [17]

(LADY MACBETH *is carried out.*)

And when we have our naked frailties hid,   90
That suffer in exposure, let us meet;
And question this most bloody piece of work,
To know it further. Fears and scruples shake us:
In the great hand of God I stand, and thence
Against the undivulged pretense I fight   95
Of treasonous malice.

MACDUFF.   And so do I.

ALL.   So all.

MACBETH. Let 's briefly put on manly readiness,[18]
And meet i' the hall together.

ALL.   Well contented.

(*Exeunt all but* MALCOLM *and* DONALBAIN.)

MALCOLM. What will you do? Let's not consort with them:
To show an unfelt sorrow is an office   100
Which the false man does easy. I'll to England.

DONALBAIN. To Ireland, I; our separated fortune
Shall keep us both safer: where we are
There's daggers in men's smiles: the near in blood,
The nearer bloody.[19]

MALCOLM.   This murderous shaft that's shot   105
Hath not yet lighted, and our safest way
Is to avoid the aim. Therefore to horse;
And let us not be dainty of leave-taking,
But shift away: there's warrant in that theft
Which steals itself when there's no mercy left   (*Exeunt.*) 110

SCENE 4—*Outside* MACBETH'S *castle.*

(*Enter* Ross *with an* OLD MAN.)

OLD MAN. Threescore and ten I can remember well:
Within the volume of which time I have seen

[16] Nor . . . motion: it is not the time to show sorrow
[17] Look to the lady: Lady Macbeth has fainted.
[18] put . . . readiness: clothe ourselves properly
[19] the . . . bloody: the closer our relations, the more likely he is to kill us

Hours dreadful and things strange, but this sore night
Hath trifled former knowings.[1]

ROSS.   Ah, good father,
Thou seest, the heavens, as troubled with man's act,   5
Threaten his bloody stage: by the clock 'tis day,
And yet dark night strangles the traveling lamp.[2]
Is 't night's predominance, or the day's shame,
That darkness does the face of earth entomb,
When living light should kiss it?

OLD MAN.   'Tis unnatural,   10
Even like the deed that's done. On Tuesday last
A falcon towering in her pride of place
Was by a mousing owl [3] hawk'd at and kill'd.

ROSS. And Duncan's horses—a thing most strange and certain—
Beauteous and swift, the minions [4] of their race,   15
Turn'd wild in nature, broke their stalls, flung out,
Contending 'gainst obedience, as they would make
War with mankind.

OLD MAN.   'Tis said they eat each other.

ROSS. They did so, to the amazement of mine eyes,
That look'd upon 't.

   (Enter MACDUFF.)
                         Here comes the good Macduff.   20
How goes the world, sir, now?

MACDUFF.   Why, see you not?

ROSS. Is 't known who did this more than bloody deed?

MACDUFF. Those that Macbeth hath slain.

ROSS.   Alas, the day!
What good could they pretend?

MACDUFF.   They were suborn'd:
Malcolm and Donalbain, the king's two sons,   25
Are stol'n away and fled, which puts upon them
Suspicion of the deed.

ROSS.   'Gainst nature still:

Scene 4:
[1] trifled . . . knowings: made all previous experience seem trivial
[2] traveling lamp: sun
[3] mousing owl: an owl whose natural prey is mice
[4] minions: favorite horses

Thriftless ambition, that wilt ravin ⁵ up
Thine own life's means! Then 'tis most like
The sovereignty will fall upon Macbeth.   30
MACDUFF. He is already named, and gone to Scone ⁶
To be invested.
ROSS.   Where is Duncan's body?
MACDUFF. Carried to Colme-kill,⁷
The sacred storehouse of his predecessors
And guardian of their bones.
ROSS.   Will you to Scone?   35
MACDUFF. No, cousin, I'll to Fife.⁸
ROSS.   Well, I will thither.
MACDUFF. Well, may you see things well done there: adieu!
Lest our old robes sit easier than our new!
ROSS. Farewell, father.
OLD MAN. God's benison ⁹ go with you, and with those   40
That would make good of bad and friends of foes!   (*Exeunt.*)

ACT III

Scene 1—Forres. *The palace.*

(*Enter* Banquo.)
BANQUO. Thou hast it now: king, Cawdor, Glamis, all,
As the weird women promised, and I fear
Thou play'dst most foully for 't: yet it was said
It should not stand in thy posterity,
But that myself should be the root and father   5
Of many kings. If there come truth from them—
As upon thee, Macbeth, their speeches shine—
Why, by the verities on thee made good,
May they not be my oracles ¹ as well

⁵ ravin up: eat up
⁶ Scone: ancient city of Scotland where the Scottish kings were crowned
⁷ Colme-kill: island of Iona where St. Columba had his cell
⁸ Fife: Macduff's castle
⁹ God's benison: God's blessing

Scene 1:
¹ oracles: prophets

And set me up in hope? But hush, no more.   10
    (*Sennet* ² *sounded. Enter* MACBETH, *as king;* LADY MACBETH *as*
      queen; LENNOX, ROSS, LORDS, LADIES, *and* ATTENDANTS.)

MACBETH. Here's our chief guest.

LADY MACBETH.   If he had been forgotten,
    It had been as a gap in our great feast,
    And all-thing unbecoming.

MACBETH. To-night we hold a solemn supper, sir,
    And I'll request your presence.

BANQUO.   Let your highness   15
    Command upon me, to the which my duties
    Are with a most indissoluble tie
    For ever knit.

MACBETH. Ride you this afternoon?

BANQUO. Aye, my good lord.   20

MACBETH. We should have else desired your good advice,
    Which still hath been both grave and prosperous,
    In this day's council; but we'll take to-morrow.
    Is 't far you ride?

BANQUO. As far, my lord, as will fill up the time   25
    'Twixt this and supper: go not my horse the better,
    I must become a borrower of the night
    For a dark hour or twain.

MACBETH.   Fail not our feast.

BANQUO. My lord, I will not.

MACBETH. We hear our bloody cousins are bestow'd   30
    In England and in Ireland, not confessing
    Their cruel parricide,³ filling their hearers
    With strange invention: ⁴ but of that to-morrow
    When therewithal we shall have cause of state
    Craving us jointly. Hie you to horse: adieu,   35
    Till you return at night. Goes Fleance with you?

BANQUO. Aye, my good lord: our time does call upon 's.

MACBETH. I wish your horses swift and sure of foot,
    And so I do commend you to their backs.
    Farewell.   (*Exit* BANQUO.)   40

---

² **sennet:** trumpet flourish to announce the arrival of a noble person
³ **parricide:** murder of a parent
⁴ **invention:** lies, falsehood

Let every man be master of his time
Till seven at night; to make society
The sweeter welcome, we will keep ourself
Till supper-time alone: while then, God be with you!
          (*Exeunt all but* MACBETH *and an* ATTENDANT.)
Sirrah,[5] a word with you: attend those men   45
Our pleasure?
ATTENDANT. They are, my lord, without the palace gate.
MACBETH. Bring them before us.   (*Exit* ATTENDANT.)
                    To be thus is nothing;
But to be safely thus: our fears in Banquo
Stick deep; and in his royalty of nature   50
Reigns that which would be fear'd: 'tis much he dares,
And, to that dauntless temper [6] of his mind,
He hath a wisdom that doth guide his valor
To act in safety. There is none but he
Whose being I do fear: and under him   55
My Genius is rebuked, as it is said
Mark Antony's was by Caesar.[7] He chid the sisters,[8]
When first they put the name of king upon me,
And bade them speak to him; then prophet-like
They hail'd him father to a line of kings: 60
Upon my head they placed a fruitless crown [9]
And put a barren scepter in my gripe,
Thence to be wrench'd with an unlineal hand,[10]
No son of mine succeeding. If 't be so,
For Banquo's issue have I filed my mind;   65
For them the gracious Duncan have I murder'd;
Put rancors in the vessel of my peace
Only for them, and mine eternal jewel [11]
Given to the common enemy of man,[12]

---

[5] sirrah: used in addressing a servant, an inferior, or a child
[6] temper: quality, disposition
[7] my genius . . . Caesar: the guiding spirit who presides over my destiny is below that of Banquo, as Antony's luck was below that of Caesar
[8] sisters: witches
[9] fruitless crown: with no royal descendants
[10] unlineal hand: no lineal descendants
[11] mine eternal jewel: my soul
[12] common enemy of man: Satan

To make them kings, the seed of Banquo kings!   70
Rather than so, come, fate, into the list,
And champion me to the utterance! Who's there?
  (*Re-enter* ATTENDANT, *with two* MURDERERS.)
Now go to the door, and stay there till we call.   (*Exit* ATTENDANT.)
Was it not yesterday we spoke together?
FIRST MURDERER. It was, so please your highness.
MACBETH.   Well then, now   75
  Have you consider'd of my speeches? Know
  That it was he in the times past which held you
  So under fortune, which you thought had been
  Our innocent self: this I made good to you
  In our last conference; pass'd in probation with you,   80
  How you were borne in hand, how cross'd, the instruments,
  Who wrought with them, and all things else that might
  To half a soul and to a notion crazed
  Say 'Thus did Banquo.'
FIRST MURDERER.   You made it known to us.
MACBETH. I did so; and went further, which is now   85
  Our point of second meeting. Do you find
  Your patience so predominant in your nature,
  That you can let this go? Are you so gospell'd,[13]
  To pray [14] for this good man and for his issue,
  Whose heavy hand hath bow'd you to the grave   90
  And beggar'd yours for ever?
FIRST MURDERER.   We are men, my liege.
MACBETH. Aye, in the catalogue ye go for men;
  As hounds and greyhounds, mongrels, spaniels, curs,
  Shoughs, water-rugs and demi-wolves, are clept [15]
  All by the name of dogs: [16] the valued file   95
  Distinguishes the swift, the slow, the subtle,
  The housekeeper, the hunter, every one
  According to the gift which bounteous nature
  Hath in him closed, whereby he does receive
  Particular addition, from the bill   100

[13] gospell'd: so submissive to the gospel message: "Love thine enemies."
[14] to pray: as to pray
[15] clept: called
[16] As hounds . . . dogs: all types of dogs are called dogs

That writes them all alike: and so of men.
Now if you have a station in the file,
Not i' the worst rank of manhood, say it,
And I will put that business in your bosoms
Whose execution takes your enemy off,   105
Grapples you to the heart and love of us,
Who wear our health but sickly in his life,
Which in his death were perfect.

SECOND MURDERER.   I am one, my liege,
Whom the vile blows and buffets of the world
Have so incensed that I am reckless what   110
I do to spite the world.

FIRST MURDERER.   And I another
So weary with disasters, tugg'd with fortune,
That I would set my life on any chance,
To mend it or be rid on 't.

MACBETH.   Both of you
Know Bonquo was your enemy.

BOTH MURDERERS.   True, my lord.   115

MACBETH. So is he mine, and in such bloody distance [17]
That every minute of his being thrusts
Against my near'st of life: and though I could
With barefaced power sweep him from my sight
And bid my will avouch it, yet I must not,   120
For certain friends that are both his and mine,
Whose loves I may not drop, but wail his fall
Who I myself struck down: and thence it is
That I to your assistance do make love,
Masking the business from the common eye   125
For sundry weighty reasons.

SECOND MURDERER.   We shall, my lord,
Perform what you command us.

FIRST MURDERER.   Though our lives—

MACBETH. Your spirits shine through you. Within this hour at most
I will advise you where to plant yourselves,   130
Acquaint you with the perfect spy o' the time,
The moment on 't; for 't must be done to-night,

[17] **bloody distance**: mortal enmity

And something [18] from the palace; always thought
That I require a clearness: [19] and with him—
To leave no rubs nor botches [20] in the work—   135
Fleance his son, that keeps him company,
Whose absence is no less material to me
Than is his father's, must embrace the fate
Of that dark hour. Resolve yourselves apart:
I'll come to you anon.

BOTH MURDERERS.   We are resolved, my lord.   140

MACBETH. I'll call upon you straight: abide within.

(Exeunt MURDERERS.*)*

It is concluded: Banquo thy soul's flight,
If it find heaven, must find it out to-night.   *(Exit.)*

SCENE 2—*The palace.*

(Enter LADY MACBETH *and a* SERVANT.*)*

LADY MACBETH. Is Banquo gone from court?

SERVANT. Aye, madam, but returns again to-night.

LADY MACBETH. Say to the king, I would attend his leisure
    For a few words.

SERVANT.   Madam, I will.   *(Exit.)*

LADY MACBETH.   Naught 's had, all 's spent,
    Where our desire is got without content: 5
    'Tis safer to be that which we destroy
    Than by destruction dwell in doubtful joy.
        (Enter MACBETH.*)*
    How now, my lord! why do you keep alone,
    Of sorriest fancies your companions making;
    Using those thoughts which should indeed have died   10
    With them they think on? Things without all remedy
    Should be without regard: what's done is done.

MACBETH. We have scotch'd [1] the snake, not kill'd it:
    She'll close and be herself, whilst our poor malice

---

[18] something: at some distance
[19] always . . . clearness: People must think that I am above suspicion
[20] rubs nor botches: flaws or defects

Scene 2:
[1] scotch'd: slashed, cut

Remains in danger of her former tooth. 15
But let the frame of things disjoint, both the worlds [2] suffer,
Ere we will eat our meal in fear, and sleep
In the affliction of these terrible dreams
That shake us nightly: better be with the dead,
Whom we, to gain our peace, have sent to peace, 20
Than on the torture of the mind to lie
In restless ecstasy. Duncan is in his grave;
After life's fitful fever he sleeps well;
Treason has done his worst: nor steel, nor poison,
Malice domestic, foreign levy,[3] nothing, 25
Can touch him further.

LADY MACBETH.   Come on;
Gentle my lord, sleek o'er your rugged looks;
Be bright and jovial among your guests to-night.

MACBETH. So shall I, love; and so, I pray, be you:
Let your remembrance apply to Banquo; 30
Present him eminence, both with eye and tongue:
Unsafe the while, that we
Must lave our honors in these flattering streams,
And make our faces vizards [4] to our hearts,
Disguising what they are.

LADY MACBETH.   You must leave this. 35

MACBETH. O, full of scorpions is my mind, dear wife!
Thou know'st that Banquo, and his Fleance, lives.

LADY MACBETH. But in them nature's copy's not eterne.[5]

MACBETH. There's comfort yet; they are assailable;
Then be thou jocund: ere the bat hath flown 40
His cloister'd flight: ere to black Hecate's summons
The shard-borne beetle with his drowsy hums
Hath rung night's yawning peal, there shall be done
A deed of dreadful note.

LADY MACBETH.   What's to be done?

MACBETH. Be innocent of the knowledge, dearest chuck, 45

[2] **both the worlds:** this world and the next
[3] **malice domestic, foreign levy:** Macbeth fears both Banquo and Macduff (domestic), and Malcolm and Donalbain (foreign levy)
[4] **vizards:** masks
[5] **But . . . eterne:** Nature has not given them an eternal lease on life, but one easy to revoke or terminate.

Till thou applaud the deed. Come, seeling [6] night,
Scarf up the tender eye of pitiful day,
And with thy bloody and invisible hand
Cancel and tear to pieces that great bond [7]
Which keeps me pale! Light thickens, and the crow   50
Makes wing to the rooky [8] wood:
Good things of day begin to droop and drowse,
Whiles night's black agents to their preys do rouse.
Thou marvel'st at my words: but hold thee still;
Things bad begun make strong themselves by ill: 55
So, prithee, go with me.   (*Exeunt.*)

SCENE 3—*A park near the palace.*

(*Enter three* MURDERERS.)

FIRST MURDERER. But who did bid thee join with us?
THIRD MURDERER.   Macbeth.
SECOND MURDERER. He needs not our mistrust; since he delivers
  Our offices, and what we have to do,
  To the direction just.
FIRST MURDERER.   Then stand with us.   5
  The west yet glimmers with some streaks of day:
  Now spurs the lated traveler apace
  To gain the timely inn, and near approaches
  The subject of our watch.
THIRD MURDERER.   Hark! I hear horses.
BANQUO. (*Within*) Give us a light there, ho!
SECOND MURDERER.   Then 'tis he: the rest   10
  That are within the note of expectation
  Already are i' the court.
FIRST MURDERER.   His horses go about.
THIRD MURDERER. Almost a mile: but he does usually—
  So all men do—from hence to the place gate
  Make it their walk.   15
SECOND MURDERER.   A light, a light!

[6] **seeling:** sewing up the eyelids of a falcon with silk thread until it is properly trained to hunt
[7] **that great bond:** the prophecy that Banquo's children shall rule
[8] **rooky:** place where rooks and crows dwell

(*Enter* BANQUO, *and* FLEANCE *with a torch.*)

THIRD MURDERER.   'Tis he.

FIRST MURDERER. Stand to 't.

BANQUO. It will be rain to-night.

FIRST MURDERER.   Let it come down.

                              (*They set upon* BANQUO.)

BANQUO. O, treachery! Fly, good Fleance, fly, fly, fly!

   Thou mayst revenge. O slave!   (*Dies.* FLEANCE *escapes.*) 20

THIRD MURDERER. Who did strike out the light?

FIRST MURDERER.   Was 't not the way?

THIRD MURDERER. There's but one down; the son is fled.

SECOND MURDERER.   We have lost

   Best half of our affair.

FIRST MURDERER. Well, let 's away and say how much is done.

                                        (*Exeunt.*)

SCENE 4—*Hall in the palace.*

(*A* banquet prepared. *Enter* MACBETH, LADY MACBETH, ROSS,
   LENNOX, LORDS, *and* ATTENDANTS.)

MACBETH. You know your own degrees;[1] sit down: at first
   And last a hearty welcome.

LORDS.   Thanks to your majesty.

MACBETH. Ourself will mingle with society
   And play the humble host.
   Our hostess keeps her state, but in best time   5
   We will require her welcome.

LADY MACBETH. Pronounce it for me, sir, to all our friends,
   For my heart speaks they are welcome.

      (*Enter first* MURDERER *to the door.*)

MACBETH. See, they encounter thee with their heart's thanks.
   Both sides are even: here I'll sit i' the midst: 10
   Be large in mirth; anon we'll drink a measure
   The table round. (*Approaching the door*) There's blood upon thy
      face.

MURDERER. 'Tis Banquo's then.

Scene 4:
[1] **degrees:** rank in sitting at table

MACBETH. 'Tis better thee without than he within.[2]
  Is he dispatch'd?   15

MURDERER. My lord, his throat is cut; that I did for him.

MACBETH. Thou art the best o' the cut-throats: yet he 's good
  That did the like for Fleance: if thou didst it,
  Thou art the nonpareil.[3]

MURDERER.   Most royal sir,
  Fleance is 'scaped.   20

MACBETH. (*Aside*) Then comes my fit again: I had else been perfect,
  Whole as the marble, founded as the rock,
  As broad and general as the casing [4] air:
  But now I am cabin'd, cribb'd, confined, bound in
  To saucy doubts and fears.—But Banquo's safe?   25

MURDERER. Aye, my good lord: safe in a ditch he bides,
  With twenty trenched gashes on his head;
  The least a death to nature.

MACBETH.   Thanks for that.
  (*Aside*) There the grown serpent lies; the worm that 's fled
  Hath nature that in time will venom breed,   30
  No teeth for the present. Get thee gone: to-morrow
  We'll hear ourselves again.   (*Exit* MURDERER.)

LADY MACBETH.   My royal lord,
  You do not give the cheer: the feast is sold [5]
  That is not often vouch'd, while 'tis a making,
  'Tis given with welcome: to feed were best at home;   35
  From thence the sauce to meat is ceremony;
  Meeting were bare without it.[6]

MACBETH.   Sweet remembrancer!
  Now good digestion wait on appetite,
  And health on both!

LENNOX.   May 't please your highness sit.
  (*The* GHOST *of* BANQUO *enters and sits in* MACBETH's *place.*)

MACBETH. Here had we now our country's honor roof'd,   40

---

[2] 'tis better . . . within: it is better on your face than in his veins
[3] nonpareil: having no equal
[4] casing: encasing; all-embracing
[5] the feast is sold: the dinner is no better than that sold at an inn
[6] From thence . . . without it: When we eat out, it is made more pleasant by added ceremonies.

Were the graced person of our Banquo present;
Who may I rather challenge for unkindness
Than pity for mischance!

ROSS.   His absence, sir,
Lays blame upon his promise. Please 't your highness
To grace us with your royal company.   45

MACBETH. The table's full.

LENNOX.   Here is a place reserved, sir.

MACBETH. Where?

LENNOX. Here, my good lord. What is 't that moves your highness?

MACBETH. Which of you have done this?

LORDS.   What, my good lord?

MACBETH. Thou canst not say I did it: never shake   50
Thy gory locks at me.

ROSS. Gentlemen, rise; his highness is not well.

LADY MACBETH. Sit, worthy friends: my lord is often thus,
And hath been from his youth: pray you, keep seat;
The fit is momentary; upon a thought   55
He will again be well: if much you note him,
You shall offend him and extend his passion:
Feed, and regard him not. Are you a man?

MACBETH. Aye, and a bold one, that dare look on that
Which might appal the devil.

LADY MACBETH.   O proper stuff! [7]   60
This is the very painting of your fear:
This is the air-drawn dagger which, you said,
Led you to Duncan. O, these flaws and starts,
Impostors to true fear, would well become
A woman's story at a winter's fire,   65
Authorized by her grandam. Shame itself!
Why do you make such faces? When all 's done,
You look but on a stool.

MACBETH. Prithee, see there! behold! look! lo! how say you?
Why, what care I? If thou canst nod, speak too.   70
If charnel-houses [8] and our graves must send

[7] O proper stuff: A fine thing this is!
[8] charnel-houses: a vault next to the church, used for storing skulls and bones found when digging new graves

Those that we bury back, our monuments
Shall be the maws of kites.[9]   (*Exit* GHOST.)
LADY MACBETH.   What, quite unmann'd in folly?
MACBETH. If I stand here, I saw him.
LADY MACBETH.   Fie, for shame!
MACBETH. Blood hath been shed ere now, i' the olden time,   75
   Ere humane statute purged the gentle weal;[10]
   Aye, and since too, murders have been perform'd
   Too terrible for the ear: the time has been,
   That, when the brains were out, the man would die,
   And there an end; but now they rise again,   80
   With twenty mortal murders[11] on their crowns,
   And push us from our stools: this is more strange
   Than such a murder is.
LADY MACBETH.   My worthy lord,
   Your noble friends do lack you.
MACBETH.   I do forget.
   Do not muse[12] at me, my most worthy friends;   85
   I have a strange infirmity, which is nothing
   To those that know me. Come, love and health to all;
   Then I'll sit down. Give me some wine, fill full.
   I drink to the general joy o' the whole table,
   And to our dear friend Banquo, whom we miss;   90
   Would he were here! to all and him we thirst,
   And all to all.
LORDS.   Our duties, and the pledge.
   (*Re-enter* GHOST.)
MACBETH. Avaunt![13] and quit my sight! let the earth hide thee!
   Thy bones are marrowless, thy blood is cold;
   Thou hast no speculation in those eyes   95
   Which thou dost glare with.
LADY MACBETH.   Think of this, good peers,
   But as a thing of custom: 'tis no other;
   Only it spoils the pleasure of the time.
MACBETH. What man dare, I dare:

[9] maws of kites: stomachs of vultures
[10] Ere . . . weal: before law cleansed society of savagery and made it gentle
[11] mortal murders: fatal wounds
[12] muse: be astonished
[13] avaunt: go away!

Approach thou like the rugged Russian bear,   100
The arm'd rhinoceros, or the Hyrcan tiger; [14]
Take any shape but that, and my firm nerves
Shall never tremble: or be alive again,
And dare me to the desert with thy sword;
If trembling I inhabit then, protest me   105
The baby of a girl. [15] Hence, horrible shadow!
Unreal mockery, hence!   (*Exit* GHOST.)
                Why, so: being gone,
I am a man again. Pray you, sit still.

LADY MACBETH. You have displaced the mirth, broke the good
   meeting,
With most admired [16] disorder.

MACBETH.   Can such things be,   110
And overcome us like a summer's cloud
Without our special wonder? You make me strange
Even to the disposition that I owe,
When now I think you can behold such sight,
And keep the natural ruby of your cheeks,   115
When mine is blanch'd with fear.

ROSS.   What sights, my lord?

LADY MACBETH. I pray you, speak not; he grows worse and worse;
Question enrages him: at once, good night:
Stand not upon the order of your going,
But go at once.

LENNOX   Good night; and better health   120
Attend his majesty!

LADY MACBETH.   A kind good night to all!
       (*Exeunt all but* MACBETH *and* LADY MACBETH.)

MACBETH. It will have blood: they say blood will have blood:
Stones have been known to move and trees to speak;
Augurs and understood relations have
By maggot-pies and choughs and rooks brought forth   125
The secret'st man of blood. [17] What is the night?

LADY MACBETH. Almost at odds with morning, which is which.

[14] Hyrcan tiger: tigers that prowled near the Caspian Sea
[15] baby of a girl: child of a very young mother
[16] admired: strange
[17] augurs . . . blood: People at one time believed that they could tell of secret crimes by the flight of magpies.

MACBETH. How say'st thou, that Macduff denies his person
  At our great bidding?
LADY MACBETH.   Did you send to him, sir?
MACBETH. I hear it by the way, but I will send: 130
  There 's not a one of them but in his house
  I keep a servant fee'd.[18] I will to-morrow,
  And betimes I will, to the weird sisters:
  More shall they speak, for now I am bent to know,
  By the worst means, the worst. For mine own good   135
  All causes shall give way: I am in blood
  Stepp'd in so far that, should I wade no more,
  Returning were as tedious as go o'er:
  Strange things I have in head that will to hand,
  Which must be acted ere they may be scann'd.   140
LADY MACBETH. You lack the season of all natures, sleep.
MACBETH. Come, we'll to sleep. My strange and self-abuse
  Is the initiate fear that wants hard use:
  We are yet but young in deed.   (*Exeunt.*)

SCENE 5—*A heath.*

(*Thunder. Enter the three* WITCHES, *meeting* HECATE.)
FIRST WITCH. Why, how now, Hecate! you look angerly.
HECATE. Have I not reason, beldams [1] as you are,
  Saucy and over-bold? How did you dare
  To trade and traffic with Macbeth
  In riddles and affairs of death;   5
  And I, the mistress of your charms,
  The close contriver of all harms,
  Was never call'd to bear my part,
  Or show the glory of our art?
  And, which is worse, all you have done   10
  Hath been but for a wayward son,
  Spiteful and wrathful; who, as others do,
  Loves for his own ends, not for you.
  But make amends now: get you gone,

[18] fee'd: Macbeth keeps a paid spy in the household of every Scottish lord.

Scene 5:
[1] beldams: belles dames; really means hags

And at the pit of Acheron [2]   15
Meet me i' the morning: thither he
Will come to know his destiny:
Your vessels and your spells provide,
Your charms and every thing beside.
I am for the air; this night I'll spend   20
Unto a dismal and a fatal end:
Great business must be wrought ere noon:
Upon the corner of the moon
There hangs a vaporous drop profound;
I'll catch it ere it comes to ground: 25
And that distill'd by magic sleights
Shall raise such artificial sprites [3]
As by the strength of their illusion
Shall draw him on to his confusion:
He shall spurn fate, scorn death, and bear   30
His hopes 'bove wisdom, grace and fear:
And you all know security [4]
Is mortals' chiefest enemy.   (*Music and a song within:* 'Come away,
come away,' &c.)

Hark! I am call'd; my little spirit, see,
Sits in a foggy cloud, and stays for me.   (*Exit.*) 35
FIRST WITCH. Come, let 's make haste; she'll soon be back again.
(*Exeunt.*)

SCENE 6—FORRES. *The palace.*

(*Enter* LENNOX *and another* LORD.)
LENNOX. My former speeches have but hit your thoughts,
    Which can interpret farther: only I say
    Things have been strangely borne.[1] The gracious Duncan
    Was pitied of Macbeth: marry,[2] he was dead:
    And the right-valiant Banquo walk'd too late;   5
    Whom, you may say, if 't please you, Fleance kill'd,

[2] Acheron: river in the underworld, Hades
[3] sprites: spirits
[4] security: excessive confidence

Scene 6:
[1] borne: managed
[2] marry: an oath meaning "By the Virgin Mary"

For Fleance fled: men must not walk too late.
Who cannot want the thought, how monstrous
It was for Malcolm and for Donalbain
To kill their gracious father? damned fact!   10
How it did grieve Macbeth! did he not straight,
In pious rage, the two delinquents tear,
That were the slaves of drink and thralls of sleep?
Was not that nobly done? Aye, and wisely too;
For 'twould have anger'd any heart alive   15
To hear the men deny 't. So that, I say,
He has borne all things well: and I do think
That, had he Duncan's sons under his key—
As, an 't ³ please heaven, he shall not—they should find
What 'twere to kill a father; so should Fleance.   20
But, peace! for from broad words, and 'cause he fail'd
His presence at the tyrant's feast, I hear,
Macduff lives in disgrace: sir, can you tell
Where he bestows himself?
LORD.   The son of Duncan,
From whom this tyrant holds the due of birth,   25
Lives in the English court, and is received
Of the most pious Edward ⁴ with such grace
That the malevolence ⁵ of fortune nothing
Takes from his high respect. Thither Macduff
Is gone to pray the holy king, upon his aid   30
To wake Northumberland and warlike Siward:
That by the help of these, with Him above
To ratify the work, we may again
Give to our tables meat, sleep to our nights,
Free from our feasts and banquets bloody knives,   35
Do faithful homage and receive free honors:
All which we pine for now: and this report
Hath so exasperate the king that he
Prepares for some attempt of war.
LENNOX.   Sent he to Macduff?
LORD. He did: and with an absolute 'Sir not I,'   40

³ an 't: if it
⁴ Edward: Edward the Confessor, saintly King of England
⁵ malevolence: evil intent, malice

The cloudy [6] messenger turns me his back,
And hums,[7] as who would say 'You'll rue the time
That clogs [8] me with this answer.'

LENNOX.   And that well might
Advise him to a caution, to hold what distance
His wisdom can provide. Some holy angel   45
Fly to the court of England and unfold
His message ere he come, that a swift blessing
May soon return to this our suffering country
Under a hand accursed!

LORD.   I'll send my prayers with him.   (*Exeunt.*)

ACT IV

SCENE 1—A *cavern. In the middle, a boiling cauldron.*

(*Thunder. Enter the three* WITCHES.)

FIRST WITCH. Thrice the brinded cat [1] hath mew'd.

SECOND WITCH. Thrice and once the hedge-pig whined.

THIRD WITCH. Harpier [2] cries ' 'Tis time, 'tis time.'

FIRST WITCH. Round about the cauldron go:
In the poison'd entrails throw.   5
Toad, that under cold stone
Days and nights has thirty one
Swelter'd [3] venom sleeping got,
Boil thou first i' the charmed pot.

ALL. Double, double toil and trouble;   10
Fire burn and cauldron bubble.

SECOND WITCH. Fillet [4] of a fenny snake,[5]
In the cauldron boil and bake;

[6] cloudy: gloomy, frowning
[7] hums: a surly murmuring sound
[8] clogs: wooden shoes which slowed down the walker; hence, makes me return with reluctant feet

Scene 1:
[1] brinded cat: striped cat
[2] Harpier: harpy; mythological creature, half woman, half bird
[3] swelter'd: coming out like sweat
[4] fillet: slice
[5] fenny snake: snake found in marsh lands

Eye of newt [6] and toe of frog,
Wool of bat and tongue of dog,   15
Adder's fork and blind-worm's sting,
Lizard's leg and howlet's [7] wing,
For a charm of powerful trouble,
Like a hell-broth boil and bubble.
ALL. Double, double toil and trouble;   20
Fire burn and cauldron bubble.
THIRD WITCH. Scale of dragon, tooth of wolf,
Witches' mummy,[8] maw and gulf [9]
Of the ravin'd salt-sea shark,
Root of hemlock digged i' the dark,   25
Liver of blaspheming Jew,
Gall of goat and slips of yew
Silver'd in the moon's eclipse,
Nose of Turk and Tartar's lips,
Finger of birth-strangled babe   30
Ditch-deliver'd by a drab,
Make the gruel thick and slab: [10]
Add thereto a tiger's chaudron,[11]
For the ingredients of our cauldron.
ALL. Double, double toil and trouble;   35
Fire burn and cauldron bubble.
SECOND WITCH. Cool it with a baboon's blood,
Then the charm is firm and good.
    (*Enter* HECATE *to the other three* WITCHES.)
HECATE. O, well done! I commend your pains;
And every one shall share i' the gains: 40
And now about the cauldron sing,
Like elves and fairies in a ring,
Enchanting all that you put in.
            (*Music and a song: 'Black spirits,' &c.* HECATE *retires.*)
SECOND WITCH. By the pricking of my thumbs,

[6] newt: lizard
[7] howlet: owlet
[8] witches' mummy: mummified witch
[9] maw and gulf: stomach and gullet
[10] slab: slimy
[11] chaudron: liver and entrails

Something wicked [12] this way comes: 45
Open, locks,
Whoever knocks!
  (*Enter* MACBETH.)

MACBETH. How now, you secret, black, and midnight hags!
  What is 't you do?

ALL.   A deed without a name.

MACBETH. I conjure you, by that which you profess,   50
  Howe'er you come to know it, answer me:
  Though you untie the winds and let them fight
  Against the churches! though the yesty [13] waves
  Confound and swallow navigation up;
  Though bladed corn be lodged and trees blown down;   55
  Though castles topple on their warders' heads;
  Though palaces and pyramids do slope
  Their heads to their foundations; though the treasure
  Of nature's germens [14] tumble all together,
  Even till destruction sicken,[15] answer me   60
  To what I ask you.

FIRST WITCH.   Speak.

SECOND WITCH.   Demand.

THIRD WITCH.   We'll answer.

FIRST WITCH. Say, if thou 'dst rather hear it from our mouths,
  Or from our masters?

MACBETH.   Call 'em, let me see 'em.

FIRST WITCH. Pour in sow's blood, that hath eaten
  Her nine farrow; [16] grease that's sweaten   65
  From the murderer's gibbet throw
  Into the flame.

ALL.   Come, high or low; [17]
  Thyself and office [18] deftly show!
    (*Thunder.* FIRST APPARITION: *an armed Head.*)

MACBETH. Tell me, thou unknown power,—

[12] **something wicked:** Macbeth
[13] **yesty:** foaming
[14] **germens:** seeds, life-germs
[15] **sicken:** is satiated
[16] **farrow:** young pigs
[17] **high or low:** wherever you are
[18] **office:** function

FIRST WITCH.   He knows thy thought:
    Hear his speech, but say thou nought.   70
FIRST APPARITION. Macbeth! Macbeth! Macbeth! beware Macduff;
    Beware the thane of Fife. Dismiss me: enough.   (*Descends.*)
MACBETH. Whate'er thou art, for thy good caution thanks;
    Thou hast harp'd [19] my fear aright: but one word more,—
FIRST WITCH. He will not be commanded: here's another,   75
    More potent than the first.
        (*Thunder.* SECOND APPARITION: *a bloody Child.*)
SECOND APPARITION. Macbeth! Macbeth! Macbeth!
MACBETH. Had I three ears, I 'ld hear thee.
SECOND APPARITION. Be bloody, bold and resolute; laugh to scorn   80
    The power of man, for none of woman born
    Shall harm Macbeth.   (*Descends.*)
MACBETH. Then live, Macduff: what need I fear of thee?
    But yet I'll make assurance doubly sure,
    And take a bond of fate: thou shalt not live;   85
    That I may tell pale-hearted fear it lies,
    And sleep in spite of thunder.
        (*Thunder.* THIRD APPARITION: *a Child crowned, with a tree in his
        hand.*)
                                          What is this,
    That rises like the issue of a king,
    And wears upon his baby-brow the round [20]
    And top of sovereignty?
ALL.   Listen, but speak not to 't.   90
THIRD APPARITION. Be lion-mettled, proud, and take no care
    Who chafes, who frets, or where conspirers are:
    Macbeth shall never vanquish'd be until
    Great Birnam wood to high Dunsinane hill
    Shall come against him.   (*Descends.*)
MACBETH.   That will never be: 95
    Who can impress [21] the forest, bid the tree
    Unfix his earth-bound root? Sweet bodements! good!
    Rebellion's head, rise never, till the wood
    Of Birnam rise, and our high-placed Macbeth

[19] harp'd: struck the string of my fear
[20] round: crown
[21] impress: force into military service

Shall live the lease of nature, pay his breath   100
To time and mortal custom.²² Yet my heart
Throbs to know one thing: tell me, if your art
Can tell so much: shall Banquo's issue ever
Reign in this kingdom?   (*Hautboys.*)
ALL.   Seek to know no more.
MACBETH. I will be satisfied: deny me this,   105
  And an eternal curse fall on you! Let me know:
  Why sinks that cauldron? and what noise is this?
FIRST WITCH. Show!
SECOND WITCH. Show!
THIRD WITCH. Show!   110
ALL. Show his eyes, and grieve his heart;
  Come like shadows, so depart!
  (*A show of eight Kings,²³ the last with a glass in his hand;
  BANQUO's Ghost following.*)
MACBETH. Thou art too like the spirit of Banquo: down!
  Thy crown does sear mine eye-balls. And thy hair,
  Thou other gold-bound brow, is like the first.   115
  A third is like the former. Filthy hags!
  Why do you show me this? A fourth! Start, eyes!
  What, will the line stretch out to the crack of doom?
  Another yet! A seventh! I'll see no more:
  And yet the eighth appears, who bears a glass ²⁴   120
  Which shows me many more; and some I see
  That two-fold balls and treble scepters carry: ²⁵
  Horrible sight! Now I see 'tis true;
  For the blood-bolter'd Banquo smiles upon me,
  And points at them for his. What, is this so?   125
                                          (*Apparitions vanish.*)
FIRST WITCH. Aye, sir, all this is so: but why
  Stands Macbeth thus amazedly?
  Come, sisters, cheer we up his sprites,
  And show the best of our delights:

²² live . . . custom: live the allotted time of his natural life and die a natural
death
²³ eight Kings: these are the eight Stuart Kings of Scotland
²⁴ glass: mirror
²⁵ twofold . . . scepters: Reference to James I who united Scotland and England.
Treble scepters refers to the triple kingdoms of Ireland, Scotland and England.

I'll charm the air to give a sound,   130
While you perform your antic round,
That this great king may kindly say
Our duties did his welcome pay.

      (*Music. The* WITCHES *dance, and then vanish, with* HECATE.)

MACBETH. Where are they? Gone? Let this pernicious hour
  Stand aye accursed in the calendar!   135
  Come in, without there!

    (*Enter* LENNOX.)

LENNOX.   What's your grace's will?
MACBETH. Saw you the weird sisters?
LENNOX.   No, my lord.
MACBETH. Came they not by you?
LENNOX.   No indeed, my lord.
MACBETH. Infected be the air whereon they ride,
  And damn'd all those that trust them! I did hear   140
  The galloping of horse: who was 't came by?
LENNOX. 'Tis two or three, my lord, that bring you word
  Macduff is fled to England.
MACBETH.   Fled to England!
LENNOX. Aye, my good lord.
MACBETH. (*Aside*) Time, thou anticipatest my dread exploits: 145
  The flighty purpose never is o'ertook
  Unless the deed go with it: from this moment
  The very firstlings of my heart shall be
  The firstlings of my hand.[26] And even now,
  To crown my thoughts with acts, be it thought and done: 150
  The castle of Macduff I will surprise;
  Seize upon Fife; give to the edge o' the sword
  His wife, his babes, and all unfortunate souls
  That trace him in his line. No boasting like a fool;
  This deed I'll do before this purpose cool: 155
  But no more sights!—Where are these gentlemen?
  Come, bring me where they are.   (*Exeunt.*)

[26] firstlings of my hand: I shall follow my first impulses.

SCENE 2—FIFE. MACDUFF's *castle*.

(*Enter* LADY MACDUFF, *her* SON, *and* ROSS.)

LADY MACDUFF. What had he done, to make him fly the land?

ROSS. You must have patience, madam.

LADY MACDUFF.   He had none:
   His flight was madness: when our actions do not,
   Our fears do make us traitors.

ROSS.   You know not
   Whether it was his wisdom or his fear.   5

LADY MACDUFF. Wisdom! to leave his wife, to leave his babes,
   His mansion and his titles in a place
   From whence himself does fly? He loves us not;
   He wants the natural touch: for the poor wren,
   The most diminutive of birds, will fight,   10
   Her young ones in her nest, against the owl.
   All is the fear and nothing is the love;
   As little is the wisdom, where the flight
   So runs against all reason.

ROSS.   My dearest coz,[1]
   I pray you, school yourself:[2] but, for your husband,   15
   He is noble, wise, judicious, and best knows
   The fits o' the season. I dare not speak much further:
   But cruel are the times, when we are traitors
   And do not know ourselves; when we hold rumor
   From what we fear, yet know not what we fear,   20
   But float upon a wild and violent sea
   Each way and move. I take my leave of you:
   Shall not be long but I'll be here again:
   Things at the worst will cease, or else climb upward
   To what they were before. My pretty cousin,   25
   Blessing upon you!

LADY MACDUFF. Father'd he is, and yet he's fatherless.

ROSS. I am so much a fool, should I stay longer,
   It would be my disgrace and your discomfort:
   I take my leave at once.   (*Exit.*)

Scene 2:
[1] coz: cousin
[2] school yourself: control yourself

LADY MACDUFF.   Sirrah, your father's dead: 30
   And what will you do now? How will you live?
SON. As birds do, mother.
LADY MACDUFF.   What, with worms and flies?
SON. With what I get, I mean; and so do they.
LADY MACDUFF. Poor bird! thou 'ldst never fear the net nor lime,[3]   35
   The pitfall nor the gin.[4]
SON. Why should I, mother? Poor birds they are not set for.
   My father is not dead, for all your saying.
LADY MACDUFF. Yes, he is dead: how wilt thou do for a father?   40
SON. Nay, how will you do for a husband?
LADY MACDUFF. Why, I can buy me twenty at any market.
SON. Then you'll buy 'em to sell again.
LADY MACDUFF. Thou speak'st with all thy wit, and yet, i' faith,   45
   With wit enough for thee.
SON. Was my father a traitor, mother?
LADY MACDUFF. Aye, that he was.
SON. What is a traitor?
LADY MACDUFF. Why, one that swears and lies.[5]   50
SON. And be all traitors that do so?
LADY MACDUFF. Every one that does so is a traitor, and must be
   hanged.
SON. And must they all be hanged that swear and lie?
LADY MACDUFF. Every one.   55
SON. Who must hang them?
LADY MACDUFF. Why, the honest men.
SON. Then the liars and swearers are fools; for there are liars and
   and swearers enow to beat the honest men and hang up them.
LADY MACDUFF. Now, God help thee, poor monkey![6]   60
   But how wilt thou do for a father?
SON. If he were dead, you 'ld weep for him: if you would not, it were
   a good sign that I should quickly have a new father.
LADY MACDUFF. Poor prattler,[7] how thou talk'st!

   (*Enter a* MESSENGER.)

[3] lime: sticky substance used to catch birds
[4] gin: traps used to catch birds
[5] one . . . lies: one that takes an oath of allegiance and then breaks it
[6] monkey: used tenderly
[7] prattler: one who talks excessively

MESSENGER. Bless you, fair dame! I am not to you known,   65
  Though in your state of honor I am perfect.
  I doubt some danger does approach you nearly:
  If you will take a homely man's advice,
  Be not found here; hence, with your little ones.
  To fright you thus, methinks I am too savage;   70
  To do worse to you were fell cruelty,
  Which is too nigh your person. Heaven preserve you!
  I dare abide no longer.   (*Exit.*)
LADY MACDUFF.   Whither should I fly?
  I have done no harm. But I remember now
  I am in this earthly world, where to do harm   75
  Is often laudable, to do good sometime
  Accounted dangerous folly: why then, alas,
  Do I put up that womanly defense,
  To say I have done no harm?—What are these faces?
    (*Enter* MURDERERS.)
FIRST MURDERER. Where is your husband?   80
LADY MACDUFF. I hope, in no place so unsanctified
  Where such as thou mayst find him.
FIRST MURDERER.   He's a traitor.
SON. Thou liest, thou shag-ear'd [8] villain!
FIRST MURDERER.   What, you egg!
                (*Stabbing him.*)
  Young fry [9] of treachery!
SON.   He has kill'd me, mother:
  Run away, I pray you!   (*Dies.*) 85
         (*Exit* LADY MACDUFF, *crying 'Murder!'*
         Exeunt MURDERERS, *pursuing her.*)

SCENE 3—ENGLAND. *Before the* KING's *palace.*

  (*Enter* MALCOLM *and* MACDUFF.)
MALCOLM. Let us seek out some desolate shade, and there
  Weep our sad bosoms empty.

---

[8] **shag-ear'd:** long shaggy hair falling over the murderer's ears reminded the boy
of a dog's ears
[9] **fry:** spawn

MACDUFF.   Let us rather
Hold fast the mortal [1] sword, and like good men
Bestride our down-fall'n birthdom: each new morn
New widows howl, new orphans cry, new sorrows   5
Strike heaven on the face, that it resounds
As if it felt with Scotland and yell'd out
Like syllable of dolor.

MALCOLM.   What I believe, I'll wail; [2]
What know, believe; and what I can redress,
As I shall find the time to friend, I will.   10
What you have spoke, it may be so perchance.
This tyrant, whose sole name blisters our tongues,
Was once thought honest: you have loved him well;
He hath not touch'd you yet. I am young; but something
You may deserve of him through me; and wisdom   15
To offer up a weak, poor, innocent lamb
To appease an angry god.

MACDUFF. I am not treacherous.

MALCOLM.   But Macbeth is.
A good and virtuous nature may recoil [3]
In an imperial charge. But I shall crave your pardon;   20
That which you are, my thoughts cannot transpose:
Angels are bright still, though the brightest [4] fell:
Though all things foul would wear the brows of grace,
Yet grace must still look so.

MACDUFF.   I have lost my hopes.

MALCOLM. Perchance even there where I did find my doubts. 25
Why in that rawness left you wife and child,
Those precious motives, those strong knots of love,
Without leave-taking? I pray you,
Let not my jealousies be your dishonors,
But mine own safeties. You may be rightly just,   30
Whatever I shall think.

MACDUFF.   Bleed, bleed, poor country:

Scene 3:
[1] mortal: deadly
[2] What . . . wail: Malcolm is testing Macduff. He fears that Macduff is a spy sent by Macbeth.
[3] recoil . . . charge: may give way under a monarch's pressure
[4] brightest: Satan

Great tyranny, lay thou thy basis sure,
For goodness dare not check thee: wear thou thy wrongs;
The title is affeer'd.⁵ Fare thee well, lord:
I would not be the villain that thou think'st   35
For the whole space that's in the tyrant's grasp
And the rich East to boot.
MALCOLM.   Be not offended:
  I speak not as in absolute fear of you.
  I think our country sinks beneath the yoke;
  It weeps, it bleeds, and each new day a gash   40
  Is added to her wounds: I think withal
  There would be hands uplifted in my right;
  And here from gracious England ⁶ have I offer
  Of goodly thousands: but for all this,
  When I shall tread upon the tyrant's head,   45
  Or wear it on my sword, yet my poor country
  Shall have more vices than it had before,
  More suffer and more sundry ways than ever,
  By him that shall succeed.
MACDUFF.   What should he be?
MALCOLM. It is myself I mean: in whom I know   50
  All the particulars of vice so grafted
  That, when they shall be open'd, black Macbeth
  Will seem as pure as snow, and the poor state
  Esteem him as a lamb, being compared
  With my confineless harms.
MACDUFF.   Not in the legions   55
  Of horrid hell can come a devil more damn'd
  In evils to top Macbeth.
MALCOLM.   I grant him bloody,
  Luxurious,⁷ avaricious, false, deceitful,
  Sudden, malicious, smacking of every sin
  That has a name: but there's no bottom, none,   60
  In my voluptuousness: your wives, your daughters,
  Your matrons, and your maids, could not fill up
  The cistern of my lust, and my desire

⁵ affeer'd: legally confirmed
⁶ gracious England: the good King of England
⁷ luxurious: lascivious

All continent [8] impediments would o'erbear,
That did oppose my will: better Macbeth   65
Then such an one to reign.
MACDUFF.   Boundless intemperance
In nature is a tyranny; it hath been
The untimely emptying of the happy throne,
And fall of many kings. But fear not yet
To take upon you what is yours: you may   70
Convey [9] your pleasures in a spacious plenty,
And yet seem cold, the time you may so hoodwink:
We have willing dames enough; there cannot be
That vulture [10] in you, to devour so many
As will to greatness dedicate themselves,   75
Finding it so inclined.
MALCOLM.   With this there grows
In my most ill-composed affection such
A stanchless avarice that, were I king,
I should cut off the nobles for their lands,
Desire his jewels and this other's house: 80
And my more-having would be as a sauce
To make me hunger more, that I should forge
Quarrels unjust against the good and loyal,
Destroying them for wealth.
MACDUFF.   This avarice
Sticks deeper,[11] grows with more pernicious root   85
Than summer-seeming lust, and it hath been
The sword of our slain kings: yet do not fear;
Scotland hath foisons [12] to fill up your will
Of your mere own: all these are portable,
With other graces weigh'd.   90
MALCOLM. But I have none: the king-becoming graces,
As justice, verity, temperance, stableness,
Bounty, perseverance, mercy, lowliness,
Devotion, patience, courage, fortitude,
I have no relish for them, but abound   95

[8] continent: restraining, holding in
[9] convey: manage secretly
[10] vulture: ravenous appetite
[11] sticks deeper: is less easily uprooted
[12] foisons: abundant supplies

In the division of each several crime,
Acting in many ways. Nay, had I power, I should
Pour the sweet milk of concord into hell,
Uproar the universal peace, confound
All unity on earth.

MACDUFF.   O Scotland, Scotland!   100

MALCOLM. If such a one be fit to govern, speak:
I am as I have spoken.

MACDUFF.   Fit to govern!
No, not to live. O nation miserable!
With an untitled tyrant bloody-scepter'd,
When shalt thou see thy wholesome days again,   105
Since that the truest issue of thy throne
By his own interdiction stands accursed,
And does blaspheme his breed? Thy royal father
Was a most sainted king: the queen that bore thee,
Oftener upon her knees than on her feet,   110
Died every day she lived.[13] Fare thee well!
These evils thou repeat'st upon thyself
Have banish'd me from Scotland. O my breast,
Thy hope ends here!

MALCOLM.   Macduff, this noble passion,
Child of integrity, hath from my soul   115
Wiped the black scruples, reconciled my thoughts
To thy good truth and honor. Devilish Macbeth
By many of these trains [14] hath sought to win me
Into his power; and modest wisdom plucks me
From over-credulous haste: but God above   120
Deal between thee and me! for even now
I put myself to thy direction, and
Unspeak mine own detraction; here abjure
The taints and blames I laid upon myself,
For strangers to my nature. I am yet   125
Unknown to woman, never was forsworn,
Scarcely have coveted what was mine own,
At no time broke my faith, would not betray
The devil to his fellow, and delight

[13] Died . . . lived: Every day she prepared for death by living a holy life.
[14] trains: tricks

No less in truth than life: my first false speaking   130
Was this upon myself: what I am truly,
Is thine and my poor country's to command:
Whither indeed, before thy here-approach,
Old Siward, with ten thousand warlike men,
Already at a point,[15] was setting forth.   135
Now we'll together, and the chance of goodness
Be like our warranted quarrel! Why are you silent?

MACDUFF. Such welcome and unwelcome things at once
'Tis hard to reconcile.
    (*Enter a* DOCTOR.)

MALCOLM. Well, more anon. Comes the king forth, I pray   140
    you?

DOCTOR. Aye, sir; there are a crew of wretched souls
    That stay his cure: [16] their malady convinces
    The great assay of art; but at his touch,
    Such sanctity hath heaven given his hand,   145
    They presently amend.

MALCOLM.   I thank you, doctor.   (*Exit* DOCTOR.)

MACDUFF. What's the disease he means?

MALCOLM.   'Tis call'd the evil:
    A most miraculous work in this good king;
    Which often, since my here-remain in England,
    I have seen him do. How he solicits heaven,   150
    Himself best knows: but strangely-visited [17] people,
    All swoln and ulcerous, pitiful to the eye,
    The mere despair of surgery, he cures,
    Hanging a golden stamp [18] about their necks,
    Put on with holy prayers: and 'tis spoken,   155
    To the succeeding royalty he leaves
    The healing benediction. With this strange virtue
    He hath a heavenly gift of prophecy,
    And sundry blessings hang about his throne
    That speak him full of grace.
        (*Enter* ROSS.)

[15] **at a point:** ready and armed
[16] **stay his cure:** await his healing power
[17] **strangely visited:** strangely afflicted
[18] **golden stamp:** golden medal

MACDUFF.   See, who comes here?   160

MALCOLM. My countryman; but yet I know him not.

MACDUFF. My ever gentle cousin, welcome hither.

MALCOLM. I know him now: good God, betimes [19] remove
   The means that makes us strangers!

ROSS.   Sir, amen.

MACDUFF. Stands Scotland where it did?

ROSS.   Alas, poor country!   165
   Almost afraid to know itself! It cannot
   Be call'd our mother, but our grave: where nothing,
   But who knows nothing, is once seen to smile;
   Where sighs and groans and shrieks that rend the air,
   Are made, not mark'd; where violent sorrow seems   170
   A modern ecstasy: the dead man's knell
   Is there scarce ask'd for who; and good men's lives
   Expire before the flowers in their caps,
   Dying or ere they sicken.

MACDUFF.   O, relation
   Too nice, and yet too true!

MALCOLM.   What's the newest grief?   175

ROSS. That of an hour's age doth hiss the speaker; [20]
   Each minute teems [21] a new one.

MACDUFF.   How does my wife?

ROSS. Why, well.

MACDUFF.   And all my children?

ROSS.   Well too.

MACDUFF. The tyrant has not batter'd at their peace?

ROSS. No; they were well at peace when I did leave 'em.   180

MACDUFF. Be not a niggard of your speech: [22] how goes 't?

ROSS. When I came hither to transport the tidings,
   Which I have heavily borne, there ran a rumor
   Of many worthy fellows that were out; [23]
   Which was to my belief witness'd the rather,   185
   For that I saw the tyrant's power a-foot:
   Now is the time of help; your eye in Scotland

[19] **betimes:** soon
[20] **hiss the speaker:** because his news is old
[21] **teems:** brings forth
[22] **Be . . . speech:** Do not spare your words.
[23] **out:** in rebellion

Would create soldiers, make our women fight,
To doff [24] their dire distresses.

MALCOLM.   Be 't their comfort
We are coming thither: gracious England hath   190
Lent us good Siward and ten thousand men;
And older and a better soldier none
That Christendom gives out.

ROSS.   Would I could answer
This comfort with the like! But I have words
That would be howl'd out in the desert air,   195
Where hearing should not latch them.

MACDUFF.   What concern they?
The general cause? or is it a fee-grief [25]
Due to some single breast?

ROSS.   No mind that's honest
But in it shares some woe, though the main part
Pertains to you alone.

MACDUFF.   If it be mine,   200
Keep it not from me, quickly let me have it.

ROSS. Let not your ears despise my tongue for ever,
Which shall possess them with the heaviest sound
That ever yet they heard.

MACDUFF.   Hum! I guess at it.

ROSS. Your castle is surprised; your wife and babes   205
Savagely slaughter'd: to relate the manner,
Were, on the quarry [26] of these murder'd deer,
To add the death of you.

MALCOLM.   Merciful heaven!
What, man! ne'er pull your hat upon your brows;
Give sorrow words: the grief that does not speak   210
Whispers the o'erfraught heart, and bids it break.

MACDUFF. My children too?

ROSS.   Wife, children, servants, all
That could be found.

MACDUFF.   And I must be from thence!
My wife kill'd too?

[24] doff: throw off
[25] fee-grief: private sorrow
[26] quarry: slaughtered bodies

ROSS.   I have said.

MALCOLM.   Be comforted:
   Let's make us medicines of our great revenge,   215
   To cure this deadly grief.

MACDUFF. He has no children. All my pretty ones?
   Did you say all? O hell-kite! ²⁷ All?
   What, all my pretty chickens and their dam
   At one fell swoop?   220

MALCOLM. Dispute it ²⁸ like a man.

MACDUFF.   I shall do so;
   But I must also feel it as a man:
   I cannot but remember such things were,
   That were most precious to me. Did heaven look on,
   And would not take their part? Sinful Macduff,   225
   They were all struck for thee! naught that I am,
   Not for their own demerits, but for mine,
   Fell slaughter on their souls: heaven rest them now!

MALCOLM. Be this the whetstone ²⁹ of your sword: let grief
   Convert to anger; blunt not the heart, enrage it.   230

MACDUFF. O, I could play the woman with mine eyes,
   And braggart with my tongue! But, gentle heavens,
   Cut short all intermission; front to front
   Bring thou this fiend of Scotland and myself;
   Within my sword's length set him; if he 'scape,   235
   Heaven forgive him too!

MALCOLM.   This tune goes manly.
   Come, go we to the king; our power ³⁰ is ready;
   Our lack is nothing but our leave.³¹ Macbeth
   Is ripe for shaking, and the powers above
   Put on their instruments. Receive what cheer you may;   240
   The night is long that never finds the day.   (*Exeunt.*)

²⁷ **hell-kite:** hellish bird of prey
²⁸ **dispute it:** resist it
²⁹ **whetstone:** stone used to sharpen daggers
³⁰ **power:** forces
³¹ **Our lack . . . leave:** Nothing remains but to say farewell to the king.

ACT V

SCENE 1—DUNSINANE. *Ante-room in the castle.*

(*Enter a* DOCTOR OF PHYSIC *and a* WAITING-GENTLEWOMAN.)

DOCTOR. I have two nights watched with you, but can perceive no truth in your report. When was it she last walked?

GENTLEWOMAN. Since his majesty went into the field,[1] I have seen her rise from her bed, throw her nightgown upon her, unlock her closet, take forth paper, fold it, write upon 't, read it, afterwards seal it, and again return to bed; yet all this while in a most fast sleep.

DOCTOR. A great perturbation in nature, to receive at once the benefit of sleep and do the effects of watching! In this slumbery agitation, besides her walking and other actual performances, what, at any time, have you heard her say?

GENTLEWOMAN. That sir, which I will not report after her.

DOCTOR. You may to me, and 'tis most meet you should.

GENTLEWOMAN. Neither to you nor any one, having no witness to confirm my speech.

(*Enter* LADY MACBETH, *with a taper.*)

Lo you, here she comes! This is her very guise, and, upon my life, fast asleep. Observe her; stand close.

DOCTOR. How come she by that light?

GENTLEWOMAN. Why, it stood by her: she has light by her continually; 'tis her command.

DOCTOR. You see, her eyes are open.

GENTLEWOMAN. Aye, but their sense is shut.

DOCTOR. What is it she does now? Look, how she rubs her hands.

GENTLEWOMAN. It is an accustomed action with her, to seem thus washing her hands: I have known her continue in this a quarter of an hour.

LADY MACBETH. Yet here's a spot.

DOCTOR. Hark! she speaks: I will set down what comes from her, to satisfy [2] my remembrance the more strongly.

Scene 1:
[1] field: led his army into the field of battle
[2] to satisfy: reinforce, confirm

LADY MACBETH. Out, damned spot! out, I say! One: two: why, then 'tis time to do 't. Hell is murky. Fie, my lord, fie! a soldier, and afeard? What need we fear who knows it, when none can call our power to account? Yet who would have thought the old man to have had so much blood in him? [3]

DOCTOR. Do you mark that?

LADY MACBETH. The thane of Fife had a wife; where is she now? What, will these hands ne'er be clean? No more o' that, my lord, no more o' that: you mar all with this starting.

DOCTOR. Go to, go to; [4] you have known what you should not.

GENTLEWOMAN. She has spoke what she should not, I am sure of that: heaven knows what she has known.

LADY MACBETH. Here's the smell of the blood still: all the perfumes of Arabia will not sweeten this little hand. Oh, oh, oh!

DOCTOR. What a sigh is there! the heart is sorely charged.

GENTLEWOMAN. I would not have such a heart in my bosom for the dignity of the whole body.

DOCTOR. Well, well, well,—

GENTLEWOMAN. Pray God it be, sir.

DOCTOR. This disease is beyond my practice: yet I have known those which have walked in their sleep who have died holily in their beds.

LADY MACBETH. Wash your hands; put on your nightgown; look not so pale: I tell you yet again, Banquo's buried; he cannot come out on 's grave.

DOCTOR. Even so?

LADY MACBETH. To bed, to bed; there's knocking at the gate: come, come, come, come, give me your hand: what's done cannot be un-done: to bed, to bed, to bed.   (*Exit.*)

DOCTOR. Will she go now to bed?

GENTLEWOMAN. Directly.

DOCTOR. Foul whisperings are abroad: unnatural deeds
    Do breed unnatural troubles: infected minds
    To their deaf pillows will discharge their secrets:
    More needs she the divine than the physician
    God, God forgive us all! Look after her;   5
    Remove from her the means of all annoyance,
    And still keep eyes upon her. So good night:

[3] **Yet . . . him:** refers to Duncan
[4] **go to:** go away

My mind she has mated [5] and amazed my sight:
I think, but dare not speak.

GENTLEWOMAN.   Good night, good doctor.   (*Exeunt.*)   10

SCENE 2—*The country near* DUNSINANE.

(*Drum and colors. Enter* MENTEITH, CAITHNESS, ANGUS, LENNOX,
    and SOLDIERS.)

MENTEITH. The English power is near, led on by Malcolm,
    His uncle Siward and the good Macduff:
    Revenges burn in them; for their dear causes
    Would to the bleeding and the grim alarm
    Excite the mortified man.[1]

ANGUS.   Near Birnam wood   5
    Shall we well meet them; that way are they coming.

CAITHNESS. Who knows if Donalbain be with his brother?

LENNOX. For certain, sir, he is not: I have a file
    Of all the gentry: there is Siward's son,
    And many unrough [2] youths, that even now   10
    Protest their first of manhood.

MENTEITH.   What does the tyrant?

CAITHNESS. Great Dunsinane he strongly fortifies:
    Some say he's mad; others, that lesser hate him,
    Do call it valiant fury: but, for certain,
    He cannot buckle his distemper'd cause   15
    Within the belt of rule.[3]

ANGUS.   Now does he feel
    His secret murders sticking on his hands;
    Now minutely revolts upbraid his faith-breach;
    Those he commands move only in command,
    Nothing in love: now does he feel his title   20
    Hang loose about him, like a giant's robe
    Upon a dwarfish thief.

MENTEITH.   Who then shall blame
    His pester'd senses to recoil and start,

[5] **mated**: bewildered

Scene 2:
[1] **mortified man**: religious, holy man
[2] **unrough**: smooth-faced, beardless
[3] **belt of rule**: make his plans go right

When all that is within him does condemn
Itself for being there?

CAITHNESS.   Well, march we on,   25
  To give obedience where 'tis truly owed:
  Meet we the medicine of the sickly weal,[4]
  And with him pour we, in our country's purge,
  Each drop of us.   (*Exeunt, marching.*)

LENNOX.   Or so much as it needs
  To dew the sovereign flower and drown the weeds.   30
  Make we our march towards Birnam.

SCENE 3—DUNSINANE. *A room in the castle.*

(*Enter* MACBETH, DOCTOR, *and* ATTENDANTS.)

MACBETH. Bring me no more reports; let them fly all:
  Till Birnam wood remove to Dunsinane
  I cannot taint with fear. What's the boy Malcolm?
  Was he not born of woman? The spirits that know
  All mortal consequences [1] have pronounced me thus: 5
  'Fear not, Macbeth; no man that's born of woman
  Shall e'er have power upon thee.' Then fly, false thanes,
  And mingle with the English epicures: [2]
  The mind I sway by and the heart I bear
  Shall never sag with doubt nor shake with fear.   10
    (*Enter a* SERVANT.)
  The devil damn thee black, thou cream-faced loon! [3]
  Where got'st thou that goose look?

SERVANT. There is ten thousand—

MACBETH.   Geese, villain?

SERVANT.   Soldiers, sir.

MACBETH. Go prick [4] thy face and over-red thy fear,
  Thou lily-liver'd boy.[5] What soldiers, patch! [6]   15

[4] medicine . . . weal: Malcolm can cure Scotland

Scene 3:
[1] **mortal consequences:** future events in human life
[2] **epicures:** people who live luxuriously
[3] **cream-faced loon:** sick, pale fool
[4] **prick:** so as to make red
[5] **lily-livered:** cowardly
[6] **patch:** fool

Death of my soul! those linen cheeks of thine
Are counselors to fear. What soldiers, whey-face!
SERVANT. The English force, so please you.
MACBETH. Take thy face hence.   (*Exit* SERVANT.)
    Seyton!—I am sick at heart,   20
    When I behold—Seyton, I say!—This push
    Will cheer me ever, or disseat me now.
    I have lived long enough: my way of life
    Is fall'n into the sear, the yellow leaf,
    And that which should accompany old age,   25
    As honor, love, obedience, troops of friends,
    I must not look to have; but, in their stead,
    Curses, not loud but deep, mouth-honor, breath,
    Which the poor heart would fain deny, and dare not.
    Seyton!   30
      (*Enter* SEYTON.)
SEYTON. What's your gracious pleasure?
MACBETH.   What news more?
SEYTON. All is confirm'd, my lord, which was reported.
MACBETH. I'll fight, till from my bones my flesh be hacked.
    Give me my armor.
SEYTON.   'Tis not needed yet.
MACBETH. I'll put it on.   35
    Send out moe [7] horses, skirr [8] the country round;
    Hang those that talk of fear. Give me mine armor.
    How does your patient, doctor?
DOCTOR.   Not so sick, my lord,
    As she is troubled with thick-coming fancies,
    That keep her from her rest.
MACBETH.   Cure her of that.   40
    Canst thou not minister to a mind diseased,
    Pluck from the memory a rooted sorrow,
    Raze out the written troubles of the brain,
    And with some sweet oblivious antidote
    Cleanse the stuff'd bosom of that perilous stuff   45
    Which weighs upon the heart?
DOCTOR.   Therein the patient

[7] moe: more
[8] skirr: scour

Must minister to himself.

MACBETH. Throw physic [9] to the dogs, I'll none of it.
Come, put mine armor on; give me my staff.
Seyton, send out. Doctor, the thanes fly from me.   50
Come, sir, dispatch. If thou couldst, doctor, cast
The water of my land, find her disease
And purge it to a sound and pristine health,
I would applaud thee to the very echo,
That should applaud again. Pull 't off,[10] I say.   55
What rhubarb, senna, or what purgative drug,
Would scour these English hence? Hear'st thou of them?

DOCTOR. Aye, my good lord; your royal preparation
Makes us hear something.

MACBETH.   Bring it after me.[11]
I will not be afraid of death and bane   60
Till Birnam forest come to Dunsinane.

DOCTOR. (*Aside*) Where I from Dunsinane away and clear,
Profit again should hardly draw me here.   (*Exeunt.*)

SCENE 4—*Country near* BIRNAM *wood.*

(*Drum and colors. Enter* MALCOLM, *old* SIWARD *and his* SON,
MACDUFF, MENTEITH, CAITHNESS, ANGUS, LENNOX, ROSS, *and*
SOLDIERS, *marching.*)

MALCOLM. Cousins, I hope the days are near at hand
That chambers will be safe.

MENTEITH.   We doubt it nothing.

SIWARD. What wood is this before us?

MENTEITH.   The wood of Birnam.

MALCOLM. Let every soldier hew him down a bough,
And bear 't before him: thereby shall we shadow [1]   5
The numbers of our host, and make discovery
Err in report of us.

SOLDIERS.   It shall be done.

[9] physic: medicine and the medical profession
[10] pull 't off: Macbeth tells his armor-bearer to take off his armor even though
he has just put it on.
[11] Bring it after me: the armor

Scene 4:
[1] shadow: disguise

SIWARD. We learn no other but the confident tyrant
    Keeps still in Dunsinane, and will endure
    Our setting down before 't.
MALCOLM.   'Tis his main hope: 10
    For where there is advantage to be given,
    Both more and less ² have given him the revolt,
    And none serve with him but constrained things
    Whose hearts are absent too.
MACDUFF.   Let our just censures
    Attend the true event, and put we on   15
    Industrious soldiership.
SIWARD.   The time approaches,
    That will with due decision make us know
    What we shall say we have and what we owe.
    Thoughts speculative their unsure hopes relate,
    But certain issue strokes must arbitrate.   20
    Towards which advance the war.   (*Exeunt, marching.*)

SCENE 5—DUNSINANE. *Within the castle.*

(*Enter* MACBETH, SEYTON, *and* SOLDIERS, *with drum and colors.*)
MACBETH. Hang out our banners on the outward walls;
    The cry is still 'They come'! Our castle's strength
    Will laugh a siege to scorn: here let them lie
    Till famine and the ague eat them up:
    Were they not forced ¹ with those that should be ours,   5
    We might have met them dareful, beard to beard,
    And beat them backward home.   (*A cry of women within.*)
                  What is that noise?
SEYTON. It is the cry of women, my good lord.   (*Exit.*)
MACBETH. I have almost forgot the taste of fears:
    The time has been, my senses would have cool'd   10
    To hear a night-shriek, and my fell of hair ²
    Would at a dismal treatise rouse and stir
    As life were in 't: I have supp'd full with horrors;

---

² **more and less:** both nobles and commoners

Scene 5:
¹ **forced:** reinforced
² **fell of hair:** scalp

Direness,[3] familiar to my slaughterous thoughts,
Cannot once start me.
  (*Re-enter* SEYTON.)

                Wherefore was that cry? 15
SEYTON. The queen, my lord, is dead.
MACBETH. She should have died hereafter;[4]
  There would have been a time for such a word.
  To-morrow, and to-morrow, and to-morrow,
  Creeps in this petty pace from day to day,
  To the last syllable of recorded time;[5] 20
  And all our yesterdays have lighted fools
  The way to dusty death. Out, out, brief candle!
  Life's but a walking shadow, a poor player
  That struts and frets his hour upon the stage 25
  And then is heard no more: it is a tale
  Told by an idiot, full of sound and fury,
  Signifying nothing.
    (*Enter a* MESSENGER.)
  Thou comest to use thy tongue; thy story quickly.
MESSENGER. Gracious my lord, 30
  I should report that which I say I saw,
  But know not how to do it.
MACBETH.   Well, say, sir.
MESSENGER. As I did stand my watch upon the hill,
  I look'd toward Birnam, and anon, methought,
  The wood began to move.
MACBETH.   Liar and slave! 35
MESSENGER. Let me endure your wrath, if 't be not so:
  Within this three mile may you see it coming;
  I say, a moving grove.
MACBETH.   If thou speak'st false,
  Upon the next tree shalt thou hang alive,
  Till famine cling[6] thee: if thy speech be sooth, 40
  I care not if thou dost for me as much.
  I pull in resolution, and begin

[3] direness: horror
[4] She . . . hereafter: She would have had to die some day.
[5] recorded time: time as opposed to eternity
[6] cling: waste away your skin till it clings to your bones

To doubt the equivocation of the fiend
That lies like truth: 'Fear not, till Birnam wood
Do come to Dunsinane!' and now a wood   45
Comes toward Dunsinane. Arm, arm, and out!
If this which he avouches does appear,
There is nor flying hence nor tarrying here.
I 'gin to be a-weary of the sun,
And wish the estate o' the world were now undone.   50
Ring the alarum-bell! Blow, wind! come, wrack!
At least we'll die with harness [7] on our back.   (*Exeunt.*)

SCENE 6—DUNSINANE. *Before the castle.*

(*Drum and colors. Enter* MALCOLM, *old* SIWARD, MACDUFF, *and
    their Army, with boughs.*)

MALCOLM. Now near enough; your leavy screens throw down,
    And show like those you are. You, worthy uncle,
    Shall, with my cousin, your right noble son,
    Lead our first battle: worthy Macduff and we
    Shall take upon 's what else remains to do,   5
    According to our order.
SIWARD.   Fare you well.
    Do we [1] but find the tyrant's power to-night,
    Let us be beaten, if we cannot fight.
MACDUFF. Make all our trumpets speak; give them all breath,
    Those clamorous harbingers of blood and death.   (*Exeunt.*) 10

SCENE 7—*Another part of the field.*

(*Alarums. Enter* MACBETH.)

MACBETH. They have tied me to a stake; [1] I cannot fly,
    But bear-like I must fight the course.[2] What's he
    That was not born of a woman? Such a one

---

[7] harness: armor

Scene 6:
[1] do we: if we do

Scene 7:
[1] stake: like a bear in the bear-pit
[2] course: the running at the bear by the dogs

Am I to fear, or none.

 (*Enter young* SIWARD.)

YOUNG SIWARD. What is thy name?

MACBETH.   Thou 'lt be afraid to hear it.   5

YOUNG SIWARD. No; though thou call'st thyself a hotter name
  Than any is in hell.

MACBETH.   My name's Macbeth.

YOUNG SIWARD. The devil himself could not pronounce a title
  More hateful to mine ear.

MACBETH.   No, nor more fearful.

YOUNG SIWARD. Thou liest, abhorred tyrant; with my sword   10
  I'll prove the lie thou speak'st.

       (*They fight, and young* SIWARD *is slain.*)

MACBETH.   Thou wast born of woman,
  But swords I smile at, weapons laugh to scorn,
  Brandish'd by man that's of a woman born.   (*Exit.*)

 (*Alarums. Enter* MACDUFF.)

MACDUFF. That way the noise is. Tyrant, show thy face!
  If thou be'st slain and with no stroke of mine,   15
  My wife and children's ghosts will haunt me still.[3]
  I cannot strike at wretched kerns,[4] whose arms
  Are hired to bear their staves: either thou, Macbeth,
  Or else my sword, with an unbatter'd edge,
  I sheathe again undeeded. There thou shouldst be;   20
  By this greater clatter, one of greatest note
  Seems bruited:[5] let me find him, fortune!
  And more I beg not.   (*Exit. Alarums.*)

 (*Enter* MALCOLM *and old* SIWARD.)

SIWARD. This way, my lord; the castle's gently render'd:
  The tyrant's people on both sides do fight;   25
  The noble thanes do bravely in the war;
  The day almost itself professes yours,
  And little is to do.

MALCOLM.   We have met with foes
  That strike beside us.

SIWARD.   Enter, sir, the castle.   (*Exit. Alarum.*)

[3] still: forever
[4] kerns: mercenary soldiers
[5] bruited: reported

SCENE 8—*Another part of the field.*

(*Enter* MACBETH.)

MABCETH. Why should I play the Roman fool,[1] and die
  On mine own sword? whiles I see lives, the gashes
  Do better upon them.

  (*Enter* MACDUFF.)

MACDUFF.   Turn, hell-hound, turn!

MACBETH. Of all men else I have avoided thee:
  But get thee back; my soul is too much charged [2]   5
  With blood of thine already.

MACDUFF.   I have no words:
  My voice is in my sword, thou bloodier villain
  Then terms can give thee out!   (*They fight.*)

MACBETH.   Thou losest labor:
  As easy mayst thou the intrenchant [3] air
  With thy keen sword impress as make me bleed: 10
  Let fall thy blade on vulnerable crests;
  I bear a charmed life, which must not yield
  To one of woman born.

MACDUFF.   Despair thy charm,
  And let the angel whom thou still hast served
  Tell thee, Macduff was from his mother's womb   15
  Untimely ripp'd.

MACBETH. Accursed be that tongue that tells me so,
  For it hath cow'd my better part of man!
  And be these juggling fiends [4] no more believed,
  That palter [5] with us in a double sense;   20
  That keep the word of promise to our ear,
  And break it to our hope. I'll not fight with thee.

MACDUFF. Then yield thee, coward,
  And live to be the show and gaze o' the time:
  We'll have thee, as our rarer monsters are,   25

Scene 8:
[1] play . . . fool: commit suicide like Brutus in *Julius Caesar*
[2] charged: loaded
[3] intrenchant: that cannot be gashed or wounded
[4] juggling fiends: the witches
[5] palter: deal dishonestly

Painted upon a pole,[6] and underwrit,
'Here may you see the tyrant.'
MACBETH.   I will not yield,
 To kiss the ground before young Malcolm's feet,
 And to be baited with the rabble's curse.
 Though Birnam wood be come to Dunsinane,   30
 And thou opposed, being of no woman born,
 Yet I will try the last: before my body
 I throw my warlike shield: lay on,[7] Macduff;
 And damn'd be him that first cries 'Hold enough!'
        (*Exeunt, fighting. Alarums.*)
 (*Retreat. Flourish. Enter, with drum and colors,* MALCOLM, *old*
  SIWARD, ROSS, *the other* THANES, *and* SOLDIERS.)
MALCOLM. I would the friends we miss were safe arrived. 35
SIWARD. Some must go off: and yet, by these I see,
 So great a day as this is cheaply bought.
MALCOLM. Macduff is missing, and your noble son.
ROSS. Your son, my lord, has paid a soldier's debt: [8]
 He only lived but till he was a man;   40
 The which no sooner had his prowess confirm'd
 In the unshrinking station where he fought,
 But like a man he died.
SIWARD.   Then he is dead?
ROSS. Aye, and brought off the field: your cause of sorrow
 Must not be measured by his worth, for then   45
 It hath no end.
SIWARD.   Had he his hurts before?
ROSS. Aye, on the front.
SIWARD.   Why then, God's soldier be he!
 Had I as many sons as I have hairs,
 I would not wish them to a fairer death:
 And so his knell is knoll'd.[9]
MALCOLM.   He's worth more sorrow, 50
 And that I'll spend for him.
SIWARD.   He's worth no more:

---

[6] painted . . . pole: your picture painted and placed on a pole at the fair
[7] lay on: strike hard
[8] a soldier's debt: since every soldier takes an oath for the cause
[9] knoll'd: knelled, tolled by the funeral bell

They say he parted well and paid his score:
And so God be with him! Here comes newer comfort.
   (*Re-enter* MACDUFF, *with* MACBETH's *head*.) [10]

MACDUFF. Hail, king! for so thou art: behold, where stands
  The usurper's cursed head: the time is free: 55
  I see thee compass'd with thy kingdom's pearl,
  That speak my salutation in their minds;
  Whose voices I desire aloud with mine:
  Hail, King of Scotland!

ALL.   Hail, King of Scotland!   (*Flourish.*)

MALCOLM. We shall not spend a large expense of time   60
  Before we reckon with your several loves,
  And make us even with you. My thanes and kinsmen,
  Henceforth be earls, the first that ever Scotland
  In such an honor named. What's more to do,
  Which would be planted newly with the time,   65
  As calling home our exiled friends abroad
  That fled the snares of watchful tyranny,
  Producing forth the cruel ministers [11]
  Of this dead butcher and his fiend-like queen,
  Who, as 'tis thought, by self and violent hands   70
  Took off her life; this, and what needful else
  That calls upon us, by the grace of Grace
  We will perform in measure, time and place:
  So thanks to all at once and to each one,
  Whom we invite to see us crown'd at Scone.   75
                      (*Flourish. Exeunt.*)

THE END

[10] with . . . head: probably on a pole or pike
[11] cruel ministers: hunting the agents Macbeth employed to do his murders

For Discussion

ACT I

Scene 1: What value does the spectacular opening of the play have? What atmosphere does it create? What effect does such a scene have on the audience? "Fair is foul, and foul is fair" the Witches say. What do they mean?

Scene 2: This is an expository scene. It is the way in which Shakespeare, the dramatist, tells about the character of Macbeth and the others. What is the political situation of Scotland? Does this situation reflect on Duncan's ability as a ruler? What good characteristics are most noticeable in Macbeth? What is Duncan's attitude toward Macbeth? What honor does he bestow on him?

Scene 3: What popular superstitions about witches are indicated in this scene? Macbeth's first words in line 38 remind us of the Witches in Scene 1. What significance do you see in this? What is Macbeth's first reaction to the prophecies? What is the dramatic significance of Ross's message in lines 104–106? Contrast Banquo's reaction to the prophecies with Macbeth's. What does this tell us about their respective characters? Macbeth's speech in lines 130–142 gives us a clue to part of his tragic flaw. What is this clue?

Scene 4: What effect does Malcolm's appointment have on Macbeth? Has Duncan acted in accord with Scottish law and custom? Macbeth's speech in lines 48–53 is most important. Has he decided to murder Duncan? Give reasons from the text for your answers.

Scene 5: Lady Macbeth possesses a quality that her husband lacks. What is it? Does Lady Macbeth plan the murder? What advice does she give her husband? Is there a genuine love between Macbeth and his wife? Is the murder firmly decided on in this scene? Give reasons for your answer.

Scene 6: What is ironic about Duncan's first words in this scene? Does Lady Macbeth's welcoming speech in lines 14–19 seem too effusive? What opportunity does Duncan's visit provide?

Scene 7: Macbeth's internal conflict is summed up in his soliloquy in lines 1–28. What motives does Macbeth offer for not killing Duncan? What very important motive does Macbeth fail to mention? What effect does Lady Macbeth's arguments have? The dramatic climax of Act I is reached in Macbeth's last speech of Scene 7. What safe plan for the murder does Lady Macbeth offer? Why must Macbeth make up his mind quickly?

ACT II

Scene 1: How is suspense created in this scene? What factors make it "a perfect night for murder"? What does Banquo mean in lines 7–9? Duncan's last act toward Lady Macbeth creates pathos. How? Macbeth's soliloquy reveals his state of conscience. What are his fears now? Why does the vision of the dagger so disturb Macbeth?

Scene 2: How is Lady Macbeth true to her character? What little note of feminine pity is noticeable in her speech in lines 9–13? How does the suspense build up in this scene? What effect is achieved by having the murder performed off-stage? What are the immediate effects of the murder on Macbeth? Are both Macbeth and his wife guilty of the crime? "A little water clears us of this deed" says Lady Macbeth. Does she really think so? What effect does the knocking at the gate produce?

Scene 3: How is relief provided by the drunken porter? Why is such relief necessary at this point? What does Lennox's speech in lines 35–42 mean? What advantage is there for Macbeth to kill the grooms? Is Lady Macbeth's fainting genuine? Why? Why do Malcolm and Donalbain flee? What advantage is there for them to flee separately?

Scene 4: In this scene we see Scotland's and nature's reactions to the crime. What do all these unnatural sights signify? Who are suspected of the murder? Is there any dramatic significance in Macduff's refusal to see Macbeth crowned? What does the old man mean in the last two lines of this scene?

ACT III

Scene 1: Is Banquo suspicious of Macbeth? What three important questions does Macbeth ask of Banquo? Why is Macbeth intent on murdering Banquo? Contrast the Macbeth of this scene with the Macbeth of Scenes 6 and 7 in Act I. What has Macbeth gained which he lacked in the first two acts of the play? What is the meaning of Macbeth's soliloquy in lines 46–71? What motive does Macbeth give the murderers? What reasons has Macbeth for not killing Banquo?

Scene 2: What seems to be Lady Macbeth's state of mind in lines 4–7? Is Macbeth suffering remorse in lines 19–25? Does Lady Macbeth know of the plans for Banquo's murder? What does this fact tell us about the change in the character of Macbeth? Is Lady Macbeth beginning to play a minor role in the plans of her husband?

Scene 3: Who is the third murderer? Tell why he has been added to the victims? Why is this scene the climax or pivotal point in the play? Why is the failure to kill Fleance a great setback for Macbeth?

Scene 4: What is Macbeth's reaction to the murderers' report? Explain the irony in lines 40–43. Is the ghost of Banquo a product of Macbeth's imagination or is it a real ghost? How does Lady Macbeth try to explain her husband's fit? How does she try to soothe her husband's fears? Explain the irony in lines 89–92. Why does Lady Macbeth cut off any answer to Lennox's question in line 116? What does Macduff's absence from the feast signify to Macbeth? Explain what Macbeth means in lines 142–144. "There's not a one of them but in his house/I keep a servant fee'd," gives us an insight into Macbeth's form of government. What does it indicate about the political atmosphere of Scotland?

Scene 5: Who is Hecate? What does she promise she'll do to Macbeth? What purpose does this scene serve? Many critics feel that this scene was not written by Shakespeare. What reasons do you think they offer for their opinion?

Scene 6: Lennox says that Fleance killed Banquo "for Fleance fled." What is the tone of his remark? Where is Macduff? What seems to be the mood of Scotland at this time? What troubles does Macbeth have to face now?

ACT IV

Scene 1: What is the atmosphere created in this scene? Instead of the apparitions throwing fear into Macbeth, what effect do they have on him? What does the first apparition represent? The "bloody child" most likely represents Macduff. Why? What does the third apparition represent? What two prophecies does Macbeth put all his confidence in? How does this add to the suspense? The eight kings represent the Stuart kings of Scotland. To what character in the play are they supposedly related? "From this moment the very firstlings of my heart shall be the firstlings of my hand" says Macbeth. What does he mean?

Scene 2: What does the ruthless murder of Lady Macduff tell us about the character of Macbeth? How is pathos created in this scene? Is the conversation between Lady Macduff and her son "natural"?

Scene 3: What purposes does this scene serve? Contrast this scene in England with the previous one in Scotland. Who have joined forces against Macbeth? Why does Malcolm appear to be testing Macduff? What purpose is served by the passage concerning the King's healing powers (lines 140–160)? What effect does the news of the murder of his wife and children have on Macduff? What does Macduff mean when he says "he has no children"? Whom does he mean? Enumerate the preparations that are being made to overthrow Macbeth. What precise events show that Macbeth's fortunes are falling?

ACT V

Scene 1: Why do the Doctor and Gentlewoman speak in prose? What other characters in the play have used prose? Contrast Lady Macbeth in this scene with Lady Macbeth in Act I, Scene 7. To what specific incidents does Lady Macbeth refer in her sleep-walking monologue? What does the Doctor think is the cause of her malady?

Scene 2: What effect does this short scene produce? What Scottish Lords have deserted Macbeth? What do they tell you about Macbeth's reign in Scotland? Who is "the medicine of the sickly weal"? What prophecy does the last line of this scene remind one of?

Scene 3: What seems to be Macbeth's attitude toward the Witches' prophecies? Point out all the words that Macbeth uses to show the fear of the servant. Is Macbeth suffering remorse? What signs of desperate valor do you find in Macbeth's words? What is Macbeth's attitude toward his sick wife? Is he more worried about Lady Macbeth or the invaders? What does this show about his character now?

Scene 4: The rebel forces are now fully united. What prophecy seems about to be fulfilled? What effect do these short scenes produce? Do they increase the action or slow it down? Explain.

Scene 5: Analyze Macbeth's speech in lines 9–15. What does he mean? What changes have come over him? Macbeth's speech, which begins "She should have died hereafter . . ." is one of the finest in the play. What emotion does it portray? Why is Macbeth so upset by the messenger's news? What does he think of the Witches now?

Scene 6: Battle orders are given before Dunsinane Castle. Who are the three rebel leaders?

Scene 7: Action is the key to battle. How is this true in this scene and the following one? What seems to be on Macbeth's mind as he battles young Seward? How is suspense created in this scene? How did the castle go over to the rebels? What does this tell about the political state of Scotland?

Scene 8: What motive prevents Macbeth from committing suicide? What surprise does Macduff have for Macbeth? Who are the "juggling fiends" in line 19? What is Macbeth's state of mind in lines 27–34? What is Seward's emotion in lines 47–50 and 51–53? Where is Macbeth killed? What effect does this have on the audience? How did Lady Macbeth die? The resolution (denouement) of the plot is achieved when we know the outcome of the play. What is the resolution of this play? How does Shakespeare prepare us for this solution? Do you think this is a fitting end for Macbeth? Explain. In a few lines, the scene of bloodshed, death, and horror is changed to one of peace and hope. Show how Shakespeare achieves this quick end. Reread the introductory remarks on *Macbeth* (pages 4–5), and show how they apply to the main character.

Reviewing the Play as a Whole

1. Each play has an atmosphere of its own. This is especially true in *Macbeth*. Show how *darkness* broods over the whole play. When the darkness of the play is relieved, it has the color of *blood*. Cite five examples of this. As a drama, *Macbeth* is full of storm and tumult. All of these details create a sense of evil which pervades the play. Explain how this is true.

2. *Irony* is a dramatic device in which a character uses words which have an ominous meaning for the audience, but which is hidden

from the speaker. *Macbeth* is filled with such ironies. Choose five and explain the added ominous meaning that the audience perceives.

3. The Witches in *Macbeth* have long been a cause of disagreement among scholars. If they are described as the goddesses of destiny, they seem to overpower Macbeth and leave him powerless to resist. Why would this explanation of the Witches damage the play? If they are only representations of Macbeth's unconscious guilt or imagination, it is hard to see what real influence they could have on Macbeth. Because of the history of Elizabethan drama and Shakespeare's sense as a dramatist, both of these interpretations leave something to be desired. Read A. C. Bradley's *Shakespearean Tragedy* (pages 271–277) for a balanced view on the Witches. Give a short report to the class on Bradley's viewpoint.

4. Ambition is Macbeth's tragic fault. Show how this is true. Lady Macbeth's fault is the same. Their ambitions are not separate but support one another. Write a short paper showing how their ambition leads to their ruin.

5. Macbeth has the imagination of a poet. When his imagination is active, we experience horror and suspense. But when his imagination "returns to normal," he becomes domineering and even brutal. Select two examples from the play which show this to be true.

6. Lady Macbeth knows her husband very well. She loves him dearly and supplements his character quite well. Give three instances in which this is true. What makes Lady Macbeth such a powerful character?

7. In the second half of the play, Lady Macbeth's influence disappears. She begins to evoke our pity. Why?

8. Banquo is an interesting character. Would you say he is completely innocent? Could he be interpreted as an ambitious character who is waiting for his chance?

9. The play leaves on its readers a deep impression of the misery of a guilty conscience and the retribution of a crime. Is this your impression? Discuss.

10. Much has been written about the "porter's scene" (Act II, Scene 3). Do you think it is necessary to the play? What purpose do you think Shakespeare had in including it?

11. Make a diagram of the action of the play. Show where the rising action begins, where the climax occurs, and where the resolution is completed.

12. Read Dryden's *An Essay of Dramatic Poesy* (pages 194–196). Do you agree with his ideas on Shakespeare?

THE SONNET

Types of Sonnets

Man is a creature of order. The poet is no exception, he is governed by *form* in his work. Besides ordering his material internally by selecting definite images and ideas, the poet also imposes an external form on his verse. One of the most famous of these is the *sonnet* form.

The sonnet originated in Italy where Petrarch told of his love for the beautiful Laura in a series of intricate fourteen-line poems. Sir Thomas Wyatt brought the sonnet form back to England where it soon became extremely popular.

As a type of lyric poetry, the sonnet must be fourteen lines in length, written in iambic pentameter, with a set structure and rhyme scheme. Two types of sonnet form are found in English poetry: the Italian and the English.

The *Italian* or Petrarchean sonnet is composed of eight lines called the *octave*, using the rhyme scheme *abba, abba,* and six lines called the *sestet*, using the rhyme arrangement of either *cd, cd, cd,* or *cde, cde*. In the Italian sonnet there is a division of thought, usually marked by the division between the octave and the sestet. The octave presents a situation and the sestet a comment; or the octave presents a question and the sestet a solution; or the octave states an idea and the sestet an example.

The *English* or Shakespearean sonnet is composed of three quatrains and a concluding couplet, rhyming *abab, cdcd, efef, gg*. Here again the thought is developed on two levels. The three quatrains for example, may present a problem and the couplet a solution, or it may present three examples and a conclusion.

The sonnet has proved effective for certain subjects and treatment. Love, death, and religion are constant themes in sonnets.

Sonnets may be grouped in a sequence or presented as single poems. They may present the development of some personal experience or merely tell a story.

86

Shakespeare's Sonnets

In 1609, about ten or fifteen years after they were written, Shakespeare's sonnets were published. Scholars have long speculated on whether these sonnets express some personal experiences or imaginary situations. Of the 154 sonnets written by Shakespeare, many of them are addressed to a young friend; others tell of the charms of a certain "dark lady" who apparently scorned the praises the poet heaped on her.

Shakespeare's sonnets are exceptional for their form and deep feeling. In them we find a remarkable awareness of both the range of human feelings and of the complexity of a single emotion. Shakespeare is keenly conscious of the tragic implications of the temporal nature of man. Many of his sonnets portray love, friendship, and poetry as defenses against the fleetingness of life.

Sonnets

18

Shall I compare thee to a summer's day?
Thou art more lovely and more temperate:
Rough winds do shake the darling buds of May,
And summer's lease hath all too short a date:
Sometime too hot the eye of heaven shines,   5
And often is his gold complexion dimmed;
And every fair from fair [1] sometime declines,
By chance or nature's changing course untrimmed; [2]
But thy eternal summer shall not fade,
Nor lose possession of that fair thou owest; [3]   10
Nor shall Death brag thou wander'st in his shade,
When in eternal lines to time thou growest: [4]
    So long as men can breathe, or eyes can see,
    So long lives this,[5] and this gives life to thee.

[1] **every . . . fair:** every beautiful thing will eventually lose part of its beauty
[2] **untrimmed:** despoiled of its beauty
[3] **owest:** own
[4] **to . . . growest:** your fame will grow with time
[5] **this:** this poem

29

When, in disgrace with fortune and men's eyes,
I all alone beweep my outcast state,
And trouble deaf heaven with my bootless [1] cries
And look upon myself and curse my fate,
Wishing me like to one more rich in hope,   5
Featured like him, like him with friends possessed,
Desiring this man's art and that man's scope,
With what I most enjoy contented least;
Yet in these thoughts myself almost despising,
Haply [2] I think on thee,—and then my state,   10
Like to the lark at break of day arising
From sullen earth, sings hymns at heaven's gate;
    For thy sweet love remembered such wealth brings
    That then I scorn to change my state with kings.

[1] bootless: useless
[2] haply: fortunately

30

When to the sessions [1] of sweet silent thought
I summon up remembrance of things past,
I sigh the lack of many a thing I sought,
And with old woes new wail my dear time's waste:
Then can I drown an eye, unused to flow,   5
For precious friends hid in death's dateless [2] night,
And weep afresh love's long since cancelled woe,
And moan the expense of many a vanished sight:
Then can I grieve at grievances foregone,[3]
And heavily from woe to woe tell o'er   10
The sad account of fore-bemoaned moan,
Which I new pay as if not paid before.
    But if the while I think on thee, dear friend,
    All losses are restored and sorrows end.

[1] sessions: The entire sonnet is cast in a legal metaphor. Notice the use of impersonal words of business and law to make a personal statement.
[2] dateless: in the legal sense, no fixed termination
[3] foregone: of the past

55

Not marble, nor the gilded monuments
Of princes, shall outlive this powerful rhyme
But you shall shine more bright in these contents [1]
Than unswept stone, besmeared with sluttish time.
When wasteful war shall statues overturn,   5
And broils [2] root out the work of masonry,
Nor Mars [3] his sword nor war's quick fire shall burn
The living record of your memory.
'Gainst death and all-oblivious enmity [4]
Shall you pace forth; your praise shall still find room   10
Even in the eyes of all posterity
That wear this world out to the ending doom.
    So, till the judgment that [5] yourself arise,
    You live in this, and dwell in lovers' eyes.

[1] **these contents:** the verses of this sonnet
[2] **broils:** brawls
[3] **Mars:** god of war
[4] **all-oblivious enmity:** war which sends all to oblivion
[5] **till the judgment that:** till the day of Judgment when

65

Since brass, nor stone, nor earth, nor boundless sea,
But sad mortality o'er-sways their power,
How with this rage shall beauty hold a plea,
Whose action is no stronger than a flower?
O, how shall summer's honey breath hold out   5
Against the wreckful siege of battering days,
When rocks impregnable are not so stout,
Nor gates of steel so strong, but Time decays?
O fearful meditation! where, alack,
Shall Time's best jewel [1] from Time's chest lie hid? 10
Or what strong hand can hold his swift foot back?
Or who his spoil of beauty can forbid?
    O, none, unless this miracle have might,
    That in black ink my love may still shine bright.

[1] **Time's best jewel:** beauty

71

No longer mourn for me when I am dead
Then you shall hear the surly sullen bell
Give warning to the world that I am fled
From this vile world, with vilest worms to dwell:
Nay, if you read this line, remember not   5
The hand that writ it; for I love you so,
That I in your sweet thoughts would be forgot
If thinking on me then should make you woe.[1]
O, if, I say, you look upon this verse,
When I perhaps compounded am with clay,   10
Do not so much as my poor name rehearse,
But let your love even with my life decay;
    Lest the wise [2] world should look into your moan
    And mock you with me after I am gone.

[1] woe: sad
[2] wise: ironically, worldly-wise

73

That time of year thou mayst in me behold
When yellow leaves, or none, or few, do hang
Upon those boughs which shake against the cold,
Bare ruined choirs, where late the sweet birds sang.
In me thou see'st the twilight of such day   5
As after sunset fadeth in the west,
Which by and by black night doth take away,
Death's second self, that seals up all in rest.
In me thou see'st the glowing of such fire
That on the ashes of his youth doth lie,   10
As the death-bed whereon it must expire,
Consumed with that which it was nourished by.[1]
    This thou perceivest, which makes thy love more strong,
    To love that well which thou must leave [2] ere long.

[1] consumed . . . nourished by: put out by the ashes of the wood that fed the fire
[2] leave: renounce

104

To me, fair friend, you never can be old,
For as you were when first your eye I eyed,
Such seems your beauty still. Three winters cold
Have from the forests shook three summers' pride,
Three beauteous springs to yellow autumn turned   5
In process of the seasons have I seen,
Three April perfumes in three hot Junes burned
Since first I saw you fresh, which yet are green,
Ah, yet doth beauty, like a dial-hand,
Steal from his figure, and no pace perceived;
So your sweet hue, which methinks still doth stand,   10
Hath motion, and mine eye may be deceived:
    For fear of which, hear this, thou age unbred:
    Ere you were born was beauty's summer dead.

116

Let me not to the marriage of true minds
Admit impediments.[1] Love is not love
Which alters when it alteration finds,
Or bends with the remover to remove.[2]
Oh, no! it is an ever-fixéd mark   5
That looks on tempests and is never shaken;
It is the star to every wandering bark,
Whose worth's unknown, although his height [3] be taken.
Love's not Time's fool,[4] though rosy lips and cheeks
Within his bending sickle's compass come;   10
Love alters not with his brief hours and weeks,
But bears it out even to the edge of doom.
    If this be error and upon me proved,
    I never writ, nor no man ever loved.

[1] **impediments:** obstacles
[2] **Or bends . . . to remove:** or ceases to love because the other has changed
[3] **height:** elevation
[4] **Love's . . . fool:** it does not change because Time makes things change

146

Poor soul, the center of my sinful earth,[1]
Thrall to these rebel powers [2] that thee array,
Why dost thou pine within and suffer dearth,
Painting thy outward walls so costly gay?
Why so large cost, having so short a lease,   5
Dost thou upon thy fading mansions spend?
Shall worms, inheritors of this excess,
Eat up thy charge? Is this thy body's end?
Then, soul, live thou upon thy servant's loss,
And let that pine to aggravate [3] thy store;   10
Buy terms divine [4] in selling hours of dross;
Within be fed, without be rich no more:
    So shalt thou feed on Death,[5] that feeds on men,
    And Death once dead, there's no more dying then.[6]

[1] **earth:** the body
[2] **rebel powers:** the lower appetites of the body
[3] **aggravate:** increase
[4] **terms divine:** eternity
[5] **feed on Death:** consume the mortal elements in yourself
[6] **Death . . . then:** because the mortal man has put on immortality

For Discussion

Sonnet 18

1. Explain why this is a Shakespearean sonnet. What do the three quatrains say? What is expressed in the couplet?
2. Why is Shakespeare's friend "more lovely and more temperate"?
3. How does Shakespeare react to the process of temporal decay in this sonnet?

Sonnet 29

1. Is the twofold division of this sonnet's thought more Italian or Shakespearean in form? Explain.
2. Contrast the mood and tone of the first eight lines with the remaining six.
3. What mood is engendered by the simile in line 11?
4. List the epithets which create the two contrasting moods in this sonnet.

Sonnet 30

1. In this sonnet Shakespeare uses the terminology of law. List the legal terms he uses to develop the analogy.
2. Make a list of the alliterations he uses. What effect does this figure of speech produce?
3. Do the epithets of this sonnet appeal primarily to the senses or to the mind? Explain.
4. Can you find a "conceit" in this sonnet?

Sonnet 55

1. In what way does the person to whom this sonnet is addressed outlive decay?
2. Good poets know that their verses will live when they and the subjects of their lines are long dead. Explain why they feel that literature is immortal.
3. Is Shakespeare more intent on his love or on the power of his verse? Explain your answer.
4. The theme of this sonnet has been expressed by many authors. Do you know of any other poems which state the same theme?

Sonnet 65

1. Compare the theme of this sonnet with Sonnet 55.
2. Why is this a Shakespearean sonnet?
3. List the epithets and images the author uses to describe beauty. Are they suitable? Why?
4. What is "time's best jewel" in line 10?

Sonnet 71

1. What is the theme of this sonnet?
2. Does it fulfill the requirements of the sonnet form mentioned on page 86? Explain.
3. Why does Shakespeare warn his love against mourning for him?
4. Explain "the surly sullen bell" in line 2. Is Shakespeare using irony in line 13 when he speaks of "the wise world"? Explain.

Sonnet 73

1. Shakespeare says he is growing old. He uses three different images to communicate this experience. Explain each figure.
2. In lines 1–4 the branches, choirs, and birds are used to convey the emotion the poet is trying to express. Explain why they are so well suited to his purpose.

3. What does Shakespeare mean by "Death's second self"? What does the poet imply in this comparison?
4. In lines 9–12 the whole experience is brought into final and complete focus with the image of fire. Explain line 12.
5. The couplet draws the conclusion and interprets the meaning of the experience of the poem. Explain.

Sonnet 104

1. Does this sonnet fulfill the requirements of the sonnet form mentioned on page 86? Explain.
2. What is the theme of this poem?
3. Explain the meaning of line 14. Explain the images used in lines 3–8. Do they sharpen the experience the poet is trying to convey? Why?

Sonnet 116

1. What is the theme of this sonnet?
2. In lines 1–4 choose the qualities of love to which Shakespeare is objecting.
3. What effect do lines 9–12 add to the first quatrain? Which quatrain is more vivid?
4. What imagery in lines 5–8 stresses the permanence of love?
5. Elizabeth Drew says that "he (Shakespeare) knows that love does alter and can be removed . . . but he will not *admit* these impediments . . ." Discuss.

Sonnet 146

1. Explain the phrase "my sinful earth" in line 1.
2. List all the epithets that Shakespeare uses to describe the body.
3. Is the solution offered in the sestet or in the couplet? Explain your answer.
4. Explain line 12.
5. Contrast this sonnet with Sonnet 71.

FRANCIS BACON

(1561–1626)

"I have taken all knowledge to be my province" Bacon once wrote to his uncle. This bold statement expresses Bacon's life-long creed. The age of specialization had not yet arrived and, in this age of versatile and well-rounded men, Francis Bacon was a giant.

His life was a long series of political offices and appointments. A lawyer by profession, he was a member of Parliament at the age of 22. In 1596 he was made Queen's counsel, and in 1603 he was knighted by James I. Within the next twelve years he had risen to the supreme position of Lord Chancellor of the Realm.

Bacon's political career, however, was secondary to his literary labors. His major works concerned the reconstruction of all knowledge on the basis of his new scientific method. This ambitious scheme was beyond his power, and he died before he could realize his project. Today Bacon is best remembered for his essays. After almost 400 years, they are still popular because of their organization, verbal economy, and worldly wisdom.

Bacon was the father of the English essay, the first to write his short impressions of men and their daily affairs. In his hands, the essay became a true literary type. His rich imagery, rhythms, and cadences assured the essay a permanent place in the halls of literature.

Of Truth

"What is truth?" said jesting Pilate,[1] and would not stay for an answer. Certainly there be that delight in giddiness,[2] and count it a bondage to fix a belief; affecting free-will in thinking, as well as in acting. And though the sects of philosophers of that kind[3] be gone, yet there remain certain discoursing wits[4] which are of the same veins, though there be not so much blood in them as was in those of

[1] **Pilate:** from Christ's trial before Pilate
[2] **giddiness:** no serious or set opinions
[3] **sects . . . kind:** the Greek Skeptics who denied that certainty was possible
[4] **discoursing wits:** talkative minds

the ancients. But it is not only the difficulty and labor which men
take in finding out of truth, nor again that when it is found it imposeth upon [5] men's thoughts, that doth bring lies in favor; but a
natural though corrupt love of the lie itself. One of the later school
of the Grecians examineth the matter, and is at a stand to think what
should be in it, that men should love lies; where neither they make
for pleasure, as with poets; [6] nor for advantage, as with the merchant; but for the lie's sake. But I cannot tell; this same truth
is a naked and open daylight, that doth not show the masques
and mummeries and triumphs of the world, half so stately and
daintily as candlelights. Truth may perhaps come to the price of
a pearl, that showeth best by day; but it will not rise to the price of a
diamond or carbuncle, that showeth best in varied lights. A mixture
of a lie doth ever add pleasure. Doth any man doubt, that if there
were taken out of men's minds vain opinions, flattering hopes, false
valuations, imaginations as one would, and the like, but it would leave
the minds of a number of men poor shrunken things, full of melancholy and indisposition, and unpleasing to themselves? One of the
Fathers,[7] in great severity, called poesy *vinum daemonum*,[8] because
it filleth the imagination, and yet it is but with the shadow of a lie.
But it is not the lie that passeth through the mind, but the lie that
sinketh in and settleth in it, that doth the hurt, such as we spake of
before. But howsoever these things are thus in men's depraved judgments and affections, yet truth, which only doth judge itself, teacheth
that the inquiry of truth, which is the love-making or wooing of it,
the knowledge of truth, which is the presence of it, and the belief of
truth, which is the enjoying of it, is the sovereign good of human
nature. The first creature of God, in the works of the days, was the
light of the sense; the last was the light of reason; and his sabbath
work, ever since, is the illumination of his Spirit. First he breathed
light upon the face of the matter or chaos; then he breathed light
into the face of man; and still he breatheth and inspireth light into
the face of his chosen. The poet [9] that beautified the sect that was
otherwise inferior to the rest, saith yet excellently well: "It is a
pleasure to stand upon the shore, and to see ships tossed upon the

[5] **imposeth upon**: restrains
[6] **poets**: Bacon follows a long-standing tradition of distrusting poets
[7] **one . . . Fathers**: St. Augustine
[8] **vinum daemonum**: wine of the devils
[9] **poet**: Lucretius, defender of Epicureanism

sea: a pleasure to stand in the window of a castle, and to see a battle and the adventures thereof below: but no pleasure is comparable to the standing upon the vantage ground of Truth (a hill not to be commanded,[10] and where the air is always clear and serene), and to see the errors, and wanderings, and mists, and tempests, in the vale below": so always that this prospect be with pity, and not with swelling or pride. Certainly, it is heaven upon earth, to have a man's mind move in charity, rest in providence, and turn upon the poles of truth.

To pass from theological and philosophical truth, to the truth of civil business: it will be acknowledged, even by those that practice it not, that clear and round dealing is the honor of man's nature; and that mixture of falsehood is like alloy in coin of gold and silver; which may make the metal work the better, but it embaseth it. For these winding and crooked courses are the goings of the serpent; which goeth basely upon the belly, and not upon the feet. There is no vice that doth so cover a man with shame as to be found false and perfidious. And therefore Montaigne [11] saith prettily, when he inquired the reason, why the word of the lie should be such a disgrace and such an odious charge? Saith he, "If it be well weighed, to say that a man lieth, is as much to say as that he is brave towards God and a coward towards men." For a lie faces God, and shrinks from man. Surely the wickedness of falsehood and breach of faith cannot possibly be so highly expressed, as in that it shall be the last peal to call the judgments of God upon the generations of men; it being foretold, that when Christ cometh, *he shall not find faith upon the earth.* [12]

[10] **commanded:** subject to attack
[11] **Montaigne:** (1533–1592), originator of the essay form, from whom Bacon took many of his ideas
[12] **he shall . . . earth:** from St. Luke

For Discussion

1. What does Bacon mean when he says that poets lie? How does a lie add pleasure to truth?
2. What Biblical references does Bacon make? Explain what he means in his reference to the creation story.
3. What examples of lying are often practiced in the business world?
4. Sum up Bacon's arguments showing that lying is morally wrong.
5. Compare this essay to "Of Studies" on the following points: (a) economy of words, (b) balance of structure, (c) subject matter.

Of Studies

Studies serve for delight, for ornament, and for ability. Their chief use for delight is in privateness and retiring; for ornament, is in discourse; and for ability, is in the judgment and disposition of business. For expert men [1] can execute, and perhaps judge of particulars, one by one; but the general counsels, and the plots and marshaling of affairs, come best from those that are learned. To spend too much time in studies is sloth; to use them too much for ornament is affectation; to make judgment wholly by their rules is the humor [2] of a scholar. They perfect nature, and are perfected by experience; for natural abilities are like natural plants, that need pruning by study; and studies themselves do give forth direction too much at large, except they be bounded in by experience. Crafty men [3] contemn studies, simple men admire them, and wise men use them; for they teach not their own use; but that [4] is a wisdom without them, and above them, won by observation. Read not to contradict and confute; nor to believe and take for granted; nor to find talk and discourse; but to weigh and consider. Some books are to be tasted, others to be swallowed, and some few to be chewed and digested; that is, some books are to be read only in parts; others to be read, but not curiously; [5] and some few to be read wholly, and with diligence and attention. Some books also may be read by deputy, [6] and extracts made of them by others; but that would be only in the less important arguments, and the meaner sort of books; else distilled books are like common distilled waters, flashy [7] things. Reading maketh a full man; conference [8] a ready [9] man; and writing an exact man. And therefore, if a man write little, he had need have a great memory; if he confer [10] little, he had need have a present wit; and if he read little, he had need have much cunning, to seem to know that he doth not. Histories make men wise; poets witty; the mathematics subtile; natural philosophy deep; moral grave;

[1] **expert men**: those who specialize, as opposed to those who have a general education   [2] **humor**: specialty, peculiarity
[3] **crafty men**: those who belonged to certain crafts; laborers
[4] **that**: the knowledge of how to use learning   [5] **curiously**: with attention to detail
[6] **read by deputy**: through reports of others   [7] **flashy**: flat, tasteless
[8] **conference**: quick-witted conversation
[9] **ready**: mentally sharp
[10] **confer**: converse

logic and rhetoric able to contend. *Abeunt studia in mores.*[11] Nay, there is no stond or impediment in the wit but may be wrought out [12] by fit studies; like as diseases of the body may have appropriate exercises. Bowling is good for the stone and reins; [13] shooting for the lungs and breast; gentle walking for the stomach; riding for the head; and the like. So if a man's wit be wandering, let him study the mathematics; for in demonstrations, if his wit be called away never so little, he must begin again. If his wit be not apt to distinguish or find differences, let him study the Schoolmen; [14] for they are *cymini sectores.*[15] If he be not apt to beat over matters, and to call up one thing to prove and illustrate another, let him study the lawyers' cases. So every defect of the mind may have a special receipt.

[11] **Abeunt studia in mores:** studies grow into habits
[12] **no stond . . . wrought out:** no lack of mental ability which cannot be straightened or remedied
[13] **stone and reins:** gallstones and similar afflictions
[14] **Schoolmen:** Scholastic philosophers who ruled the universities during the Middle Ages
[15] **cymini sectores:** hairsplitters; they argued on minute and obscure points

For Discussion

1. Bacon was one of the most learned men of his age. Choose a few sentences from this essay which show his learning.
2. In the first part of this essay, Bacon is explaining the use and place of studies in a man's life. Which one of the three purposes he mentions strikes you as most important? Why?
3. In the second half of this essay, Bacon states that different subjects develop different faculties of our mind. Do you agree with this theory? Are there any subjects which you are studying now that exemplify his theory? Discuss.
4. Bacon is famous for his *verbal economy*. Every word counts and no extra word is tolerated. Choose three examples of this verbal economy. Another feature of Bacon's style is *balance*. Point out three examples from this essay.
5. An analogy is a comparison between two unlike objects. What is the meaning of the analogy which Bacon uses in the sentence "Nay, there is no stond . . . appropriate exercises"? Do you agree with the medical part of this analogy? Discuss.
6. Give examples of books that may be read by deputy. Can all books be read in this "distilled" method? Discuss.

Of Travel

Travel, in the younger sort, is a part of education, in the elder, a part of experience. He that travelleth into a country before he hath some entrance into the language, goeth to school, and not to travel. That young men travel under some tutor, or grave servant, I allow well; so that he be such a one that hath the language, and hath been in the country before; whereby he may be able to tell them what things are worthy to be seen in the country where they go; what acquaintances they are to seek; what exercises or discipline the place yieldeth. For else young men shall go hooded, and look abroad little. It is a strange thing, that in sea voyages, where there is nothing to be seen but sky and sea, men should make diaries; but in land-travel, wherein so much is to be observed, for the most part they omit it; as if chance were fitter to be registered than observation. Let diaries therefore be brought in use. The things to be seen and observed are: the courts of princes, specially when they give audience to ambassadors; the courts of justice, while they sit and hear causes; and so of consistories ecclesiastic; the churches and monasteries, with the monuments which are therein extant; the walls and fortifications of cities and towns, and so the havens and harbors; antiquities and ruins; libraries; colleges, disputations,[1] and lectures, where any are; shipping and navies; houses and gardens of state and pleasure, near great cities; armories; arsenals; magazines; exchanges; burses;[2] warehouses; exercises of horsemanship, fencing, training of soldiers, and the like; comedies, such whereunto the better sort of persons do resort; treasuries of jewels and robes; cabinets and rarities; and, to conclude, whatsoever is memorable in the places where they go. After all which the tutors or servants ought to make diligent inquiry. As for triumphs, masks, feasts, weddings, funerals, capital executions, and such shows, men need not to be put in mind of them; yet are they not to be neglected. If you will have a young man to put his travel into a little room, and in short time to gather much, this you must do. First, as was said, he must have some entrance into the language before he goeth. Then he must have such a servant or tutor as knoweth the country, as was likewise

---

[1] **disputations:** formal debates held in the medieval universities
[2] **burses:** stock exchanges

said. Let him carry with him also some card [3] or book describing the country where he travelleth; which will be a good key to his inquiry. Let him keep also a diary. Let him not stay long in one city or town; more or less as the place deserveth, but not long; nay, when he stayeth in one city or town, let him change from one end and part of the town to another; which is a great adamant [4] of acquaintance. Let him sequester himself from the company of his countrymen, and diet in such places where there is good company of the nation where he travelleth. Let him, upon his removes from one place to another, procure recommendation to some person of quality residing in the place whither he removeth; that he may use his favor in those things he desireth to see or know. Thus he may abridge his travel with much profit. As for the acquaintance which is to be sought in travel; that which is most of all profitable is acquaintance with the secretaries and employed men of ambassadors; for so in travelling in one country he shall suck the experience of many. Let him also see and visit eminent persons in all kinds, which are of great name abroad; that he may be able to tell how the life agreeth with the same. For quarrels, they are with care and discretion to be avoided. They are commonly for mistresses, healths, place, and words. And let a man beware how he keepeth company with choleric and quarrelsome persons; for they will engage him into their own quarrels. When a traveller returneth home, let him not leave the countries where he hath travelled altogether behind him; but maintain a correspondence by letters with those of his acquaintance which are of most worth. And let his travel appear rather in his discourse than in his apparel or gesture; and in his discourse let him be rather advised in his answers, than forward to tell stories; and let it appear that he doth not change his country manners [5] for those of foreign parts; but only prick in some flowers of that he hath learned abroad into the customs of his own country.

[3] card: chart or map
[4] adamant: magnet, loadstone
[5] country manners: those of his own country

For Discussion

1. What validity does Bacon's first sentence have? Discuss.
2. What would be our modern counterpart of a "tutor or grave servant"?
3. Why is a knowledge of the native tongue of the place where you travel so important? Do modern Americans follow Bacon's advice on this matter? Why?

4. Find evidence in the essay to prove that only the wealthy traveled in Bacon's time. Is this still true?
5. What wise advice does Bacon offer to the returning traveler? Is such advice still pertinent today? Explain.

For Composition:

1. Bacon is on the side of a *liberal education,* an education that teaches us *how* to live. Newman held the same view in his essay on liberal education. Is this attitude still tenable in the twentieth century? Write a short composition expressing your views on the subject.
2. Write a letter to a friend, telling him your ideas on what he should see and do in visiting your city or town.

BEN JONSON

(1573–1637)

An outstanding figure of the Renaissance, Ben Jonson was the center of a literary group which included Shakespeare, Bacon, and John Donne. Both a playwright and an actor, Jonson is best known for his comedies, such as *Volpone*, in which he portrayed and emphasized the eccentricities and weaknesses of people. *Every Man in His Humor*, his first success, was produced in 1589 with Shakespeare in the cast.

Under James I, Jonson was in high favor at the court as a writer of *masques*, which were elaborate pageants composed of song and dance. A gifted writer of unbounded vitality, Jonson was deeply loved by many and exerted a great influence on younger writers of his day. In fact, his influence extends down to our present day in such writers as Yeats, Auden, and Eliot.

Jonson, like most of his contemporaries, had great respect for the classical tradition. Yet, he managed to maintain a sturdy independence at all times which gives his poetry an idiomatic and popular flavor. This is very noticeable if you compare him to Milton, perhaps the greatest classical poet of English literature.

SONG TO CELIA

Drink to me only with thine eyes,
    And I will pledge with mine;
Or leave a kiss but in the cup,
    And I'll not look for wine.
The thirst that from the soul doth rise   5
    Doth ask a drink divine;
But might I of Jove's [1] nectar [2] sup,
    I would not change for thine.

I sent thee late a rosy wreath,
    Not so much honoring thee   10

[1] **Jove:** Jupiter, the father of the gods
[2] **nectar:** a sweet drink prepared only for the gods

As giving it a hope, that there
 It could not withered be.
But thou thereon didst only breathe,
 And sent'st it back to me;
Since when it grows, and smells, I swear,   **15**
 Not of itself, but thee.

HYMN TO CYNTHIA

Queen and huntress,[1] chaste and fair,
Now the sun is laid to sleep,
Seated in thy silver chair,
State in wonted manner keep:
 Hesperus [2] entreats thy light,   **5**
 Goddess, excellently bright.

Earth, let not thy envious shade
Dare itself to interpose;
Cynthia's shining orb was made
Heaven to clear,[3] when day did close: **10**
 Bless us then with wishèd sight,
 Goddess, excellently bright.

Lay thy bow of pearl [4] apart,
And thy crystal-shining quiver;
Give unto the flying hart [5]   **15**
Space to breathe, how short soever:
 Thou that mak'st a day of night,
 Goddess, excellently bright.

ON MY FIRST SON

(In 1603, the plague carried off Jonson's first son when the child was
only seven years old.)

 Farewell, thou child of my right hand, and joy;
 My sin was too much hope of thee, loved boy.

[1] **Queen and huntress:** Diana or Cynthia, goddess of the moon and a huntress
[2] **Hesperus:** the evening star   [3] **clear:** make bright
[4] **bow of pearl:** referring to Cynthia's bow, arrows, and quiver
[5] **hart:** deer which Cynthia is traditionally portrayed as hunting

Seven years thou wert lent to me, and I thee pay,
Exacted by thy fate, on the just day.
O, I could lose all father now. For why   5
Will man lament the state he should envy?
To have so soon 'scaped world's, and flesh's, rage,
And if no other misery, yet age?
Rest in soft peace, and, asked, say here doth lie
Ben Jonson, his best piece of poetry.   10
For whose sake, henceforth, all his vows be such,
As what he loves may never like too much.

For Discussion

"To Celia"

1. What emotion is the poet trying to communicate?
2. Do the first 8 lines refer to an actual thirst? Explain.
3. Explain the reference in lines 1–2. Explain lines 15–16.
4. Is this song in a sonnet form? Explain your answer.
5. What are the two basic images used by the poet?

"Hymn to Cynthia"

1. What does line 3 modify? Explain the use of the adjective "silver" in line 3.
2. What lines apply to Cynthia as "moon-goddess"?
3. Explain the use of the epithets, *pearl* and *crystal-shining* in lines 13–14. Explain the meaning of lines 13–16.

"On My First Son"

1. What is the poet's emotion? Is it genuine? Explain.
2. Show that Jonson exercises great restraint in the poem.
3. Explain lines 2, 5, and 10. Explain the figure of speech in lines 3–4.
4. Why should man *envy* this child?
5. What lesson does the poet seem to learn in his sorrow?

THE CAVALIER POETS

The first half of the seventeenth century—from 1600 to 1660—saw the decline of the glories of the Renaissance. More and more, men were becoming occupied with the religious conflict which had originated with the Reformation and which finally broke out into open war between the Puritans, led by Oliver Cromwell, and the supporters of Charles I.

The drama, which had been the chief form of Elizabethan literature was fading. Lyric poetry in England continued into the seventeenth century, but it took more diverse forms than before.

Under the leadership of Ben Jonson, there arose a group of poets called the "tribe of Ben," who had an important effect on the poetry of the time. These young poets were witty and clever and admirers of the classical poets, such as Horace and Catullus. The spirit of these new poets was a pagan one—love of life for the moment. Horace had spoken of *carpe diem*—make the most of today. This idea is echoed in the expression "Eat, drink and be merry for tomorrow we die."

A number of these poets were part of the court of Charles I, and because of their loyal support of the king, they came to be known as the "Cavalier poets." Their main theme was love, not the love professed by the Elizabethans but a realistic love, based on the *carpe diem* of the Roman poets. Their message was: Beauty in women and in nature fades, so make the most of it while it lasts.

Although the Cavalier poets had individual styles, their verse has certain qualities in common—grace, ease, elegance, and wit. At times the Cavaliers charm us with their music and imagery. At other times it is their simplicity and sadness which stirs our hearts.

One of the chief poets of this group was Robert Herrick, who was not, however, a court poet. He celebrated the delights found in nature, in May-Day celebrations, and in country dances. Two other outstanding Cavalier poets were Sir John Suckling and Robert Lovelace, both of whom lived short, dramatic lives, involved as they were in the turbulent politics of the time. They are remembered today, however, for their few beautiful lyrics.

ROBERT HERRICK

(1591–1674)

The outstanding member of the "tribe of Ben" was Robert Herrick. At the age of 40 he became a clergyman. We find in him the quintessence of the Cavalier spirit. The spirit of *carpe diem* runs through most of his poetry. But he occasionally disarms us with a simplicity and charm we would hardly expect in a man of his nature. This is evident in "A Child's Grace" and "To Daffodils."

The subject matter of his poems is clearly indicated by Herrick in the introduction to *Hesperides*, a collection of his secular verses.

> "I sing of brooks, of blossoms, birds and bowers,
>   Of April, May, June and July-flowers;
> I sing of May-poles, hock-carts, wassails, wakes,
>   Of bridegrooms, brides, and bridal-cakes;
> I write of youth, of love, and have access
> By these, to sing of clearly wantonness;
>
>   .   .   .
>
> I write of Hell; I sing and ever shall,
> Of Heaven, and hope to have it after all."

TO THE VIRGINS TO MAKE MUCH OF TIME

> Gather ye rose-buds while ye may,
>   Old Time is still a-flying:
> And this same flower that smiles today,
>   Tomorrow will be dying.
>
> The glorious lamp of heaven, the Sun,   5
>   The higher he's a-getting
> The sooner will his race be run,
>   And nearer he's to setting.
>
> That age is best which is the first,
>   When youth and blood are warmer;   10

107

But being spent, the worse, and worst
    Times, still succeed the former.

Then be not coy, but use your time;
    And while ye may, go marry:
For having lost but once your prime,   15
    You may for ever tarry.

CORINNA'S GOING A-MAYING

Get up, get up for shame, the blooming morn
Upon her wings presents the god unshorn.[1]
    See how Aurora [2] throws her fair
    Fresh-quilted [3] colors through the air:
    Get up, sweet slug-a-bed, and see   5
    The dew bespangling herb and tree.
Each flower has wept and bowed toward the east
Above an hour since: yet you not dressed;
    Nay; not so much as out of bed?
    When all the birds have matins said   10
    And sung their thankful hymns, 'tis sin,
    Nay, profanation, to keep in,
Whenas [4] a thousand virgins on this day
Spring, sooner than the lark, to fetch in May.[5]

Rise, and put on your foliage, and be seen   15
To come forth, like the spring-time, fresh and green,
    And sweet as Flora. Take no care
    For jewels for your gown or hair:
    Fear not; the leaves will strew
    Gems in abundance upon you: 20
Besides, the childhood of the day has kept,
Against [6] you come, some orient [7] pearls unwept;

[1] **god unshorn**: Apollo, god of the sun
[2] **Aurora**: goddess of the dawn
[3] **fresh-quilted**: mixed like colors in a new-made quilt
[4] **whenas**: when
[5] **May**: hawthorne blossoms
[6] **against**: until
[7] **orient**: shining

Come and receive them while the light
Hangs on the dew-locks of the night:
And Titan [8] on the eastern hill   25
Retires himself, or else stands still
Till you come forth. Wash, dress, be brief in praying:
Few beads [9] are best when once we go a-Maying.

Come, my Corinna, come; and, coming, mark
How each field turns a street, each street a park   30
Made green and trimmed with trees; see how
Devotion gives each house a bough
Or branch: each porch, each door ere this
An ark,[10] a tabernacle is,
Made up of white-thorn, neatly interwove;   35
As if here were those cooler shades of love.
Can such delights be in the street
And open fields and we not see't?
Come, we'll abroad; and let's obey
The proclamation made for May: 40
And sin no more, as we have done, by staying;
But, my Corinna, come, let's go a-Maying.

There's not a budding boy or girl this day
But is got up, and gone to bring in May.
A deal of youth, ere this, is come   45
Back, and with white-thorn laden home.
Some have despatched their cakes and cream
Before that we have left [11] to dream:
And some have wept, and wooed, and plighted troth,
And chose their priest, ere we can cast off sloth: 50
Many a green-gown [12] has been given;
Many a kiss, both odd and even:
Many a glance too has been sent
From out the eye, love's firmament;

[8] Titan: sun
[9] beads: prayers of the rosary
[10] ark: basket
[11] left: ceased
[12] many a green-gown: a gown made green by being rolled in the fresh grass

Many a jest told of the keys betraying   55
This night, and locks picked, yet we're not a-Maying.

Come, let us go while we are in our prime;
And take the harmless folly of the time.
    We shall grow old apace, and die
    Before we know our liberty.   60
    Our life is short, and our days run
    As fast away as does the sun;
And, as a vapor or a drop of rain,
Once lost, can ne'er be found again,
    So when or you or I are made   65
    A fable, song, or fleeting shade,
    All love, all liking, all delight
    Lies drowned with us in endless night.

ANOTHER GRACE FOR A CHILD

    Here a little child I stand,
    Heaving up my either hand;
    Cold as paddocks [1] though they be,
    Here I lift them up to Thee,
    For a benison [2] to fall   5
    On our meat, and on us all.
        Amen.

[1] paddocks: frogs
[2] benison: blessing

TO DAFFODILS

    Fair daffodils, we weep to see
    You haste away so soon;
    As yet the early-rising sun
    Has not attained his noon.
      Stay, stay,   5
    Until the hasting day
      Has run
    But to the evensong; [1]

[1] evensong: evening prayers; vespers

And, having prayed together, we
　　Will go with you along.　　　　　　　　10

We have short time to stay, as you,
　　We have as short a spring;
As quick a growth to meet decay,
　　As you, or anything.
　　　　　We die,　　　　　　　　15
　　　As hours do, and dry
　　　　　Away,
　　Like to the summer's rain;
Or as the pearls of morning's dew,
　　Ne'er to be found again.　　　　　　20

For Discussion

"To the Virgins to Make Much of Time"

1. What do the rosebuds in the first stanza symbolize? How does line 3 fit in with the basic image of roses?
2. What does the course of day symbolize? Is the feeling of stanza 2 the same as that of stanza 1? Explain.
3. What does stanza 3 mean? Does it interpret the symbols of rosebuds and course of day?
4. What are the "worse and worst times"?
5. Read the poem again and see who is really dying.
6. Does the last stanza settle the meaning of the symbols or does it only offer one application? Explain.

"Corinna's Going A-Maying"

1. Explain the mythological references in the first four lines.
2. What image do lines 7–8 present?
3. The May-Day ritual is presented as a religious rite. What words indicate the interpretation?
4. The description of Corinna herself suggests that she is a part of nature as are the flowers, birds, and trees. Show how this is true in the second and third stanzas.
5. Herrick says that the season of spring cannot and ought not be denied. Not to respond to spring is a "sin" against nature. What does he mean?
6. Explain the "dew" metaphor in the first 2 stanzas. What significance do the dewdrops symbolize? Show how it has so much significance in lines 63–64.

"A Child's Grace"

1. Paddocks are toads or frogs. Why is this simile so apt?
2. What picture of this child does your imagination create?

"To Daffodils"

1. What is the mood of this poem? What do the daffodils symbolize?
2. What do personification and direct address add to this poem? Would Herrick have achieved the same effect if he did not use them? Explain.
3. What comparison does Herrick make in the second stanza? Is it valid? Why?
4. What does the "hasting day" symbolize? What does the use of "evensong" add to the personification?
5. The shortness of lines 5 and 7 is paralleled by lines 15 and 17. Why are these lines important? Are these lines read more slowly than others? Why? Explain the effect they create.

SIR JOHN SUCKLING

(1609–1642)

Sir John Suckling and Richard Lovelace are the two outstanding Cavalier poets of the time. Followers of Charles I, they expressed the spirit of an age of gaiety. They sing of love and youth and the beauty found in transient nature.

Suckling's short life was packed with adventure and romance. As a gentleman of the court of Charles I, he produced plays that dazzled the court audience. He also fought in the King's campaign against rebels in Scotland. He is remembered today, however, for his lyrics which gracefully and humorously reflect the Cavalier spirit.

THE CONSTANT LOVER

Out upon it, I have loved
    Three whole days together!
And am like to love three more,
    If it prove fair weather.

Time shall moult away his wings   5
    Ere he shall discover
In the whole wide world again
    Such a constant lover.

But the spite on 't is, no praise
    Is due at all to me: 10
Love with me had made no stays,
    Had it any been but she.

Had it any been but she,
    And that very face,
There had been at least ere this   15
    A dozen dozen in her place.

WHY SO PALE AND WAN?

Why so pale and wan, fond lover?
    Prithee, why so pale?
Will, when looking well can't move her,
    Looking ill prevail?
    Prithee, why so pale?   5

Why so dull and mute, young sinner?
    Prithee, why so mute?
Will, when speaking well can't win her,
    Saying nothing do 't?
    Prithee, why so mute?   10

Quit, quit for shame! This will not move;
    This cannot take her.
If of herself she will not love,
    Nothing can make her:
    The devil take her!   15

For Discussion

"The Constant Lover"

1. Explain the effect of line 4.
2. What image of time is created in line 5?
3. What has made the poet so "constant" in his new-found love? Explain.
4. Explain the last stanza.

"Why So Pale and Wan?"

1. What is the tone of this poem? What is the effect of the last line?
2. How does this poem fulfill the definition of Cavalier poetry?

RICHARD LOVELACE

(1618–1658)

Richard Lovelace was the epitome of the Cavalier spirit—a soldier, gentle-man, and lover. He was reputed to be the handsomest man in England. After the fall of Charles I, he petitioned the Puritan Parliament to restore the King and the Anglican Church. The boldness of his request won him a prison term. It was during his prison sentence that he whiled away his time by writing poems, such as "To Althea, from Prison," which has made him famous.

TO ALTHEA, FROM PRISON

When Love with unconfinèd wings
   Hovers within my gates,
And my divine Althea brings
   To whisper at the grates;
When I lie tangled in her hair   5
   And fettered to her eye,
The birds that wanton in the air
   Know no such liberty.

When flowing cups run swiftly round
   With no allaying Thames,   10
Our careless heads with roses bound,
   Our hearts with loyal flames;
When thirsty grief in wine we steep,
   When healths and draughts go free,
Fishes that tipple in the deep   15
   Know no such liberty.

When, like committed [1] linnets, I
   With shriller throat shall sing

[1] committed: captured

The sweetness, mercy, majesty,
 And glories of my king;   **20**
When I shall voice aloud how good
 He is, how great should be,
Enlargèd winds, that curl the flood,
 Know no such liberty.

Stone walls do not a prison make,   **25**
 Nor iron bars a cage;
Minds innocent and quiet take
 That for an hermitage;
If I have freedom in my love
 And in my soul am free,   **30**
Angels alone, that soar above,
 Enjoy such liberty.

TO LUCASTA, GOING TO THE WARS

Tell me not, Sweet, I am unkind,
 That from the nunnery
Of thy chaste breast and quiet mind
 To war and arms I fly.

True, a new mistress now I chase,   **5**
 The first foe in the field;
And with a stronger faith embrace
 A sword, a horse, a shield.

Yet this inconstancy is such
 As thou too shalt adore;   **10**
I could not love thee, Dear, so much,
 Loved I not Honor more.

For Discussion

"To Althea, from Prison"

1. What does the first stanza mean? Is Althea actually present in the prison?
2. Explain the meaning of line 10.
3. How does the third stanza portray Lovelace as a loyal Cavalier?

4. What does he mean when he compares himself to "committed linnets"?
5. Stanza 4 is famous. What general truth does it express? Explain lines 28, 29, and 32.

"To Lucasta, Going to the Wars"

1. The proper choice of words is important in poetry. Explain the use of "nunnery" in line 2. Why are "chaste" and "quiet" so apt in line 3? What words in line 4 contrast with "chaste" and "quiet"?
2. What is the implied comparison in lines 5–6? Explain the use of the word "chase" in line 5. Why does he choose the word "embrace" in line 7? Is this an apt word? Explain.
3. How does the word "inconstancy" in line 9 fit into the basic image of the poem?
4. How are the last two lines a compliment to Lucasta?

EDMUND WALLER

(1606–1687)

Edmund Waller began writing poetry during the reign of Charles I and continued as a poet during the stormy days of Cromwell down to the Restoration period. His life was the perfect example of moderation in all things. Writing on the average of four pages of verse a year, he polished and refined them until he was satisfied with every word. Alexander Pope praised his smooth and sweet style. In "Go, Lovely Rose" Waller has blended the sense of the second stanza of Ben Jonson's "Song to Celia" (page 103) and Herrick's "To the Virgins to Make Much of Time" (page 107).

GO, LOVELY ROSE!

Go, lovely Rose!
Tell her that wastes her time and me,
   That now she knows,
When I resemble her to thee,
How sweet and fair she seems to be.   5

Tell her that's young,
And shuns to have her graces spied,
   That hadst thou sprung
In deserts, where no men abide,
Thou must have uncommended died.   10

Small is the worth
Of beauty from the light retired;
   Bid her come forth,
Suffer herself to be desired,
And not blush so to be admired.   15

Then die! that she
The common fate of all things rare
   May read in thee;

How small a part of time they share
That are so wondrous sweet and fair!   20

For Discussion

1. Does the first stanza seem closer to Jonson's thought or to Herrick's? Explain.
2. What is the point Waller makes in the second stanza?
3. Compare lines 8–12 with lines 53–56 of Gray's "Elegy Written in a Country Churchyard." Which poet is correct? Explain.
4. "Then die" in line 16 is addressed to the rose. What effect do these words have on the tone of the poem? Explain.
5. Does the last stanza seem closer to Jonson's thought or to Herrick's? Explain.

THE METAPHYSICAL POETS

The poetry of the Elizabethan and Cavalier poets had a common basis. That basis presumed that sensuous and sensual imagery was the only way in which the likeness between different objects could be expressed. Certain words and images were proper to poetry because they carried definite emotional overtones. The "tribe of Ben" was constantly using the images of flowers, nature, and drink. These were the classical images of the poets of Greece and Rome, and so were adopted by these poets. This was really an anti-intellectual approach to poetry which stemmed from the excessive spirit of the Renaissance.

The Metaphysical poets of the seventeenth century deliberately sought to change this poetic basis. They expressed experience as it was molded by the *intellect*. The perceived likeness between different objects was more *logical* than sensuous for them. They compared the concrete with the abstract, the sublime with the commonplace. In their attempt to find intellectual equivalents for the emotions, they chose *detached* words—words that did not have emotional overtones. They preferred the words and terms of commerce, science, war, and theology.

In the scientific spirit of their day, the Metaphysical poets were quite analytic. They were very conscious of their own nature, thoughts, and moods, and they attempted to express these thoughts and feelings in their own unique way. Although their imagery is sometimes strange and obscure, it is always challenging.

The term "metaphysical" applies more to the style of these poets than to their subject matter. They, too, are concerned with love, death, nature, and God. But their intellectual bent governed not only their choice of words and images, but also their choice of form and rhythm. For example, the strict logical form of the sonnet and other complicated lyrics appealed to them.

The poetry of the Metaphysical school has exerted a great influence on modern poets. There is a closer connection between today's poets and these seventeenth-century poets than any other school of poetry.

JOHN DONNE

(1573–1631)

John Donne was born of a wealthy London merchant and related through
his mother to St. Thomas More. He was a man whose worldly behavior
and poetic genius were mingled with a deeply religious nature. Though
educated at Oxford and Cambridge, he received a degree from neither
university because of his Catholic faith. Yet in his day, the only road
to advancement lay in the profession of the Anglican faith. After an
intense spiritual struggle, he chose Anglicanism. But his earlier faith
and training in Catholic philosophy appear in many of his later works.

In 1615 he was ordained in the Anglican church and was later made
Dean of St. Paul's in London. His sermons and meditations given during
these years endeared him to both the king and the common people.

Like Ben Jonson, Donne had a great influence on the younger poets
of his day. Ben Jonson influenced the Cavalier poets; Donne influenced
the Metaphysical poets, including George Herbert, Richard Crashaw, and
Henry Vaughan. In their approach to poetry, their ideas, and their
startling concepts, these men were much like their master, John Donne.

Donne's poetry was clearly a revolt against Elizabethan poetry, with
its smooth and often elegant lyricism. His poetry is frequently rough,
angular, abrupt, and involved. It is also powerful, intense, and original.

In many respects Donne's poetry comes close to the ideas of our
modern poets. It is not surprising, therefore, to find him hailed today as
a leading poet of the English language. Gerard Manley Hopkins, T.S.
Eliot, and W.H. Auden have followed in the Donne tradition.

THE CANONIZATION

For God's sake hold your tongue, and let me love,
    Or [1] chide my palsy, or my gout,
My five gray hairs, or ruined fortune flout,
    With wealth your state, your mind with arts improve,
      Take you a course, get you a place,
      Observe [2] his honour, or his grace,   5

[1] or: either   [2] observe: be attentive to

Or the king's real, or his stampèd face.[3]
  Contemplate; what you will, approve,[4]
  So [5] you will let me love.

Alas, alas, who's injured by my love?   10
  What merchant's ships have my sighs drowned?
Who says my tears have overflowed his ground? [6]
  When did my colds a forward spring remove? [7]
    When did the heats which my veins fill
    Add one more to the plaguey bill?   15
Soldiers find wars, and lawyers find out still
  Litigious men, which quarrels move,[8]
  Though she and I do love.

Call us what you will, we are made such by love;
  Call her one, me another fly,[9]   20
We are tapers too, and at our own cost die,
  And we in us find the eagle and the dove.[10]
    The phoenix [11] riddle hath more wit
    By us, we two being one, are it.
So to one neutral thing both sexes fit,   25
  We die and rise the same, and prove
  Mysterious by this love.

We can die by it, if not live by love,
  And if unfit for tombs and hearse
Our legend be, it will be fit for verse;   30
  And if no piece of chronicle we prove,
    We'll build in sonnets pretty rooms; [12]
    As well a well-wrought urn becomes
The greatest ashes, as half-acre tombs,

[3] stamped face: on a coin
[4] approve: experience
[5] so: if only
[6] overflowed . . . ground: ruined a farm by flooding
[7] forward . . . remove: prevent an early spring
[8] which . . . move: stir up quarrels
[9] me . . . fly: the lovers appear to be aimlessly wheeling around each other like two flies
[10] eagle and dove: the types for fierceness and humility
[11] phoenix: a mythical bird which rises from its own ashes
[12] sonnets pretty rooms: sonnets here mean love poems; "rooms" is a literal translation of the Italian word "stanza"

And by these hymns, all shall approve [13]   35
Us *canonized* for love;

And thus invoke us: 'You whom reverend love
Made one another's hermitage;
You to whom love was peace, that now is rage;
Who did the whole world's soul contract, and drove   40
Into the glasses of your eyes [14]
(So made such mirrors, and such spies,
That they did all to you epitomize),
Countries, towns, courts: beg from above
A pattern of your love!' [15]   45

[13] approve: confirm, or prove
[14] drove . . . eyes: made yourselves fully aware of the world, since everything in the world is to be found in each of you
[15] beg . . . love: ask God to give us a pattern of your love so that others may love as you did

SONG

Go and catch a falling star,
    Get with child a mandrake root,[1]
Tell me where all past years are,
    Or who cleft the Devil's foot;
Teach me to hear mermaids [2] singing,   5
Or to keep off envy's stinging,
        And find
        What wind
Serves to advance an honest mind.

If thou be'st born to strange sights,   10
    Things invisible to see,
Ride ten thousand days and nights
    Till Age snow white hairs on thee;
Thou, when thou return'st, wilt tell me
All strange wonders that befell thee,   15
        And swear
        No where
Lives a woman true and fair.

[1] get with . . . root: the forked root of the mandrake which suggests the form of the human body
[2] mermaids: the sirens who lured men to death with their songs

If thou find'st one, let me know;
    Such a pilgrimage were sweet.   20
Yet do not; I would not go,
    Though at next door we might meet.
Though she were true when you met her,
And last till you write your letter,
        Yet she   25
        Will be
False, ere I come, to two or three.

A HYMN TO GOD THE FATHER

Wilt Thou forgive that sin where I begun,
    Which was my sin, though it were done before? [1]
Wilt Thou forgive that sin, through which I run,
    And do run still, though still I do deplore?
        When Thou hast done, Thou hast not done,   5
        For I have more. [2]

Wilt Thou forgive that sin which I have won
    Others to sin, and made my sin their door?
Wilt Thou forgive that sin which I did shun
    A year, or two: but wallowed in, a score? [3]   10
        When Thou hast done, Thou hast not done,
        For I have more.

I have a sin of fear, that when I have spun
    My last thread, I shall perish on the shore;
But swear by Thy self, that at my death Thy Son   15
    Shall shine as He shines now, and heretofore;
        And, having done that, Thou hast done;
        I fear no more.

[1] that sin ... before: original sin which we inherit from Adam and Eve
[2] For ... more: I have more sins to be forgiven.
[3] score: twenty years

DEATH, BE NOT PROUD

Death, be not proud, though some have callèd thee
Mighty and dreadful, for thou art not so,
For those whom thou think'st thou dost overthrow

Die not, poor Death, nor yet canst thou kill me.
From rest and sleep, which but thy pictures be,   5
Much pleasure, then from thee much more must flow;
And soonest our best men with thee do go—
Rest of their bones and souls' delivery!
Thou'rt slave to fate, chance, kings and desperate men,
And dost with poison, war, and sickness dwell,   10
And poppy or charms can make us sleep as well,
And better than thy stroke; why swell'st [1] thou then?
One short sleep past, we wake eternally,
And Death shall be no more: Death, thou shalt die!

[1] swell'st: with pride

AT THE ROUND EARTH'S IMAGINED CORNERS

At the round earth's imagined corners blow
Your trumpets, angels, and arise, arise
From death, you numberless infinities
Of souls, and to your scattered bodies go,
All whom the flood did, and fire shall o'erthrow,   5
All whom war, dearth, age, agues, tyrannies,
Despair, law, chance, hath slain, and you whose eyes
Shall behold God, and never taste death's woe.
But let them sleep, Lord, and me mourn a space;
For, if above all these my sins abound,   10
'Tis late to ask abundance of Thy grace,
When we are there. Here on this lowly ground,
Teach me how to repent, for that's as good
As if Thou hadst sealed my pardon with Thy blood.

BATTER MY HEART, THREE-PERSON'D GOD

Batter my heart, three-person'd God; for, you
As yet but knock, breathe, shine, and seek to mend;
That I may rise, and stand, o'erthrow me, and bend
Your force, to break, blow, burn and make me new.
I, like an usurp'd [1] town, to another due,   5
Labour to admit you, but Oh, to no end,

[1] usurp'd: captured

Reason your viceroy [2] in me, me should defend,
But is captiv'd, and proves weak or untrue.
Yet dearly I love you, and would be loved fain,
But am betroth'd [3] unto your enemy: 10
Divorce me, untie, or break that knot again,
Take me to you, imprison me, for I
Except you enthrall me, never shall be free,
Nor ever chaste, except you ravish me.

[2] **viceroy**: one who takes the place of the king or other high official
[3] **betroth'd**: wed

MEDITATION XVII

Nunc lento sonitu dicunt, morieris.
Now, this bell tolling softly for another, says to me: Thou must die.

(Confined to bed with a serious illness, the author hears the bells of his nearby church and is reminded of death and the vanity of human existence.)

Perchance he for whom this bell tolls may be so ill, as that he knows not it tolls for him; and perchance I may think myself so much better than I am, as that they who are about me, and see my state, may have caused it to toll for me, and I know not that. The church is Catholic, universal, so are all her actions; all that she does belongs to all. When she baptizes a child, that action concerns me; for that child is thereby connected to that body which is my head too, and ingrafted into that body whereof I am a member. And when she buries a man, that action concerns me: all mankind is of one author, and is one volume; when one man dies, one chapter is not torn out of the book, but translated into a better language; and every chapter must be so translated; God employs several translators; some pieces are translated by age, some by sickness, some by war, some by justice; but God's hand is in every translation, and his hand shall bind up all our scattered leaves again for that library where every book shall lie open to one another. As therefore the bell that rings to a sermon calls not upon the preacher only, but upon the congregation to come, so this bell calls us all; but how much more me, who am brought so near the door by this sickness. There was a contention as far as a suit (in which both piety and dignity, religion and estimation, were mingled), which of the religious orders should ring to prayers first in the morning; and it was determined, that they should ring first that rose earliest. If we understand aright the dignity of this bell that tolls for our evening prayer, we would be glad to make it ours by rising early, in that application, that it might be ours as well as his, whose indeed it is. The bell doth toll for him that thinks it doth; and though it intermit again, yet from that minute that that occasion wrought upon him, he is united to God. Who casts not up his eye to the sun when it rises? but who takes off his eye from a comet when that breaks out? Who bends not his ear to any bell which upon any occasion rings? but who can remove it from that bell which is passing a piece of himself out of this world? No man is an island, entire of itself; every man is a piece of the continent, a part of the main. If a clod be washed away by the sea, Europe is the less, as well as if a promontory were, as well as if a manor of thy friend's or of thine own were: any man's death diminishes me, because I am involved in mankind, and therefore never send to know for whom the bell tolls; it tolls for thee. Neither can we call this a begging of misery, or a borrowing of misery, as though we were not miserable enough of ourselves, but must fetch in more from the next house, in taking upon us the misery of our neighbours. Truly it were an excusable covetousness if we did, for affliction is a treaure, and scarce any man hath enough of it. No man hath affliction enough that is not matured and ripened by it, and made fit for God by that affliction. If a man carry treasure in bullion, or in a wedge of gold, and have none coined into current money, his treasure will not defray him as he travels. Tribulation is treasure in the nature of it, but it is not current money in the use of it, except we get nearer and nearer our home, heaven, by it. Another man may be sick too, and sick to death, and this affliction may lie in his bowels, as gold in a mine, and be of no use to him; but this bell, that tells me of his affliction, digs out and applies that gold to me: if by this consideration of another's danger I take mine own into contemplation, and so secure myself, by making my recourse to my God, who is our only security.

For Discussion

"The Canonization"

Here Donne daringly treats profane love as if it were divine love. The canonization does not concern a pair of saints, but rather a pair of lovers who have renounced the world.

1. What is the tone in the first stanza?

2. Who might the person addressed in the poem be? What does the person represent?

3. Explain lines 6–7. What two categories of worldly success does the poet summarize in these lines?

4. There is a conflict between the real, practical world and the lovers' world, which dominates the second stanza. Choose the significant details of stanza 2 which accentuate this conflict.

5. Explain the Phoenix myth and show how it fits the meaning of the third stanza.

6. Does the poet seriously intend the metaphors he uses in the last two stanzas? Explain.

7. The word "legend" in line 30 meant "the life of a saint" in Donne's time. Show how this fits the idea of stanza 4 on canonization.

8. The last stanza states that the lovers have renounced the world but have really gained the world and each other. Show how this is treated by Donne.

9. What Catholic doctrine is implied in lines 44–45? Explain how it is used by Donne.

10. What is the poet's tone in the concluding stanza? Compare this to stanza 1.

"Song"

1. What is the mood of the first stanza? What is the point of the commands Donne issues? How do these details accentuate the mood?

2. What details in the second stanza show the futility of the search for "a woman true and fair"?

3. What does the word "pilgrimage" suggest (line 20)?

4. Why does the poet say "Yet do not; I would not go" (line 21)?

"A Hymn to God the Father"

1. What two kinds of sin does Donne refer to in the first stanza? Through what Sacraments are these sins forgiven?

2. Explain the pun in lines 5, 11, and 17.

3. Explain the poet's meaning in line 8, "And made my sin their door."

4. Explain the figure of speech in lines 13–14.

5. What is the tone of this poem? Do you think it is a good religious poem? Explain.

6. What aspect of metaphysical poetry is stressed in this poem?

"Death, Be Not Proud"

1. What effect does the poet achieve by addressing Death directly?

2. What type of personality is Death? Show how the poet's argument with Death proves your answer.

3. What is the paradox on which the poem is built?
4. Why are "rest" and "sleep" called *pictures* of death in line 5?
5. How is death a "slave to fate, chance, kings and desperate men"?
6. Show how this poem fulfills the definition of a sonnet.

"At the Round Earth's Imagined Corners"

1. Compare line 1 with *Apocalypse* 7:1. What aspect of metaphysical poetry is noticeable in this line?
2. To what event does the octave refer? Choose the significant details which account for the various modes of death.
3. What does the poet request in the sestet? What Christian experience does he communicate? Explain.
4. Compare this sonnet to "A Hymn to God the Father." What theme is found in both poems? How does the development of the theme vary in each poem?

"Batter My Heart, Three Person'd God"

1. What is the theme of this sonnet? Contrast its mood with that of "At the Round Earth's Imagined Corners."
2. What metaphor is used in lines 1–4? Select all the words which refer to a blacksmith and his forge.
3. Explain in detail the simile "like a usurped town" (line 5). Why is it so apt in the context of this poem?
4. The terminology of love and marriage is often used by the Metaphysical poets to express spiritual life and love. Show how this is true in the sestet.

"Meditation XVII"

1. Donne's explanation of the Church is quite orthodox. What Catholic doctrines on the Church are contained in this meditation?
2. Who is the "head" of which Donne speaks? Whose body is Donne a member of? Does Donne's explanation agree with St. Paul's doctrine?
3. Explain what Donne means when he says "No man is an island entire of itself. . . ."? How does this fit in with your own ideas on the nature of man?
4. Explain why "affliction is a treasure." Paraphrase Donne's words about tribulation in the last section of the meditation.
5. How does Donne's meditation compare with the modern sermons you hear? Which do you prefer? Why?

GEORGE HERBERT

(1593–1633)

John Donne was a friend of George Herbert's family, and he had a great influence on the young poet. Like Donne, Herbert's imagery is based on the intellect rather than the senses, and the structure of his poems is extremely logical. Yet there is a simplicity in Herbert's poetry that is not often found in Donne. There is an air of peace and satisfaction about Herbert's poems, which comes from his saintly life. In 1630 he was ordained an Anglican minister and served his flock with a devotion and reverence that made him famous throughout England.

In his poetry, he often treats of the inadequacy of earthly love. "The Pulley" is a good example of Herbert's quiet, devotional poetry. "The Collar" is in quite another mood. Here he describes his service to God as a bondage against which he rebels until he suddenly realizes that the freedom he seeks is freedom from God's love.

THE COLLAR

I struck the board,[1] and cried, No more.
I will abroad.
What? shall I ever sigh and pine?
My lines and life are free; free as the road,
    Loose as the wind, as large as store.[2]   5
Shall I be still in suit? [3]
Have I no harvest but a thorn
To let me blood, and not restore
What I have lost with cordial [4] fruit?
    Sure there was wine   10
Before my sighs did dry it: there was corn
    Before my tears did drown it.

[1] **board:** table
[2] **store:** as large as abundance itself
[3] **in suit:** in attendance, as a suitor, for preferment or reward
[4] **cordial:** restorative

Is the year only lost to me?
Have I no bays [5] to crown it?
No flowers, no garlands gay? all blasted?   15
All wasted?
Not so, my heart: but there is fruit,
And thou hast hands.
Recover all thy sigh-blown age
On double pleasures: leave thy cold dispute   20
Of what is fit, and not. Forsake thy cage,
Thy rope of sands,[6]
Which petty thoughts have made, and made to thee
Good cable, to enforce and draw,
And be thy law,   25
While thou didst wink and wouldst not see.
Away; take heed:
I will abroad.
Call in thy death's head there: tie up thy fears.
He that forbears   30
To suit and serve his need,
Deserves his load.
But as I raved and grew more fierce and wild
At every word,
Methought I heard one calling, *Child*.   35
And I replied, *My Lord*.

[5] **bays:** laurel wreath used as a crown
[6] **rope of sands:** the Church's teachings as they appear to a brash young man

THE PULLEY

When God at first made man,
Having a glass of blessings standing by,
Let us (said He) pour on him all we can.
Let the world's riches, which dispersèd lie,
Contract into a span.   5

So strength first made a way,
Then beauty flowed, then wisdom, honour, pleasure.
When almost all was out, God made a stay,

Perceiving that alone of all His treasure
    Rest [1] in the bottom lay.   10

    For if I should (said He)
Bestow this jewel also on My creature,
  He would adore My gifts instead of Me,
And rest in Nature, not the God of Nature.
    So both should losers be.   15

    Yet let him keep the rest,
But keep them with repining restlessness.
  Let him be rich and weary, that at least,
If goodness lead him not, yet weariness
    May toss him to My breast.   20

[1] rest: peacefulness (The poet plays on this word in the remaining two stanzas.)

For Discussion

"The Collar"

1. What effect do the opening 2 lines create?
2. What does the poet mourn over in the first 16 lines? Explain the metaphors he uses.
3. What change of tone is apparent in line 17? What suggests these thoughts to Herbert?
4. Explain the last 4 lines of the poem. What is their tone? What solution do they offer to the poet's problem?
5. Why is this a metaphysical poem?

"The Pulley"

1. Explain what the pulley symbolizes. In what way is this a typical metaphysical device?
2. The key to the poem's understanding is the word "rest." Explain. Show how Herbert plays on this word in lines 14 and 16.
3. Compare the tone of the opening lines with those of "The Collar."
4. Write a prose paraphrase of this poem.

HENRY VAUGHAN

(1622–1695)

Born in Wales, Henry Vaughan studied at Oxford and eventually devoted himself to the study of medicine. In 1647 he returned to his home and practiced among his own people. His guide in religion and literature was George Herbert.

Vaughan brought to his poetry a deep love of nature. He was the only one of the followers of Donne who contemplated nature so carefully. In this he is a forerunner of William Wordsworth. Though Vaughan may have lacked Donne's vigor and virility, and Herbert's delicacy and sense of form, he brought a new lightness and lyricism to his poetry which neither of these poets possessed.

Like the other Metaphysical writers, Vaughan brings together the temporary and the eternal. For him, all creation had one author, one meaning, and one end.

THE WORLD

I saw Eternity the other night
Like a great *Ring* of pure and endless light,
    All calm, as it was bright,
And round beneath it, Time in hours, days, years
      Driv'n by the spheres   5
Like a vast shadow moved, in which the world
    And all her train were hurled; [1]
The doting lover in his quaintest [2] strain
    Did there complain,
Near him, his lute, his fancy, and his flights,   10
    Wit's sour delights,
With gloves, and knots, [3] the silly snares of pleasure;
    Yet his dear treasure

[1] **hurled:** the poet is contrasting the beauty of the heavenly skies with the useless and vain activities of earthly life.
[2] **quaintest:** fanciest
[3] **knots:** love knots

133

All scattered lay, while he his eyes did pour
    Upon a flower.   15

The darksome statesman,[4] hung with weights and woe
Like a thick midnight-fog moved there so slow
    He did not stay, nor go;
Condemning thoughts (like sad Eclipses) scowl
    Upon his soul,   20
And clouds of crying witnesses without
    Pursued him with one shout.
Yet digged the mole, and lest his ways be found
    Worked under ground,
Where he did clutch his prey, but one did see   25
    That policy;[5]
Churches and altars fed him,[6] perjuries
    Were gnats and flies,[7]
It rained about him blood and tears, but he
    Drank them as free.[8]   30

The fearful miser on a heap of rust
Sat pining all his life there, did scarce trust
    His own hands with the dust,
Yet would not place one piece [9] above, but lives
    In fear of thieves.   35
Thousands there were as frantic as himself
    And hugged each one his pelf;
The downright epicure placed heaven in sense
    And scorned pretence
While others, slipped into a wide excess,   40
    Said little less;
The weaker sort slight, trivial wares enslave
    Who think them brave,[10]
And poor, despisèd Truth sat counting by [11]
    Their victory.   45

[4] darksome statesman: probably Cromwell
[5] policy: stratagem
[6] Churches . . . him: a reference to the abolition of the Bishops by Parliament in 1642
[7] were . . . flies: were of as little importance as gnats and flies
[8] as free: as liberally as they rained about him
[9] place one piece: invest one coin
[10] brave: beautiful
[11] counting by: observing

Yet some, who all this while did weep and sing,
And sing, and weep, soared up into the *Ring*,
But most would use no wing.
O fools (said I) thus to prefer dark night
Before true light,   50
To live in grots, and caves, and hate the day
Because it shews the way,
The way which from this dead and dark abode
Leads up to God,
A way where you might tread the Sun, and be   55
More bright than he.
But as I did their madness so discuss
One whispered thus,
*This Ring the Bridegroom did for none provide
But for his bride.*[12]   60

[12] **Bridegroom . . . bride:** reference to Christ and His Church

THE RETREAT

Happy those early days! when I
Shined in my angel-infancy:
Before I understood this place
Appointed for my second race,
Or taught my soul to fancy ought   5
But a white, celestial thought;
When yet I had not walked above
A mile, or two, from my first love,
And looking back (at that short space,)
Could see a glimpse of his bright-face;   10
When on some gilded cloud, or flower
My gazing soul would dwell an hour,
And in those weaker glories spy
Some shadows of eternity;
Before I taught my tongue to wound   15
My conscience with a sinful sound,
Or had the black art to dispense
A sev'ral sin to ev'ry sense,
But felt through all this fleshly dress [1]
Bright shoots of everlastingness.   20

[1] **fleshly dress:** body

O how I long to travel back
And tread again that ancient track!
That I might once more reach that plain,
Where first I left my glorious train,
From whence the enlightened spirit sees   25
That shady city of palm trees;
But (ah!) my soul with too much stay
Is drunk, and staggers in the way.
Some men a forward motion love,
But I by backward steps would move,   30
And when this dust falls to the urn
In that state I came return.

For Discussion

"The World"

1. What setting does the poet present in the first 8 lines? What does this setting reveal about the personality of Vaughan?
2. Describe "the doting lover" (line 8). What does "strain" mean (line 9)? Paraphrase lines 13–14.
3. Briefly describe "the darksome statesman." What type of person does the poet portray in his description?
4. Point out the vivid details which describe the "fearful miser."
5. Who are the people described in the last stanza? Explain the last 2 lines of the poem. Who are the Bridegroom and his bride?

"The Retreat"

1. Explain the title of this poem. Does it hint at the theme? Explain.
2. "My second race" (line 4) refers to our earthly existence. Explain why this is an apt comparison. What would be our first race?
3 Explain lines 11–14. Why are they typical of Vaughan? What sins does the poet refer to in lines 15–18?
4. What image does line 22 recreate? What does line 26 mean?
5. Choose all the words and expressions which repeat the title of this poem. What effect does this repetition create? Explain.
6. Do you think the poet expresses a common human experience? Discuss.

RICHARD CRASHAW

(c. 1613–1649)

Crashaw is the only Catholic Metaphysical poet of the seventeenth century. At Cambridge, while still a Protestant, Crashaw learned Spanish and Italian. He was then able to read the writings of the Spanish mystics and especially the biography of the recently canonized St. Theresa of Avila. These works deeply influenced his religious thought and poetic style. Having lost his fellowship at Cambridge because of his Anglican leanings, he eventually embraced the Roman Catholic faith.

The most mystical of the Metaphysical poets, Crashaw has combined the traits of the school of Donne with his own sensual imagery. In Crashaw the senses are dominant and suggest a whole series of images and emotions. His religious lyrics are marked by their fervor, sincerity, and verbal energy.

HYMN ON THE GLORIOUS ASSUMPTION
OF OUR BLESSED LADY

Hark! she is call'd, the parting hour is come;
Take thy farewell, poor World, Heaven must go home.
A piece of heav'nly earth, purer and brighter
Than the chaste stars, whose choice lamps come to light her
Whilst through the crystal orbs, clearer than they   5
She climbs, and makes a far more Milky Way.
She's call'd! Hark, how the dear immortal dove
Sighs to his silver mate: Rise up, my love!
Rise up, my fair, my spotless one,
The winter's past, the rain is gone,   10
    The spring is come, the flow'rs appear,
No sweets (save thou) are wanting here.
                Come away, my love,
                Come away, my dove,
                    Cast off delay;   15

137

The court of heav'n is come
To wait upon thee home;
Come, come away.

The flowers appear,
Or quickly would, wert thou once here.   20
The spring is come, or if it stay
'Tis to keep time with thy delay.
The rain is gone, except so much as we
Detain in needful tears to weep the want of thee.

The winter's past,   25
Or if he makes less haste

His answer is, why she does so,
If summer come not, how can winter go?

Come away, come away!

The shrill winds chide, the waters weep thy stay;   30
The fountains murmur; and each loftiest tree
Bows low'st his leafy top, to look for thee.

Come away, my love,
Come away, my dove, etc.

She's call'd again. And will she go?   35
When heav'n bids come, who can say no?
Heaven calls her, and she must away,
Heav'n will not, and she cannot, stay.
Go then, go glorious.

On the golden wings   40

Of the bright youth of Heav'n,[1] that sings
Under so sweet a burthen.   Go,
Since thy dread son will have it so:
And while thou goest, our song and we
Will, as we may, reach after thee.   45
Hail, Holy Queen of humble hearts!
We in thy praise will have our parts.
And though thy dearest looks must now give light
To none but the blest heavens, whose bright
Beholders, lost in sweet delight,   50
Feed for ever their fair sight
With those divinest eyes, which we
And our dark world no more shall see.

---

[1] **youth of Heav'n:** cherubim; the young angels

Though our poor eyes are parted so,
Yet shall our lips never let go   55
Thy gracious name, but to the last,
Our loving song shall hold it fast.
    Thy precious name shall be
    Thyself to us; and we
       With holy care will keep it by us,   60
          We to the last
          Will hold it fast,
And no Assumption shall deny us.
    All the sweetest showers
    Of our fairest flowers   65
    Will we strow upon it.
Though our sweets cannot make
It sweeter, they can take
Themselves new sweetness from it.

Mary, men and angels sing,   70
Maria Mother of our King.
Live rosy Princess, live, and may the bright
Crown of a most incomparable light
Embrace thy radiant brows. O may the best
Of everlasting joys bathe thy white breast.   75
Live our chaste love, the holy mirth
Of heaven, the humble pride of earth.
Live crown of women, queen of men,
Live mistress of our song; and when
Our weak desires have done their best,   80
Sweet angels come, and sing the rest.

For Discussion

"Hymn on the Glorious Assumption of Our Blessed Lady"

1. What is the tone of this poem? What details strengthen and heighten the tone?
2. Who is "the dear immortal dove" mentioned in line 7? Who is "his silver mate"? Explain the meaning.
3. Lines 8–12 are a paraphrase of the *Canticle of Canticles* often applied to Christ and His Church. How does Crashaw use this salutation?

4. What effect will Our Lady's arrival produce in Heaven? Why is Our Lady so honored?

5. Who are the "bright youth of Heaven" (line 30)? Who is "thy dread son" (line 41)?

6. What effect will Our Lady's departure produce here on earth? Why is Mary "the humble pride of earth" (line 65)?

7. Meter plays an important role in this poem. How does it suggest movement? Give examples of lines in which the meter suggests ascent, speed, sorrow, joy.

8. In what way does Crashaw communicate the doctrine of Our Lady's Assumption? What means does he use which you do not find in your religion textbook?

For Composition:

1. Contrast the Metaphysical poets with their contemporaries, the Cavalier poets. Write a report on their respective attitudes toward love, nature, life, and religion. Which group appeals more to you? Why?

2. Many of the poems in this section have been religious in nature. Write a short essay on religious poetry, showing that such poetry has a human significance.

JOHN MILTON

(1608–1674)

Milton was born in London of parents who had a great love for music and literature. This love they passed on to their son. Trained at Cambridge, Milton was raised in the classical tradition of the day—a curriculum of Latin, Greek, and foreign languages. Choosing literature as his vocation, he began his long literary career with poems that show little evidence of his later Puritan convictions.

After traveling on the Continent, he became an ardent follower of the Puritans, and served as Latin Secretary to the Commonwealth under Cromwell. His duty was to translate Latin letters from foreign governments and to write answers in the same tongue. This work seriously weakened his eyes.

This was the period of his most controversial writings. In his *Areopagitica*, he championed freedom of the press, but denied such freedom to Catholics. At this time, he also advocated divorce, a position which may have resulted from his unhappy married life. No published poetry came from his busy pen during this period. It was an age of pamphlets, debates, and political upheaval. Finally, in 1652, Milton became blind.

After Charles I was executed in 1649, Oliver Cromwell, with the help of the Parliament, set up a new form of government. Although civil liberty was promised, the leaders of this government were most intolerant and the people yearned once again for a king. In their zeal, the Puritan reformers almost wrecked the Anglican Church and destroyed many of the ecclesiastical treasures of England. Finally Cromwell became absolute ruler. In one of the ironies of history, Cromwell, who rose to end the tyranny of the Stuart kings, had become a tyrant himself. After the death of Oliver Cromwell in 1658, his son Richard took the reins of government. General unrest and popular clamor for the monarchy brought Charles II to the throne in 1660.

Charles II did not press the punishment of all those responsible for his father's death in 1649. Thus Milton escaped death and lived on to produce his greatest poetry and the best poem to rise from the Puritan spirit, *Paradise Lost*.

ON HIS BLINDNESS

When I consider how my light [1] is spent [2]
   Ere half my days in this dark world and wide,
   And that one talent [3] which is death to hide
   Lodged with me useless, though my soul more bent [4]
To serve therewith my Maker, and present   5
   My true account, lest He returning chide;
   "Doth God exact day-labor, light denied?"
   I fondly [5] ask. But patience, to prevent
That murmur, soon replies, "God doth not need
   Either man's work or his own gifts. Who best   10
   Bear his mild yoke, they serve him best. His state
Is kingly: thousands at his bidding speed,
   And post o'er land and ocean without rest;
   They also serve who only stand and wait."

[1] **light**: sight
[2] **is spent**: used up
[3] **talent**: his writing ability
[4] **bent**: desirous, willing
[5] **fondly**: foolishly

ON SHAKESPEARE

What needs my Shakespeare for his honored bones
The labour of an age in piléd stones?
Or that his hallowed reliques [1] should be hid
Under a star-ypointing [2] pyramid?
Dear son of memory, great heir of fame,   5
What need'st thou such weak witness of thy name?
Thou in our wonder and astonishment
Hast built thyself a livelong monument.
For whilst, to the shame of slow-endeavoring art
Thy easy numbers [3] flow, and that each heart   10
Hath from the leaves of thy unvalued [4] book

[1] **reliques**: remains
[2] **star-ypointing**:star-pointing; "y" is affixed to the present participle here for the sake of the rhythm
[3] **numbers**: songs and poems
[4] **unvalued**: invaluable

Those Delphic [5] lines with deep impression took,
Then thou, our fancy of itself bereaving,
Dost make *us* marble with too much conceiving,[6]
And so sepúlchred in such pomp dost lie   15
That kings for such a tomb would wish to die.

[5] **Delphic:** inspired by Apollo, the god of poetry, whose shrine was at Delphi
[6] **conceiving:** thinking, imagining

ON HIS HAVING ARRIVED AT THE
AGE OF TWENTY-THREE

How soon hath time, the subtle thief of youth,
   Stolen on his wing my three and twentieth year!
   My hasting days fly on with full career,
   But my late spring no bud or blossom show'th.
Perhaps my semblance [1] might deceive the truth,   5
   That I to manhood am arrived so near,
   And inward ripeness doth much less appear,
   That some more timely-happy [2] spirits endu'th.[3]
Yet be it [4] less or more, or soon or slow,
   It shall be still [5] in strictest measure even [6]   10
   To that same lot, however mean or high,
Toward which time leads me, and the will of Heaven.
   All [7] is, if I have grace to use it so,
   As ever in my great Task-master's eye.

[1] **semblance:** outward appearance
[2] **timely-happy:** happy in the early maturity of their powers
[3] **endu'th:** endows with intellectual vigor
[4] **it:** inward ripeness
[5] **still:** always
[6] **even:** conformable to
[7] **all:** all the affairs of life

For Discussion

"On His Blindness"

1. Read *St. Matthew's Gospel* 25:14–30. How did this parable influence Milton's sonnet?
2. The first 7½ lines state the problem. Restate it briefly in your own words. The solution to the problem is offered in the remainder of

the poem. What is the solution that "patience" offers? Does "patience" directly answer Milton's complaint? Explain.

3. Would you say that the solution offered in the sestet is a Christian one? Why?

4. What effect do the short, monosyllabic words create? How does this effect the mood of the poem? Explain.

5. Line 14 is one of the famous lines in literature. Discuss how this line is an expression of the Christian attitude on suffering.

"On Shakespeare"

1. What is the theme of this poem? Explain the meaning of lines 7–8.

2. What would we call "piled stone" (line 2) and "a star-y pointing pyramid" (line 4)? What allusion does line 4 contain?

3. Why does Milton address Shakespeare as "son of memory" and "heir of fame" (line 5)?

4. What does "numbers" mean in line 10? Explain the meaning of lines 13–16 and why they are considered a "conceit."

"On His Having Arrived at the Age of Twenty-three"

1. Milton wrote this poem for a friend who has chided him for dreaming away his years in studious retirement. What answer does the poem offer to such a charge?

2. Explain why the poet calls Time "the subtle thief of youth." What does line 4 mean? Explain the metaphor it contains.

3. What do lines 5–6 tell us of Milton's appearance at this time?

4. Does Milton give the impression of being a religious young man? Explain.

5. What attitude toward God is revealed in the term "Great Taskmaster" (line 14)? Would this be a Puritanical idea of God? Explain.

6. This poem is a sonnet. Explain why.

THE EPIC

Introduction

We have already noted that Milton was educated in the great classical tradition of Western Europe. His ability to read Latin, Greek, and Italian brought him in contact with the greatest epic poems in the literature of the world. In Greek he read the *Iliad* and the *Odyssey*, the two outstanding epics of Homer. Latin brought him into contact with the *Aeneid* of Virgil, a national epic of wide scope. His Italian enabled him to read Boccaccio's *Teseida* and Dante's *Divine Comedy*, thought by many to be the greatest epic of them all.

Even as a youth, Milton thought he had "a commission" to write a great religious epic. As we saw in his sonnet *On His Blindness*, he was totally blind at 45 with his great work unwritten. It was in his years of solitude after the accession of Charles II that he undertook his greatest and most difficult literary task. During those last years he produced the only great epic in English.

An *epic* is a narrative poem of great length which deals with events of grandeur and importance arising from a life of action, especially of violent action, such as war. The events and persons of an epic strengthen our belief in the worth and dignity of man and his achievements. The epic spirit, which began with Homer, continued down to Milton. The characteristics of an epic found in Milton's *Paradise Lost* can be traced back to their classical origins. These characteristics can be briefly listed as follows:

1. The *plot* is a unified narrative. The action of the plot usually begins in the middle of the narrative and then goes back to the beginning of the story. The main action of the plot is short, but it usually implies action on a much broader scale.
2. The *hero* is a character of superhuman stature who performs mighty deeds, and overcomes all odds for an ideal. He usually personifies the ideals of his age, his race, and his nation.
3. The *setting* is usually in the distant past, either in legend or early history. This enforces the heroic dimensions of the hero.
4. The *mood* of an epic is solemn and dignified. Because the

hero and the action are on such a lofty plain, the mood created
is, naturally, sublime.

5. The *literary devices* traditionally used by Homer and the
   other classical epic poets are retained to strengthen the mood,
   ennoble the hero, and sweep the action along. Among these
   literary devices are found:

   (a) A brief statement of *theme* or central idea.

   (b) An *invocation* to the Muse of epic poetry for inspiration
       and guidance in telling such a great tale.

   (c) A *roll-call* of important characters who take part in the
       action.

   (d) *Lofty speeches* by the hero and other leading characters,
       used to enhance their importance and add to their
       stature.

Paradise Lost

Milton intended to pattern his great work after past epics and
also to surpass them. Having read and mastered his classical models,
he wanted to take the best of these works and make it into something new. Each of the characteristics of the epic is found in *Paradise Lost* in a new way.

The *action* is war, but not human war. Other epics concern war
for earthly ends, like the founding of Rome in the *Aeneid*. But
Milton's war is a struggle between good and evil. The issues and
outcome of this war are far more important. It is a war between
the Son of God and Satan, between the descendants of Adam and
the fallen Angels.

Milton's *hero*, in the literary sense, is Adam. The actions of
Adam give unity to the epic; his fate is its chief subject. He is
devoted to God and to Eve. The conflict in Adam arises from these
two loves. The power that starts the crisis is Satan, and eventually
Adam falls. His sin is disobedience to God, as Milton says in the
very first line of *Paradise Lost*. Adam, like all his descendants, stands
between God and Satan.

Against God, who stands for order, wisdom, and love, Milton
sets Satan who stands for disorder, passion, and hatred. Pride caused
Satan's fall as Milton describes it in Book One. Satan's fall leads to
his hatred of God and all God's creatures and his eventual desire
for revenge by ending the happiness of Adam and Eve. Satan is an

impressive character in *Paradise Lost,* but his evil motives and actions bring about a gradual decay until all his angelic qualities are corrupted or lost.

The *setting* of *Paradise Lost* was created by a blind man. It is a world created out of Milton's memories of the past and transformed into a new world to replace the one he no longer saw. His descriptions of Heaven, Hell, and the Garden of Eden are of places we have never seen.

The *mood* of *Paradise Lost* is the most solemn and sublime we have in our language. There is an organ-roll to Milton's style which raises it to new heights. His choice of words and sentence structure elevates his style far above everyday speech. There is an imaginative power in Milton's epic that haunts the reader and sustains the mood.

Among the *literary devices* which Milton used in a new way we might mention his *invocation.* He addresses a divine power instead of a pagan Muse. He calls for divine inspiration not only to compose but actually to supply him with his words. This Heavenly Muse is a divine voice, close to the Holy Spirit, whom in his opening lines he invokes immediately after her. Hers is the voice that spoke to Moses, and Milton asks to be heard with special attention because he repeats what the voice of God has told him.

Paradise Lost is a poem that will repay careful reading. Its long sentences, Latinized vocabulary, and classical allusions may make your first reading a slow and studious process. But a second reading should begin to bear rewards and demonstrate the fact that "Milton is the last great practitioner of literary epic. With him it found a finality which forbade any extension of its scope."

Paradise Lost

BOOK ONE

ARGUMENT: This First Book proposes, first in brief, the whole subject—man's disobedience, and the loss thereupon of Paradise, wherein he was placed: then touches the prime cause of his fall—the serpent, or rather Satan in the serpent; who, revolting from God, and drawing to his side many legions of angels, was, by the command of God, driven out of heaven, with all his crew, into the great deep. Which action passed over, the Poem hastes into the midst of things; presenting Satan, with his angels, now fallen into hell—described here not in the center (for heaven and earth may be supposed as yet not made, certainly not yet accursed), but in a place of utter darkness, fitliest called chaos. Here Satan, with his angels lying on the burning lake, thunderstruck and astonished, after a certain space recovers, as from confusion; calls up him who, next in order and dignity, lay by him: they confer of their miserable fall. Satan awakens all his legions, who lay till then in the same manner confounded. They rise: their numbers; array of battle; their chief leaders named, according to the idols known afterwards in Canaan and the countries adjoining. To these Satan directs his speech; comforts them with hope yet of regaining heaven; but tells them, lastly, of a new world and new kind of creature to be created, according to an ancient prophecy, or report, in heaven—for that angels were long before this visible creation was the opinion of many ancient Fathers. To find out the truth of this prophecy, and what to determine thereon, he refers to a full council. What his associates thence attempt. Pandemonium, the palace of Satan, rises, suddenly built out of the Deep: the infernal Peers there sit in council.

> Of man's first disobedience, and the fruit
> Of that forbidden tree whose mortal [1] taste
> Brought death into the world, and all our woe,
> With loss of Eden, till one greater Man

[1] mortal: deadly

148

Restore us, and regain the blissful seat,[2]   5
Sing, Heavenly Muse,[3] that, on the secret top
Of Oreb, or of Sinai,[4] didst inspire
That Shepherd [5] who first taught the chosen seed
In the beginning how the heavens and earth
Rose out of chaos: [6] or, if Sion hill [7]   10
Delight thee more, and Siloa's brook that flowed
Fast by [8] the oracle [9] of God, I thence
Invoke thy aid to my adventrous song,
That with no middle flight intends to soar
Above the Aonian mount,[10] while it pursues   15
Things unattempted yet in prose or rhyme.
And chiefly Thou, O Spirit,[11] that dost prefer
Before all temples the upright heart and pure,
Instruct me, for Thou know'st; Thou from the first
Wast present, and, with mighty wings outspread,   20
Dove-like [12] sat'st brooding on the vast Abyss,
And mad'st it pregnant: what in me is dark
Illumine, what is low raise and support;
That, to the highth of this great argument,
I may assert [13] Eternal Providence,   25
And justify the ways of God to men.
    Say first—for heaven hides nothing from thy view,
Nor the deep tract of hell—say first what cause
Moved our grand [14] Parents, in that happy state,
Favored of heaven so highly, to fall off   30
From their Creator, and transgress his will
For one restraint, lords of the world besides.

[2] seat: abode
[3] Heavenly Muse: the Holy Spirit
[4] Oreb . . . Sinai: mountains where Moses received the message of God
[5] that Shepherd: Moses
[6] in the beginning . . . chaos: Moses wrote the first five books of the Old Testament
[7] Sion hill: where Jerusalem was built
[8] fast by: close to
[9] the oracle: the temple of Solomon
[10] the Aonian mount: Helicon where the Muses of classic poets dwelt
[11] Spirit: the Holy Spirit of the New Testament
[12] dove-like: the Spirit is represented in art as a dove
[13] assert: vindicate
[14] grand: first, original

Who first seduced them to that foul revolt?
   The infernal serpent; [15] he it was whose guile,
Stirred up with envy and revenge, deceived   35
The mother of mankind, what time [16] his pride
Had cast him out from heaven, with all his host
Of rebel angels, by whose aid, aspiring
To set himself in glory above his peers,[17]
He trusted to have equalled the Most High,   40
If he opposed, and, with ambitious aim
Against the throne and monarchy of God,
Raised impious war in heaven and battle proud,
With vain attempt. Him the Almighty Power
Hurled headlong flaming from the ethereal sky,   45
With hideous ruin and combustion, down
To bottomless perdition, there to dwell
In adamantine chains and penal fire,
Who durst defy the Omnipotent to arms.
   Nine times [18] the space that measures day and night   50
To mortal men, he, with his horrid crew,
Lay vanquished, rolling in the fiery gulf,
Confounded, though immortal. But his doom [19]
Reserved him to more wrath; for now the thought
Both of lost happiness and lasting pain   55
Torments him: round he throws his baleful [20] eyes,
That witnessed huge affliction and dismay,
Mixed with obdurate pride and steadfast hate.
At once, as far as angel's ken,[21] he views
The dismal situation waste and wild.   60
A dungeon horrible, on all sides round,
As one great furnace flamed; yet from those flames
No light; but rather darkness visible
Served only to discover sights of woe,
Regions of sorrow, doleful shades, where peace   65

[15] **the infernal serpent:** Satan
[16] **what time:** at the time when
[17] **his peers:** his equals, the other archangels
[18] **nine times:** the angels fell for nine days
[19] **doom:** judgment on him
[20] **baleful:** full of pain
[21] **ken:** know

And rest can never dwell, hope never comes
That comes to all, but torture without end
Still urges,[22] and a fiery deluge, fed
With ever-burning sulphur unconsumed.
Such place Eternal Justice had prepared   70
For those rebellious; here their prison ordained
In utter [23] darkness, and their portion set,
As far removed from God and light of heaven
As from the center thrice to the utmost pole.
Oh, how unlike the place from whence they fell!   75
There the companions of his fall, o'erwhelmed
With floods and whirlwinds of tempestuous fire,
He soon discerns; and, weltering [24] by his side,
One next himself in power, and next in crime,
Long after known in Palestine, and named   80
Beëlzebub. To whom the arch-enemy,
And thence in heaven called *Satan*,[25] with bold words
Breaking the horrid silence, thus began:—
    "If thou beest he—but Oh, how fallen! how changed
From him!—who, in the happy realms of light,   85
Clothed with transcendent brightness, didst outshine
Myriads, though bright—if he whom mutual league,
United thoughts and counsels, equal hope
And hazard in the glorious enterprise,
Joined with me once, now misery hath joined   90
In equal ruin; into what pit thou seest
From what highth fallen: so much the stronger proved
He [26] with this thunder: and till then who knew
The force of those dire arms? Yet not for those,
Nor what the potent victor in his rage   95
Can else inflict, do I repent, or change,
Though changed in outward lustre, that fixed mind,
And high disdain from sense of injured merit,
That with the mightiest raised me to contend,
And to the fierce contention brought along   100

[22] urges: presses on
[23] utter: outer
[24] weltering: rolling about
[25] Satan: in Hebrew the name means "adversary"
[26] He: God

Innumerable force of spirits armed,
That durst dislike his reign, and, me preferring,
His utmost power with adverse power opposed
In dubious battle on the plains of heaven,
And shook his throne. What though the field be lost?   105
All is not lost—the unconquerable will,
And study of revenge, immortal hate,
And courage never to submit or yield:
And what is else not to be overcome;
That glory never shall his wrath or might   110
Extort from me. To bow and sue for grace
With suppliant knee, and deify his power
Who, from the terror of this arm, so late
Doubted his empire—that were low indeed;
That were an ignominy and shame beneath   115
This downfall; since, by fate, the strength of gods,
And this empyreal substance, cannot fail;
Since, through experience of this great event,
In arms not worse, in foresight much advanced,
We may with more successful hope resolve   120
To wage by force or guile eternal war,
Irreconcilable to our grand Foe,
Who now triumphs, and in the excess of joy
Sole reigning holds the tyranny of heaven."
    So spake the apostate angel, though in pain,   125
Vaunting aloud, but racked with deep despair;
And him thus answered soon his bold compeer:—[27]
    "O prince, O chief of many thronèd powers
That led the embattled seraphim [28] to war
Under thy conduct, and, in dreadful deeds   130
Fearless, endangered heaven's perpetual King,
And put to proof his high supremacy,
Whether upheld by strength, or chance, or fate!
Too well I see and rue the dire event [29]
That, with sad overthrow and foul defeat,   135
Hath lost us heaven, and all this mighty host

[27] compeer: companion
[28] seraphim: the highest order of angels
[29] event: outcome

In horrible destruction laid thus low,
As far as gods and heavenly essences [30]
Can perish: for the mind and spirit remains
Invincible, and vigor soon returns,   140
Though all our glory extinct, and happy state
Here swallowed up in endless misery.
But what if He our Conqueror (whom I now
Of force [31] believe almighty, since no less
Than such could have o'erpowered such force as ours)   145
Have left us this our spirit and strength entire,
Strongly to suffer and support our pains,
That we may so suffice [32] his vengeful ire,
Or do him mightier service as his thralls
By right of war, whate'er his business be,   150
Here in the heart of hell to work in fire,
Or do his errands in the gloomy deep? [33]
What can it then avail though yet we feel
Strength undiminished, or eternal being
To undergo eternal punishment?"   155
　　Whereto with speedy words the arch-fiend replied:—
"Fallen cherub,[34] to be weak is miserable,
Doing or suffering: but of this be sure—
To do aught good never will be our task,
But ever to do ill our sole delight,   160
As being the contrary to His high will
Whom we resist. If then his providence
Out of our evil seek to bring forth good,
Our labor must be to pervert that end,
And out of good still to find means of evil;   165
Which ofttimes may succeed so as perhaps
Shall grieve him, if I fail [35] not, and disturb
His inmost counsels from their destined aim.
But see! the angry victor hath recalled
His ministers of vengeance and pursuit   170

[30] essences: beings
[31] of force: of necessity
[32] suffice: satisfy
[33] deep: chaos
[34] cherub: next to the seraphim in rank
[35] fail: mistake

Back to the gates of heaven: the sulphurous hail,
Shot after us in storm, o'erblown hath laid
The fiery surge that from the precipice
Of heaven received us falling; and the thunder,
Winged with red lightning and impetuous rage,   175
Perhaps hath spent his [36] shafts, and ceases now
To bellow through the vast and boundless deep.
Let us not slip [37] the occasion, whether scorn
Or satiate fury yield it from our Foe.
Seest thou yon dreary plain, forlorn and wild,   180
The seat of desolation, void of light,
Save what the glimmering of these livid flames
Casts pale and dreadful? Thither let us tend
From off the tossing of these fiery waves;
There rest, if any rest can harbor there;   185
And, re-assembling our afflicted [38] powers,
Consult how we may henceforth most offend [39]
Our Enemy, our own loss how repair,
How overcome this dire calamity,
What reinforcement we may gain from hope,   190
If not what resolution from despair."
    Thus Satan, talking to his nearest mate,
With head uplift above the wave, and eyes
That sparkling blazed; his other parts besides
Prone on the flood, extended long and large,   195
Lay floating many a rood, in bulk as huge
As whom the fables name of monstrous size,
Titanian [40] or earth-born, that warred on Jove,
Briareos [41] or Typhon,[42] whom the den
By ancient Tarsus held, or that sea-beast   200
Leviathan,[43] which God of all his works
Created hugest that swim the ocean-stream.

[36] his: its
[37] slip: miss
[38] afflicted: overthrown
[39] offend: do violence to
[40] Titans: the older Greek gods who ruled before Jupiter usurped their power
[41] Briareos: a hundred-handed monster
[42] Typhon: a hundred-headed monster
[43] Leviathan: a biblical monster, much like a whale

Him, haply slumbering on the Norway foam,
The pilot of some small night-foundered [44] skiff,
Deeming some island, oft, as seamen tell,   205
With fixèd anchor in his scaly rind,
Moors by his side under the lee,[45] while night
Invests the sea, and wishèd morn delays.
So stretched out huge in length the arch-fiend lay,
Chained on the burning lake; nor ever thence   210
Had risen, or heaved his head, but that the will
And high permission of all-ruling heaven
Left him at large to his own dark designs,
That with reiterated crimes he might
Heap on himself damnation, while he sought   215
Evil to others, and enraged might see
How all his malice served but to bring forth
Infinite goodness, grace, and mercy, shewn
On man by him seduced, but on himself
Treble confusion, wrath, and vengeance poured.   220
    Forthwith upright he rears from off the pool
His mighty stature; on each hand the flames
Driven backward slope their pointing spires, and, rolled
In billows, leave i' the midst a horrid vale.
Then with expanded wings he steers his flight   225
Aloft, incumbent [46] on the dusky air,
That felt unusual weight; till on dry land
He lights—if it were land that ever burned
With solid, as the lake with liquid fire,
And such appeared in hue as when the force   230
Of subterranean wind transports a hill
Torn from Pelorus,[47] or the shattered side
Of thundering Aetna,[48] whose combustible
And fuelled entrails, thence conceiving fire,
Sublimed [49] with mineral fury, aid the winds,   235
And leave a singèd bottom all involved

[44] night-foundered: overtaken by night
[45] lee: the sheltered side
[46] incumbent: lying upon
[47] Pelorus: a mountain in Sicily
[48] Aetna: the volcano, Etna
[49] sublimed: turned to flame

With stench and smoke. Such resting found the sole
Of unblest feet. Him followed his next [50] mate;
Both glorying to have scaped the Stygian flood
As gods, and by their own recovered strength,   240
Not by the sufferance [51] of supernal power.
    "Is this the region, this the soil, the clime,"
Said then the lost archangel, "this the seat
That we must change for heaven?—this mournful gloom
For that celestial light? Be it so, since He   245
Who now is sovran can dispose and bid
What shall be right: farthest from Him is best,
Whom reason hath equalled,[52] force hath made supreme
Above his equals. Farewell, happy fields,
Where joy for ever dwells! Hail, horrors! hail,   250
Infernal world! and thou, profoundest [53] hell,
Receive thy new possessor—one who brings
A mind not to be changed by place or time.
The mind is its own place, and in itself
Can make a heaven of hell; a hell of heaven.   255
What matter where, if I be still the same,
And what I should be, all but less than he [54]
Whom thunder hath made greater? Here at least
We shall be free; the Almighty hath not built
Here for his envy, will not drive us hence: 260
Here we may reign secure; and, in my choice,
To reign is worth ambition, though in hell:
Better to reign in hell than serve in heaven.
But wherefore let we then our faithful friends,
The associates and co-partners of our loss,   265
Lie thus astonished [55] on the oblivious [56] pool,
And call them not to share with us their part
In this unhappy mansion, or once more

---

[50] **next:** nearest
[51] **sufferance:** permission
[52] **whom reason hath equalled:** Satan believes that he is equal to God in everything except power
[53] **profoundest:** lowest
[54] **all . . . he:** second only to God
[55] **astonished:** dazed, thunderstruck
[56] **oblivious:** producing forgetfulness

With rallied arms to try what may be yet
Regained in heaven, or what more lost in hell?"   270
    So Satan spake; and him Beëlzebub
Thus answered:—"Leader of those armies bright
Which, but the Omnipotent, none could have foiled!
If once they hear that voice, their liveliest pledge
Of hope in fears and dangers—heard so oft   275
In worst extremes, and on the perilous edge
Of battle, when it raged, in all assaults
Their surest signal—they will soon resume
New courage and revive, though now they lie
Grovelling and prostrate on yon lake of fire,   280
As we erewhile, astounded and amazed;
No wonder, fallen such a pernicious [57] highth!"
    He scarce had ceased when the superior fiend
Was moving toward the shore; his ponderous shield,
Ethereal temper, massy, large, and round,   285
Behind him cast. The broad circumference
Hung on his shoulders like the moon, whose orb
Through optic glass [58] the Tuscan artist [59] views
At evening, from the top of Fesolè, [60]
Or in Valdarno, to descry new lands,   290
Rivers, or mountains, in her spotty globe.
His spear—to equal which the tallest pine
Hewn on Norwegian hills, to be the mast
Of some great admiral, [61] were but a wand—
He walked with, to support uneasy steps   295
Over the burning marle, [62] not like those steps
On heaven's azure; and the torrid clime
Smote on him sore besides, vaulted with fire.
Nathless [63] he so endured, till on the beach
Of that inflamèd sea he stood, and called   300
His legions—angel forms, who lay entranced

[57] **pernicious:** destructive
[58] **optic glass:** telescope
[59] **Tuscan artist:** Galileo
[60] **Fesole:** a hill overlooking Florence
[61] **admiral:** flagship
[62] **marle:** soil
[63] **nathless:** nevertheless

Thick as autumnal leaves that strow the brooks
In Vallombrosa,[64] where the Etrurian shades
High over-arched embower; or scattered sedge
Afloat, when with fierce winds Orion [65] armed   305
Hath vexed the Red-Sea coast, whose waves o'erthrew
Busiris [66] and his Memphian [67] chivalry,
While with perfidious hatred they pursued
The sojourners of Goshen,[68] who beheld
From the safe shore their floating carcases   310
And broken chariot-wheels. So thick bestrown,
Abject [69] and lost, lay these, covering the flood,
Under amazement of their hideous change.
He called so loud that all the hollow deep
Of hell resounded:—"Princes, potentates,   315
Warriors, the flower of heaven—once yours; now lost,
If such astonishment as this can seize
Eternal spirits! Or have ye chosen this place
After the toil of battle to repose
Your wearied virtue,[70] for the ease you find   320
To slumber here, as in the vales of heaven?
Or in this abject posture have ye sworn
To adore the Conqueror, who now beholds
Cherub and seraph rolling in the flood
With scattered arms and ensigns, till anon   325
His swift pursuers from heaven-gates discern
The advantage, and, descending, tread us down
Thus drooping, or with linkèd thunderbolts
Transfix us to the bottom of this gulf?—
Awake, arise, or be for ever fallen!"   330
    They heard, and were abashed, and up they sprung
Upon the wind, as when men wont to watch,
On duty sleeping found by whom they dread,

---

[64] **Vallombrosa**: the Shady Valley near Florence
[65] **Orion**: a constellation whose appearance supposedly signified the coming of storms
[66] **Busiris**: a legendary ruler of Egypt
[67] **Memphian**: from Memphis, the capital of Egypt
[68] sojourners from Goshen: the Israelites
[69] abject: hurled down
[70] virtue: bravery

Rouse and bestir themselves ere well awake.
Nor did they not perceive the evil plight 335
In which they were, or the fierce pains not feel;
Yet to their general's voice they soon obeyed
Innumerable. As when the potent rod
Of Amram's son,[71] in Egypt's evil day,
Waved round the coast, up-called a pitchy [72] cloud 340
Of locusts, warping [73] on the eastern wind,
That o'er the realm of impious Pharaoh hung
Like night, and darkened all the land of Nile;
So numberless were those bad angels seen
Hovering on wing under the cope [74] of hell, 345
'Twixt upper, nether, and surrounding fires;
Till, as a signal given, the uplifted spear
Of their great sultan waving to direct
Their course, in even balance down they light
On the firm brimstone, and fill all the plain: 350
A multitude like which the populous north
Poured never from her frozen loins to pass
Rhene or the Danaw,[75] when her barbarous sons
Came like a deluge on the south, and spread
Beneath Gibraltar to the Libyan sands. 355
Forthwith, from every squadron and each band,
The heads and leaders thither haste where stood
Their great commander—godlike shapes, and forms
Excelling human; princely dignities;
And powers that erst in heaven sat on thrones, 360
Though of their names in heavenly records now
Be no memorial, blotted out and rased [76]
By their rebellion from the books of life.
Nor had they yet among the sons of Eve
Got them new names, till, wandering o'er the earth, 365
Through God's high sufferance for the trial of man,
By falsities and lies the greatest part

[71] **Amram's son:** Moses
[72] **pitchy:** black as pitch
[73] **warping:** undulating
[74] **cope:** covering
[75] **Rhene . . . Danaw:** Rhine . . . Danube
[76] **rased:** erased

Of mankind they corrupted to forsake
God their Creator, and the invisible
Glory of Him that made them to transform   370
Oft to the image of a brute, adorned
With gay religions [77] full of pomp and gold,
And devils to adore for deities:
Then were they known to men by various names,
And various idols through the heathen world.   375
    Say, Muse, their names then known, who first, who last,
Roused from the slumber on that fiery couch,
At their great emperor's call, as next in worth
Came singly where he stood on the bare strand,
While the promiscuous crowd stood yet aloof.   380
    The chief were those who, from the pit of hell
Roaming to seek their prey on earth, durst fix
Their seats, long after, next the seat of God,
Their altars by His altar, gods adored
Among the nations round, and durst abide   385
Jehovah thundering out of Sion, throned
Between the cherubim; yea, often placed
Within His sanctuary itself their shrines,
Abominations; and with cursèd things
His holy rites and solemn feasts profaned,   390
And with their darkness durst affront His light.
First, *Moloch*,[78] horrid king, besmeared with blood
Of human sacrifice, and parents' tears;
Though, for the noise of drums and timbrels loud,
Their children's cries unheard that passed through fire   395
To his grim idol. Him the Ammonite
Worshiped in Rabba [79] and her watery plain
In Argob and in Basan,[80] to the stream
Of utmost Arnon.[81] Nor content with such
Audacious neighborhood, the wisest heart   400
Of Solomon he led by fraud to build

[77] **religions:** religious rites
[78] **Moloch:** a sun god who was worshipped in the form of a bull; the Ammonites sacrificed their children to him
[79] **Rabba:** capital of the Ammonites
[80] **Argob . . . Basan:** regions east of the Jordan River
[81] **Arnon:** a river flowing into the Dead Sea

His temple right against the temple of God
On that opprobrious hill,[82] and made his grove
The pleasant valley of Hinnon, Tophet thence
And black Gehenna [83] called, the type of hell.   405
Next *Chemos*,[84] the obscene dread of Moab's sons,
From Aroar to Nebo and the wild
Of southmost Abarim; in Hesebon
And Horonaim, Seon's [85] realm, beyond
The flowery dale of Sibma clad with vines,   410
And Elealè to the Asphaltic Pool: [86]
Peor his other name, when he enticed
Israel in Sittim, on their march from Nile,
To do him wanton rites, which cost them woe.
Yet thence his lustful orgies he enlarged   415
Even to that hill of scandal, by the grove
Of Moloch homicide, lust hard by hate,
Till good Josiah drove them thence to hell.
With these came they who, from the bordering flood
Of old Euphrates to the brook that parts   420
Egypt from Syrian ground, had general names
Of *Baalim* and *Ashtaroth* [87]—those male,
These feminine. For spirits, when they please,
Can either sex assume, or both; so soft
And uncompounded is their essence pure,   425
Not tied or manacled with joint or limb,
Nor founded on the brittle strength of bones,
Like cumbrous flesh; but, in what shape they choose,
Dilated or condensed, bright or obscure,
Can execute their aery purposes,   430
And works of love or enmity fulfil.
For those the race of Israel oft forsook
Their living strength, and unfrequented left

[82] that opprobrious hill: Mount of Olives where pagan shrines had been built
[83] Hinnon . . . Gehenna: a valley formerly used in pagan rites which was turned into a place for burning garbage
[84] Chemos: another form of Moloch
[85] Seon's: Seon, a king of the Ammonites
[86] Sibma . . . Pool: names of mountains and towns near the Dead Sea, which Milton calls the Asphaltic Pool
[87] Baalim . . . Ashtaroth: pagan gods

His righteous altar, bowing lowly down
To bestial gods; for which their heads, as low   435
Bowed down in battle, sunk before the spear
Of despicable foes. With these in troop
Came *Astoreth*, whom the Phœnicians called
Astarte, queen of heaven, with crescent horns;
To whose bright image nightly by the moon   440
Sidonian [88] virgins paid their vows and songs;
In Sion also not unsung, where stood
Her temple on the offensive mountain, built
By that uxorious king [89] whose heart, though large,
Beguiled by fair idolatresses, fell   445
To idols foul. *Thammuz* [90] came next behind,
Whose annual wound in Lebanon allured
The Syrian damsels to lament his fate
In amorous ditties all a summer's day,
While smooth Adonis [91] from his native rock   450
Ran purple to the sea, supposed with blood
Of Thammuz yearly wounded: the love-tale
Infected Sion's daughters with like heat,
Whose wanton passions in the sacred porch
Ezekiel saw, when, by the vision led,   455
His eye surveyed the dark idolatries
Of alienated Judah. Next came one
Who mourned in earnest, when the captive Ark
Maimed his brute image,[92] head and hands lopt off,
In his own temple, on the grunsel-edge,[93]   460
Where he fell flat and shamed his worshipers:
Dagon his name, sea-monster, upward man
And downward fish; yet had his temple high
Reared in Azotus, dreaded [94] through the coast
Of Palestine, in Gath and Ascalon,   465
And Acaron and Gaza's frontier bounds

[88] **Sidonian:** Phoenician, people of Sidon
[89] **uxorious king:** Solomon
[90] **Thammuz:** a Phoenician Adonis
[91] **Adonis:** a Phoenician river named after the god
[92] **his brute image:** Dagon the fish god
[93] **grunsel-edge:** threshold
[94] **dreaded:** worshipped

Him followed *Rimmon*,[95] whose delightful seat
Was fair Damascus, on the fertile banks
Of Abbana and Pharphar, lucid streams.
He also against the house of God was bold: 470
A leper [96] once he lost, and gained a king—
Ahaz, his sottish conqueror, whom he drew
God's altar to disparage and displace
For one of Syrian mode, whereon to burn
His odious offerings, and adore the gods   475
Whom he had vanquished. After these appeared
A crew who, under names of old renown—
Osiris, Isis, Orus,[97] and their train—
With monstrous shapes and sorceries abused
Fanatic Egypt and her priests to seek   480
Their wandering gods disguised in brutish forms
Rather than human. Nor did Israel scape
The infection, when their borrowed gold composed
The calf in Oreb; and the rebel king [98]
Doubled that sin in Bethel and in Dan,   485
Likening his Maker to the grazèd ox—
Jehovah, who, in one night, when he passed
From Egypt marching, equalled [99] with one stroke
Both her first-born [100] and all her bleating gods.
Belial [101] came last; than whom a Spirit more lewd   490
Fell not from heaven, or more gross to love
Vice for itself. To him no temple stood
Or altar smoked; yet who more oft than he
In temples and at altars, when the priest
Turns atheist, as did Eli's sons, who filled   495
With lust and violence the house of God?
In courts and palaces he also reigns,
And in luxurious [102] cities, where the noise

---

[95] Rimmon: worshipped by the Syrians
[96] leper: Naaman the leper in the Book of Kings
[97] Osiris, Isis, Orus: chief Egyptian deity
[98] the rebel king: Jeroboam, who made two calves of gold
[99] equalled: struck down
[100] her first-born: reference to the tenth plague sent down on the Egyptians
[101] Belial: a god of the Assyrians
[102] luxurious: lewd

Of riot ascends above their loftiest towers,
And injury and outrage; and, when night   500
Darkens the streets, then wander forth the sons
Of Belial, flown [103] with insolence and wine.
Witness the streets of Sodom, and that night
In Gibeath, when the hospitable door
Exposed a matron, to avoid worse rape.   505
    These were the prime [104] in order and in might:
The rest were long to tell; though far renowned
The Ionian gods—of Javan's issue held [105]
Gods, yet confessed later than heaven and earth,
Their boasted parents;—*Titan*, heaven's first-born,   510
With his enormous brood, and birthright seized
By younger *Saturn:* he from mightier Jove,
His own and Rhea's son, like measure [106] found;
So *Jove* usurping reigned. These, first in Crete
And Ida [107] known, thence on the snowy top   515
Of cold Olympus ruled the middle air,
Their highest heaven; or on the Delphian cliff,
Or in Dodona,[108] and through all the bounds
Of Doric [109] land; or who with Saturn old
Fled over Adria [110] to the Hesperian fields,[111]   520
And o'er the Celtic [112] roamed the utmost isles.[113]
    All these and more came flocking; but with looks
Downcast and damp; yet such wherein appeared
Obscure some glimpse of joy to have found their chief
Not in despair, to have found themselves not lost   525
In loss itself; which on his countenance cast
Like doubtful hue. But he, his wonted pride

---

[103] flown: flushed
[104] prime: chief
[105] Javan . . . held: the Ionians, or Greeks, were considered to be the descendants of Javan, son of Japhat
[106] measure: treatment
[107] Ida: Mt. Ida in Crete
[108] Dodona: temple of Zeus in Epirus
[109] Doric: Greek
[110] Adria: the Adriatic Sea
[111] Hesperian fields: the fields of the West, Italy
[112] Celtic: France and northwest Europe
[113] utmost isles: British Isles

Soon recollecting, with high words, that bore
Semblance of worth, not substance, gently raised
Their fainting courage, and dispelled their fears: 530
Then straight commands that, at the warlike sound
Of trumpets loud and clarions, be upreared
His mighty standard. That proud honor claimed
Azazel as his right, a cherub tall:
Who forthwith from the glittering staff unfurled   535
The imperial ensign; which, full high advanced,[114]
Shone like a meteor streaming to the wind,
With gems and golden lustre rich emblazed,
Seraphic arms and trophies; all the while
Sonorous metal blowing martial sounds: 540
At which the universal host up-sent
A shout that tore hell's concave, [115] and beyond
Frighted the reign [116] of Chaos and old Night.
All in a moment through the gloom were seen
Ten thousand banners rise into the air,   545
With orient [117] colors waving: with them rose
A forest huge of spears; and thronging helms
Appeared, and serried [118] shields in thick array
Of depth immeasurable. Anon they move
In perfect phalanx to the Dorian mood   550
Of flutes and soft recorders [119]—such as raised
To highth of noblest temper heroes old
Arming to battle, and instead of rage
Deliberate valor breathed, firm, and unmoved
With dread of death to flight or foul retreat;   555
Nor wanting power to mitigate and swage [120]
With solemn touches troubled thoughts, and chase
Anguish and doubt and fear and sorrow and pain
From mortal or immortal minds. Thus they,
Breathing united force with fixèd thought,   560

[114] advanced: uplifted
[115] concave: vault, dome
[116] reign: realm
[117] orient: shining
[118] serried: interlocked
[119] recorders: musical instruments called flageolets
[120] swage: assuage

Moved on in silence to soft pipes that charmed
Their painful steps o'er the burnt soil. And now
Advanced in view they stand—a horrid [121] front
Of dreadful length and dazzling arms, in guise
Of warriors old, with ordered spear and shield,   565
Awaiting what command their mighty chief
Had to impose. He through the armèd files
Darts his experienced eye, and soon traverse [122]
The whole battalion views—their order due,
Their visages and stature as of gods;   570
Their number last he sums. And now his heart
Distends with pride, and, hardening in his strength,
Glories: for never, since created man,
Met such embodied [123] force, as named with [124] these,
Could merit more than that small infantry [125]   575
Warred on by cranes—though all the giant brood
Of Phlegra [126] with the heroic race were joined
That fought at Thebes and Ilium, on each side
Mixed with auxiliar gods; and what resounds
In fable or romance of Uther's son,[127]   580
Begirt with [128] British and Armoric [129] knights;
And all who since, baptized or infidel,
Jousted in Aspramont, or Montalban,
Damasco, or Marocco, or Trebisond,
Or whom Biserta sent from Afric shore   585
When Charlemain with all his peerage fell
By Fontarabbia.[130] Thus far these beyond
Compare of mortal prowess, yet observed [131]
Their dread commander. He, above the rest

[121] horrid: bristling
[122] traverse: cross
[123] embodied: collected
[124] named with: compared with
[125] small infantry: the pygmies whose battle with the cranes is told by Homer
[126] Phlegra: the place where the giants were conquered by the gods
[127] Uther's son: Arthur
[128] begirt with: surrounded by
[129] Armoric: Brittany
[130] Aspramont . . . Fontarabbia: these names come from the chivalric romances
of the Middle Ages
[131] observed: did homage to

In shape and gesture proudly eminent,   590
Stood like a tower. His form had yet not lost
All her [132] original brightness, nor appeared
Less than archangel ruined, and the excess
Of glory obscured: as when the sun new-risen
Looks through the horizontal misty air   595
Shorn of his beams, or, from behind the moon,
In dim eclipse, disastrous twilight sheds
On half the nations, and with fear of change
Perplexes monarchs. Darkened so, yet shone
Above them all the archangel: but his face   600
Deep scars of thunder had intrenched, and care
Sat on his faded cheek, but under brows
Of dauntless courage, and considerate [133] pride
Waiting revenge. Cruel his eye, but cast
Signs of remorse and passion, to behold   605
The fellows of his crime, the followers rather
(Far other once beheld in bliss), condemned
For ever now to have their lot in pain—
Millions of spirits for his fault amerced [134]
Of heaven, and from eternal splendors flung   610
For his revolt—yet faithful how they stood,
Their glory withered; as, when heaven's fire
Hath scathed the forest oaks or mountain pines,
With singèd top their stately growth, though bare,
Stands on the blasted heath. He now prepared   615
To speak; whereat their doubled ranks they bend
From wing to wing, and half enclose him round
With all his peers: attention held them mute,
Thrice he assayed,[135] and thrice, in spite of scorn,
Tears, such as angels weep, burst forth: at last   620
Words interwove with sighs found out their way:—
   "O myriads of immortal spirits! O Powers
Matchless, but with the Almighty!—and that strife
Was not inglorious, though the event [136] was dire,

[132] **her:** its
[133] **considerate:** deliberate
[134] **amerced:** punished by loss
[135] **assayed:** tried
[136] **event:** outcome

As this place testifies, and this dire change,   625
Hateful to utter. But what power of mind,
Foreseeing or presaging, from the depth
Of knowledge past or present, could have feared
How such united force of gods, how such
As stood like these, could ever know repulse?   630
For who can yet believe, though after loss,
That all these puissant legions, whose exile
Hath emptied heaven, shall fail to reascend,
Self-raised, and re-possess their native seat?
For me, be witness all the host of heaven,   635
If counsels different, or danger shunned
By me, have lost our hopes. But he who reigns
Monarch in heaven till then as one secure
Sat on his throne, upheld by old repute,
Consent or custom, and his regal state   640
Put forth at full, but still his strength concealed—
Which tempted our attempt, and wrought our fall.
Henceforth his might we know, and know our own,
So as not either to provoke, or dread
New war provoked: our better part [137] remains   645
To work [138] in close design, by fraud or guile,
What force effected not; that he no less
At length from us may find, Who overcomes
By force hath overcome but half his foe.
Space may produce new worlds: whereof so rife [139]   650
There went a fame [140] in heaven that He ere long
Intended to create, and therein plant
A generation whom his choice regard
Should favor equal to the sons of heaven.
Thither, if but to pry, shall be perhaps   655
Our first eruption—thither, or elsewhere;
For this infernal pit shall never hold
Celestial spirits in bondage, nor the abyss
Long under darkness cover. But these thoughts

[137] **better part:** wiser course of action
[138] **work:** bring about
[139] **rife:** commonly reported
[140] **fame:** rumor

Full counsel must mature. Peace is despaired;   660
For who can think submission? War, then, war
Open or understood [141] must be resolved."
    He spake; and, to confirm his words, outflew
Millions of flaming swords, drawn from the thighs
Of mighty cherubim; the sudden blaze   665
Far round illumined hell. Highly they raged
Against the Highest and fierce with graspèd arms
Clashed on their sounding shields the din of war,
Hurling defiance toward the vault of heaven.
    There stood a hill not far, whose grisly top   670
Belched fire and rolling smoke; the rest entire
Shone with a glossy scurf [142]—undoubted sign
That in his womb was hid metallic ore,
The work of sulphur. Thither, winged with speed,
A numerous brigad hastened: as when bands   675
Of pioneers,[143] with spade and pickaxe armed,
Forerun the royal camp, to trench a field,
Or cast a rampart. Mammon [144] led them on—
Mammon, the least erected spirit that fell
From heaven; for even in heaven his looks and thoughts   680
Were always downward bent, admiring more
The riches of heaven's pavement, trodden gold,
Than aught divine or holy else enjoyed
In vision beatific. By him first
Men also, and by his suggestion taught,   685
Ransacked the center,[145] and with impious hands
Rifled the bowels of their mother earth
For treasures better hid. Soon had his crew
Opened into the hill a spacious wound,
And digged out ribs of gold. Let none admire   690
That riches grow in hell; that soil may best
Deserve the precious bane.[146] And here let those
Who boast in mortal things, and wondering tell

[141] understood: among ourselves, secret
[142] scurf: covering
[143] pioneers: miners
[144] Mammon: a Chaldean god
[145] center: the earth is the center of the universe in the Ptolemaic system
[146] bane: blight, evil

Of Babel, and the works of Memphian Kings,[147]
Learn how their greatest monuments of fame,   695
And strength, and art, are easily outdone
By spirits reprobate, and in an hour
What in an age they, with incessant toil
And hands innumerable, scarce perform.
Nigh on the plain, in many cells prepared,   700
That underneath had veins of liquid fire
Sluiced from the lake, a second multitude
With wondrous art founded [148] the massy ore,
Severing each kind, and scummed the bullion-dross.[149]
A third as soon had formed within the ground   705
A various mould, and from the boiling cells
By strange conveyance filled each hollow nook;
As in an organ, from one blast of wind,
To many a row of pipes the sound-board breathes.
Anon out of the earth a fabric huge   710
Rose like an exhalation, with the sound
Of dulcet symphonies and voices sweet—
Built like a temple, where pilasters round
Were set, and Doric pillars overlaid
With golden architrave; nor did there want   715
Cornice or frieze, with bossy [150] sculptures graven:
The roof was fretted gold. Not Babylon
Nor great Alcairo [151] such magnificence
Equalled in all their glories, to enshrine
Belus or Serapis [152] their gods, or seat   720
Their kings, when Egypt with Assyria strove
In wealth and luxury. The ascending pile
Stood fixed her stately highth; and straight the doors,
Opening their brazen folds, discover, wide
Within, her ample spaces o'er the smooth   725
And level pavement: from the archèd roof,
Pendent by subtle magic, many a row

[147] works . . . kings: the pyramids
[148] founded: melted at a foundry
[149] bullion-dross: slag
[150] bossy: embossed with figures and designs
[151] Alcairo: Cairo
[152] Belus . . . Serapis: Baal, the Egyptian god of the underworld

Of starry lamps and blazing cressets,[153] fed
With naphtha and asphaltus, yielded light
As from a sky. The hasty multitude   730
Admiring entered; and the work some praise,
And some the architect. His hand was known
In heaven by many a towered structure high,
Where sceptred angels held their residence,
And sat as princes, whom the supreme King   735
Exalted to such power, and gave to rule,
Each in his hierarchy, the orders bright.
Nor was his name unheard or unadored
In ancient Greece; and in Ausonian [154] land
Men called him Mulciber; and how he fell   740
From heaven they fabled, thrown by angry Jove
Sheer o'er the crystal battlements: from morn
To noon he fell, from noon to dewy eve,
A summer's day, and with the setting sun
Dropt from the zenith, like a falling star,   745
On Lemnos, the Aegean isle. Thus they relate,
Erring; for he with this rebellious rout [155]
Fell long before; nor aught availed him now
To have built in heaven high towers; nor did he scape
By all his engines,[156] but was headlong sent,   750
With his industrious crew, to build in hell.
    Meanwhile the wingèd heralds, by command
Of sovran power, with awful ceremony
And trumpet's sound, throughout the host proclaim
A solemn counsel forthwith to be held   755
At Pandemonium,[157] the high capital
Of Satan and his peers. Their summons called
From every band and squarèd regiment
By place or choice the worthiest: they anon
With hundreds and with thousands trooping came   760
Attended. All access was thronged; the gates

[153] cressets: hanging lamps
[154] Ausonian: Italian
[155] rout: crew
[156] engines: devices
[157] Pandemonium: the place of "all the devils"

And porches wide, but chief the spacious hall
(Though like a covered field, where champions bold
Wont ride in armed, and at the Soldan's [158] chair
Defied the best of panim [159] chivalry   765
To mortal combat, or career with lance),
Thick swarmed, both on the ground and in the air,
Brushed with the hiss of rustling wings. As bees
In spring-time, when the sun with Taurus [160] rides,
Pour forth their populous youth about the hive   770
In clusters; they among fresh dews and flowers
Fly to and fro, or on the smoothèd plank,
The suburb of their straw-built citadel,
New rubbed with balm, expatiate, and confer
Their state-affairs: so thick the aerie crowd   775
Swarmed and were straitened; [161] till, the signal given,
Behold a wonder! They but now who seemed
In bigness to surpass earth's giant sons,
Now less than smallest dwarfs, in narrow room
Throng numberless—like that pygmean race   780
Beyond the Indian mount; or faery elves,
Whose midnight revels, by a forest-side
Or fountain, some belated peasant sees,
Or dreams he sees, while overhead the moon
Sits arbitress,[162] and nearer to the earth   785
Wheels her pale course: they, on their mirth and dance
Intent, with jocund music charm his ear;
At once with joy and fear his heart rebounds.
Thus incorporeal spirits to smallest forms
Reduced their shapes immense, and were at large,[163]   790
Though without number still, amidst the hall
Of that infernal court. But far within,
And in their own dimensions like themselves,
The great seraphic lords and cherubim
In close recess and secret conclave sat,   795

[158] **Soldan's**: Sultan's
[159] **panim**: pagan
[160] **Taurus**: the sign of the Bull in the zodiac
[161] **straitened**: crowded together
[162] **arbitress**: witness
[163] **at large**: uncrowded

A thousand demi-gods on golden seats,
Frequent [164] and full. After short silence then,
And summons read, the great consult [165] began.

[164] frequent: crowded
[165] consult: consultation

For Discussion

1. Lines 1-5 state Milton's theme. Express it in your own words.
2. The *Book of Exodus* in your Bible tells the story of Moses shepherding Jethro's flocks on Horeb (Oreb). Read Chapter 3 and see where Milton obtained his background.
3. Who are "the chosen seed" in line 10? Why are they called "chosen"?
4. Lines 20-21 are an allusion to *Genesis* 1:2. Explain their meaning.
5. Explain Milton's purpose as stated in lines 25-26.
6. Lines 27-33 pose specific questions that turn our attention to the cause of disobedience. Show how this is true. Who is the cause of "that foul revolt"?
7. Briefly explain the revolt in Heaven that is portrayed in lines 34-49.
8. Lines 50-81 portray Satan and his followers in Hell. Point to details which make this setting unearthly. How does the lack of sharp, specific details make the situation remote?
9. Satan's speech to Beelzebub (lines 84-124) is a typical, formal speech of epic poetry. What effect does such a speech produce on the reader?
10. What qualities does Satan display in this first speech? Is he a proud liar?
11. Beelzebub's answer to Satan (lines 127-155) is shorter than Satan's speech. Why is this fitting? What do you think of the character of Beelzebub?
12. Satan's speech in lines 156-191 leads one to expect a creature of great vigor. His vigor is motivated by deep hatred and bitter defeat. Show how this is true in lines 156-191.
13. Satan's size is reflected in the long sentence that runs from line 192 to 220. What epic qualities does a sentence like this show?
14. The first action of the epic begins with line 221. What characteristics of epic action are noticeable in this section (lines 221-242)?
15. One of Satan's most powerful speeches is in lines 242-263. Do you think this speech shows Milton's keen insight into the way people can feel? Explain.

16. In what way is Satan's leadership apparent in lines 331–375? What kind of leader is he?

17. What classical epic devices are noticeable in lines 381–521? Explain your answer.

18. What ignoble qualities of Satan are shown in lines 522–622? Could he ever be considered a hero? Why or why not?

19. Satan's speech in lines 622–663 outlines his strategy. Why will he avoid provoking a new war with the "Monarch in Heaven"? What plan of attack does he propose?

20. Lines 664–751 contain many Biblical and classical allusions. Make a list of each and explain the poetic effect they produce.

21. The scene at Pandemonium (lines 752–798) is of majestic scope. In your own words describe the scene.

22. Reread the section of the Introduction which defines the epic and its characteristics (page 145). Show how each pertains to Book One of *Paradise Lost*.

23. Read Addison's "A Consideration of Milton's *Paradise Lost*" (pages 236–240). Express your opinion of his ideas.

For Composition: Write a short essay comparing *Paradise Lost* with *Beowulf*. What differences strike you immediately? What is the distinction between a *folk epic* and a *literary epic*? How does such a distinction apply to *Paradise Lost* and *Beowulf*?

SAMUEL PEPYS

(1633–1703)

Often a diary can give a more vivid insight into history than many other kinds of books. As an eye-witness account of history and everyday life, it can affect us much more than learned essays of later generations. This is true, for example, of *Anne Frank: A Diary of a Young Girl*, part of which you read in ninth grade. To a lesser degree, the same is true of a famous diary written by Samuel Pepys between the years 1660–1699.

Written in a system of obscure shorthand, Pepys' *Diary* was intended for his own private records and never meant for the eyes of the public. Yet he did not destroy it in later years, but bequeathed it to Magdalene College, his Alma Mater. There it lay undeciphered and unread, until an Oxford undergraduate began to transcribe it in 1820. When finished, the *Diary* totalled 9,325 pages and gave a magnificent account of colorful London life in the first years of the Restoration. In the following excerpts, we can share the panic and fear of the Great Fire of London and the noise and manners of the London theater. Here is history come to life as told by a man who was there!

from *Pepys' Diary*

THE FIRE OF LONDON

SEPTEMBER 2, 1666 (LORD'S DAY)

Some of our maids sitting up late last night to get things ready against our feast today, Jane called us up about three in the morning, to tell us of a great fire they saw in the city. So I rose and slipped on my night-gown, and went to her window; and thought it to be on the back-side of Marke-lane at the farthest; but, being unused to such fires as followed, I thought it far enough off; and so went to bed again, and to sleep. About seven rose again to dress myself, and there looked out at the window, and saw the fire not so much as it was, and further off. So to my closet to set things to rights, after yesterday's cleaning. By and by Jane comes and tells me that she hears that above 300 houses have been burned down tonight by the fire we saw, and that it is now burning down all Fish Street, by London Bridge. So I made myself ready presently, and walked to the Tower; [1] and there got up upon one of the high places, Sir J. Robinson's little son going up with me; and there I did see the houses at that end of the bridge all on fire, and an infinite great fire on this and the other side the end of the bridge; which, among other people, did trouble me for poor little Michell and our Sarah on the bridge. So down with my heart full of trouble, to the Lieutenant of the Tower, who tells me that it begun this morning in the King's baker's house in Pudding-lane, and that it hath burned St. Magnus's Church and most part of Fish Street already. So I down to the water-side, and there got a boat, and through bridge and there saw a lamentable fire. Poor Michell's house, as far as the Old Swan, already burned that way, and the fire running further, that, in a very little time, it got as far as the Steele-yard, while I was there. Everybody endeavoring to remove their goods, and flinging into the river, or bringing them into lighters that lay off; poor people staying in their houses as long as till the very fire touched them, and then running into boats or clambering from one pair of stairs, by the water-side, to another. And, among other things, the poor pigeons, I perceive, were loth to leave their houses, but hovered about the windows and balconies, till some of them burned their wings, and fell down. Having stayed, and in an hour's time seen the fire rage every way; and nobody, to my sight, endeavoring to quench it, but to remove their goods, and leave all to the fire, and having seen it get as far as the Steele-yard, and the wind mighty high, and driving it into the city: and everything, after so long a drought, proving combustible, even the very stones of churches; and, among other things, the poor steeple by which pretty Mrs. ——— lives, and whereof my old schoolfellow Elborough is parson, taken fire in the very top, and there burned till it fell down; I to White Hall,[2] with a gentleman with me who desired to go off from the Tower, to see the fire, in my boat; to White Hall, and there up to the King's closet in the Chapel, where people came about me, and I did give them an account dismayed them all, and word was carried into the King. So I was called for, and did tell the King and Duke

---

[1] **Tower:** the Tower of London
[2] **White Hall:** the royal palace

of York [3] what I saw; and, that unless his Majesty did command houses to be pulled down, nothing could stop the fire. They seemed much troubled, and the King commanded me to go to my Lord Mayor from him, and command him to spare no houses, but to pull down before the fire every way. The Duke of York bid me tell him, that if he would have any more soldiers, he shall; and so did my Lord Arlington afterwards, as a great secret. Here meeting with Captain Cocke, I in his coach, which he lent me, and Creed with me to Paul's; [4] and there walked along Watling Street, as well as I could, every creature coming away loaden with goods to save, and, here and there, sick people carried away in beds. Extraordinary good goods carried in carts and on backs. At last met my Lord Mayor in Canning Street, like a man spent, with a handkercher about his neck. To the King's message, he cried like a fainting woman, "Lord! what can I do? I am spent; people will not obey me. I have been pulling down houses; but the fire overtakes us faster than we can do it." That he needed no more soldiers; and that, for himself, he must go and refresh himself, having been up all night. So he left me, and I him, and walked home, seeing people all almost distracted, and no manner of means used to quench the fire. The houses, too, so very thick thereabouts, and full of matter for burning, as pitch and tar, in Thames Street; and warehouses of oil, and wines, and brandy, and other things. Here I saw Mr. Isaake Houblon, the handsome man, prettily dressed and dirty at his door at Dowgate, receiving some of his brothers' things, whose houses were on fire; and, as he says, have been removed twice already; and he doubts, as it soon proved, that they must be, in a little time, removed from his house also, which was a sad consideration. And to see the churches all filling with goods by people who themselves should have been quietly there at this time. By this time, it was about twelve o'clock; and so home, and there find my guests, which was Mr. Wood and his wife Barbary Shelden, and also Mr. Moone; she mighty fine, and her husband, for aught I see, a likely man. But Mr. Moone's design and mine, which was to look over my closet, and please him with the sight thereof, which he hath long desired, was wholly disappointed; for we were in great trouble and disturbance at this fire, not knowing what to think of it. However, we had an extraordinary good dinner,

[3] **Duke of York:** brother of Charles II, afterwards King James II
[4] **Paul's:** St. Paul's Cathedral

and as merry as at this time we could be. While at dinner, Mrs. Batelier came to enquire after Mr. Woolfe and Stanes, who, it seems, are related to them, whose houses in Fish Street are all burned, and they in a sad condition. She would not stay in the fright. Soon as dined, I and Moone away, and walked through the city, the streets full of nothing but people and horses and carts loaden with goods, ready to run over one another, and removing goods from one burned house to another. They now removing out of Canning Street, which received goods in the morning, into Lumbard Street, and further; and among others, I now saw my little goldsmith Stokes receiving some friend's goods, whose house itself was burned the day after. We parted at Paul's; he home, and I to Paul's Wharf, where I had appointed a boat to attend me, and took in Mr. Carcasse and his brother, whom I met in the street, and carried them below and above bridge too and again to see the fire, which was now got further, both below and above, and no likelihood of stopping it. Met with the King and Duke of York in their barge, and with them to Queenhithe, and there called Sir Richard Browne to them. Their order was only to pull down houses apace, and so below bridge at the waterside; but little was or could be done, the fire coming upon them so fast. Good hopes there was of stopping it at the Three Cranes above, and at Buttulph's Wharf below bridge, if care be used; but the wind carries it into the city, so as we know not, by the waterside, what it do there. River full of lighters [5] and boats taking in goods, and good goods swimming in the water; and only I observed that hardly one lighter or boat in three that had the goods of a house in, but there was a pair of virginals [6] in it. Having seen as much as I could now, I away to White Hall by appointment, and there walked to St. James's Park; and there met my wife, and Creed, and Wood, and his wife, and walked to my boat; and there upon the water again, and to the fire up and down, it still encreasing, and the wind great. So near the fire as we could for smoke; and all over the Thames, with one's face in the wind, you were almost burned with a shower of fire-drops. This is very true; so as houses were burned by these drops and flakes of fire, three or four, nay, five or six houses, one from another. When we could endure no more upon the water, we to a little ale-house on the Bankside, over against the Three Cranes, and

[5] lighters: barges
[6] virginals: small pianos

there stayed till it was dark almost and saw the fire grow; and, as it grew darker, appeared more and more; and in corners and upon steeples, and between churches and houses, as far as we could see up the hill of the city, in a most horrid, malicious, bloody flame, not like the fine flame of an ordinary fire. Barbary and her husband away before us. We stayed till, it being darkish, we saw the fire as only one entire arch of fire from this to the other side the bridge, and in a bow up the hill for an arch of above a mile long; it made me weep to see it. The churches, houses, and all on fire, and flaming at once; and a horrid noise the flames made, and the cracking of houses at their ruin. So home with a sad heart, and there find everybody discoursing and lamenting the fire; and poor Tom Hater come with some few of his goods saved out of his house, which was burned upon Fish Street Hill. I invited him to lie at my house, and did receive his goods; but was deceived in his lying there, the news coming every moment of the growth of the fire; so as we were forced to begin to pack up our own goods, and prepare for their removal; and did by moonshine, it being brave, dry, and moonshine and warm weather, carry much of my goods into the garden; and Mr. Hater and I did remove my money and iron chests into my cellar, as thinking that the safest place. And got my bags of gold into my office, ready to carry away, and my chief papers of accounts also there, and my tallies into a box by themselves. So great was our fear, as Sir W. Batten hath carts come out of the country to fetch away his goods this night. We did put Mr. Hater, poor man! to bed a little but he got but very little rest, so much noise being in my house, taking down of goods.

SEPTEMBER 5, 1666.

I lay down in the office again upon W. Hewer's quilt, being mighty weary, and sore in my feet with going till I was hardly able to stand. About two in the morning my wife calls me up, and tells me of new cries of fire, it being come to Barking Church, which is the bottom of our lane. I up; and finding it so, resolved presently to take her away, and did, and took my gold, which was about £2350,[7] W. Hewer and Jane down by Proundy's boat to Woolwich, but, Lord! what a sad sight it was by moonlight, to see the whole city almost on fire, that you might see it plain at Woolwich, as if you were by it.

[7] £2350: about $27,000.

There, when I come, I find the gates shut, but no guard kept at all; which troubled me, because of discourse now begun, that there is plot in it, and that the French had done it. I got the gates open, and to Mr. Shelden's, where I locked up my gold, and charged my wife and W. Hewer never to leave the room without one of them in it, night or day. So back again, by the way seeing my goods well in the lighters at Deptford, and watched well by people. Home, and whereas I expected to have seen our house on fire, it being now about seven o'clock, it was not. But to the fire, and there find greater hopes than I expected; for my confidence of finding our office on fire was such, that I durst not ask anybody how it was with us, till I come and saw it not burned. But, going to the fire, I find, by the blowing up of houses, and the great help given by the workmen out of the King's yards, sent up by Sir W. Pen,[8] there is a good stop given to it, as well as at Marke Lane end as ours; it having only burned the dial of Barking Church, and part of the porch, and was there quenched. I up to the top of Barking steeple, and there saw the saddest sight of desolation that I ever saw; everywhere great fires, oil-cellars, and brimstone, and other things burning. I became afeard to stay there long, and therefore down again as fast as I could, the fire being spread as far as I could see it; and to Sir W. Pen's, and there eat a piece of cold meat, having eaten nothing since Sunday, but the remains of Sunday's dinner. Here I met with Mr. Young and Whistler; and, having removed all my things, and received good hopes that the fire at our end is stopped, they and I walked into the town, and find Fenchurch Street, Gracious Street, and Lumbard Street all in dust. The Exchange a sad sight, nothing standing there, of all the statues or pillars, but Sir Thomas Gresham's picture in the corner. Walked into Moorfields, our feet ready to burn, walking through the town among the hot coals, and find that full of people, and poor wretches carrying their goods there, and everybody keeping his goods together by themselves; and a great blessing it is to them that it is fair weather for them to keep abroad night and day; drank there, and paid twopence for a plain penny loaf. Thence homeward, having passed through Cheapside, and Newgate Market, all burned; and seen Anthony Joyce's house in fire; and took up, which I keep by me, a piece of glass of Mercer's Chapel in the street, where much more was, so melted and

[8] Sir W. Pen: prominent figure in 17th-century naval affairs

buckled with the heat of the fire like parchment. I also did see a poor cat taken out of a hole in a chimney, joyning to the wall of the Exchange, with the hair all burned off the body, and yet alive. So home at night, and find there good hopes of saving our office; but great endeavors of watching all night, and having men ready; and so we lodged them in the office, and had drink and bread and cheese for them. And I lay down and slept a good night about midnight; though, when I rose, I heard that there had been a great alarm of French and Dutch being risen, which proved nothing. But it is a strange thing to see how long this time did look since Sunday, having been always full of variety of actions, and little sleep, that it looked like a week or more, and I had forgot almost the day of the week.

THE THEATER

JANUARY 3, 1661.

Early in the morning to the Exchequer, where I told over what money I had of my Lord's [1] and my own there, which I found to be £970. Thence to Will's [2] where Spicer and I did eat our dinner of a roasted leg of pork which Will did give us, and after that to the Theater, where was acted *Beggars' Bush*, it being very well done; and here the first time I ever saw a woman come upon the stage.

JANUARY 28, 1661.

At the office all morning; dined at home, and after dinner to Fleet Street, with my sword to Mr. Brigden (lately made Captain of the Auxiliaries) to be refreshed, and with him to an ale-house, where I met Mr. Davenport, and after some talk of Cromwell, Ireton, and Bradshaw's bodies being taken out of their graves [3] today, I went to Mr. Crew's and thence to the Theater, where I saw again *The Lost Lady*, which do now please me better than before; and here I sitting behind in a dark place, a lady spit backward upon me by a mistake, not seeing me, but after seeing her to be a very pretty lady, I was not troubled at it at all.

[1] **my Lord**: the Earl of Sandwich
[2] **Will's**: famous coffeehouse
[3] **out of their graves**: the bodies were to be dug up, hanged, and reburied under the gallows

MARCH 1, 1662.

This morning I paid Sir W. Batten £40, which I have owed him this half year having borrowed it of him. Then to the office all the morning, so dined at home, and after dinner comes my uncle Thomas, with whom I had some high words of difference, but ended quietly, though I fear I shall do no good by fair means upon him. Thence my wife and I by coach, first to see my little picture that is a drawing, and thence to the Opera, and there saw *Romeo and Juliet*, the first time it was ever acted; but it is a play of itself the worst that ever I heard in my life, and the worst acted that ever I saw these people do, and I am resolved to go no more to see the first time of acting, for they were all of them out more or less.

SEPTEMBER 29, 1662 (MICHAELMAS DAY).

So we parted, and in the park Mr. Cooke by appointment met me, to whom I did give my thoughts concerning Tom's [4] match and their journey tomorrow, and did carry him by water to Tom's, and there taking up my wife, maid, dog, and him, did carry them home, where my wife is much pleased with my house, and so am I fully. I sent for some dinner and there dined, Mrs. Margaret Pen being by, to whom I had spoke to go along with us to a play this afternoon, and then to the King's Theater, where we saw *Midsummer's Night's Dream*, which I had never seen before, nor shall ever again, for it is the most insipid ridiculous play that ever I saw in my life. I saw, I confess, some good dancing, and some handsome women, which was all my pleasure.

MARCH 2, 1667.

After dinner with my wife to the King's house to see *The Maiden Queen*, a new play of Dryden's, mightily commended for the regularity of it, and the strain and wit: and the truth is, there is a comical part done by Nell,[5] which is Florimell, that I never can hope ever to see the like done again by man or woman. The King and Duke of York were at the play. But so great performance of a comical part was never, I believe, in the world before as Nell do this, both as a mad girl, then most and best of all when she comes in like a young gallant; and hath the motions and carriage of a spark the most that ever I saw any man have. It makes me, I confess, admire her.

[4] Tom's: Tom is Pepys' brother
[5] Nell: Nell Gwyn, the actress

For Discussion

"The Fire of London"

1. Read the description of "The Fire of London" in your history book. Compare it with Pepys' diary account. Which version has more human interest? What does the diary account tell you about its author? What does your history book account tell about its author?
2. A diary should reveal the personal, intimate character of its author. What kind of person was Samuel Pepys? Was he a curious person? What good effects does such a character produce? What seemed to be Pepys' main concern and worries during the fire?
3. Richard D. Altick has told of the detective work involved in deciphering Pepys' *Diary*. Read the chapter entitled "Secrets in Cipher" in his book *The Scholar Adventurers*.

For Composition: From Pepys' account of the fire of London, write a newspaper story of the event as if you were a reporter on the scene.

"The Theater"

1. What details of the theater do we learn from Pepys' account?
2. What impression does Pepys give us of the acting profession of his day?
3. Pepys had an eye for pretty women. What details show this to be true?

JOHN DRYDEN

(1631–1700)

John Dryden reflected in his life the complexities and conflicting elements of the latter part of the seventeenth century. Born a Puritan during Cromwell's rule, he became an Anglican under Charles II, and later a Catholic under James II. Much that he wrote was involved with the political and religious discussions of the period.

Dryden was a master of all the literary forms of his day and rose to become the most important writer of his time. in the fields of poetry, drama, and criticism. It was Dryden who established the *heroic couplet* as the chief poetic form that was to prevail for nearly a hundred years in England. His clear, crisp essays and prefaces served as a model for later writers, and had a marked influence on English prose style. One of the keenest of critics, he was the first to justly evaluate and appreciate the Elizabethan writers.

Some of Dryden's best poetry and prose are satirical, a reflection of this period, which was more interested in reason and craftsmanship in literature than in imagination. His finest lyrics, however, are serious and convey a true emotion, though expressed in neatly rhymed iambic pentameter couplets. His translations of Homer, Virgil, and other classical poets did much to familiarize English readers with the literature of Greece and Rome.

In honor of its patron saint, the St. Cecilia Society of London issued an ode as an annual commemoration. Dryden's two odes on this theme were printed ten years apart and are among his noblest efforts. The first of these poems, "A Song for Saint Cecilia's Day," records the history of music and its zenith in the supposed invention of the organ by St. Cecilia.

"Alexander's Feast" is based on the same theme. At a feast celebrating his conquest of Persia, Alexander and Thais listen to Timotheus playing his lyre. The power of this music excites the audience and finally, in a fit of revenge, the audience leap up, seize torches and set fire to the city. In the final stanza, St. Cecilia is acclaimed for her invention of the organ which surpasses the lyre of Timotheus. Both "Alexander's Feast" and "A Song for St. Cecilia's Day" show Dryden's ability to write easily in forms other than the heroic couplet.

A SONG FOR SAINT CECILIA'S DAY

From harmony, from heavenly harmony
    This universal frame began;
  When Nature underneath a heap
    Of jarring atoms lay,
And could not heave her head,   5
The tuneful voice was heard from high,
    Arise, ye more than dead.
Then cold and hot and moist and dry [1]
    In order to their stations leap,
      And Music's power obey.   10
From harmony, from heavenly harmony
    This universal frame began;
      From harmony to harmony
Through all the compass of the notes it ran,
The diapason [2] closing full in Man.   15

What passion cannot Music raise and quell?
      When Jubal [3] struck the corded shell,
  His listening brethren stood around,
      And, wondering, on their faces fell
To worship that celestial sound.   20
Less than a god they thought there could not dwell
    Within the hollow of that shell,
    That spoke so sweetly, and so well.
What passion cannot Music raise and quell?

    The trumpet's loud clangor   25
      Excites us to arms
    With shrill notes of anger
      And mortal alarms.
    The double, double, double beat
      Of the thundering drum   30
      Cries, "Hark! the foes come;
  Charge, charge, 'tis too late to retreat!"

[1] cold . . . dry: the qualities of the four elements in nature, according to the ancient philosophers
[2] diapason: full, rich stop on the pipe-organ; here, full harmony
[3] Jubal: in Genesis called the "father of all who handle the harp and organ"

The soft complaining flute
In dying notes discovers
The woes of hopeless lovers,   35
Whose dirge is whispered by the warbling lute.

Sharp violins proclaim
Their jealous pangs and desperation,
Fury, frantic indignation,
Depth of pains and height of passion,   40
For the fair, disdainful dame.

But, oh! what art can teach,
What human voice can reach
The sacred organ's praise?
Notes inspiring holy love,   45
Notes that wing their heavenly ways
To mend the choirs above.

Orpheus [4] could lead the savage race,
And trees unrooted left their place,
Sequacious [5] of the lyre;   50
But bright Cecilia raised the wonder higher;
When to her organ vocal breath was given,
An angel heard, and straight appeared,
Mistaking earth for heaven.

GRAND CHORUS

As from the power of sacred lays [6]   55
The spheres began to move,[7]
And sung the great Creator's praise
To all the blest above;
So when the last and dreadful hour
This crumbling pageant shall devour,   60

[4] Orpheus: in Greek mythology, a poet and musician whose lyre charmed beasts
and moved trees and rocks
[5] sequacious: following after
[6] lays: poems, music
[7] spheres . . . move: a common belief in ancient times that the stars made
music as they revolved in their spheres

The trumpet shall be heard on high,
The dead shall live, the living die,
And Music shall untune the sky.

EPIGRAM ON MILTON

These lines were printed under the engraved portrait of Milton in the folio edition of *Paradise Lost*, 1688. The three poets referred to are Homer, Virgil, and Milton.

Three poets, in three distant ages born,
Greece, Italy, and England did adorn.
The first in loftiness of thought surpassed,
The next in majesty, in both the last.
The force of Nature could no farther go;   5
To make a third she joined the former two.

ALEXANDER'S FEAST; OR, THE POWER OF MUSIC

An Ode in Honor of St. Cecilia's Day

'Twas at the royal feast,[1] for Persia won
   By Philip's [2] warlike son:
    Aloft in awful state
    The godlike hero sate
     On his imperial throne: 5
  His valiant peers were placed around;
Their brows with roses and with myrtles bound:
  (So should desert in arms be crowned).
The lovely Thais [3] by his side,
Sate like a blooming Eastern bride   10
In flower of youth and beauty's pride.
    Happy, happy, happy pair!
     None but the brave,
     None but the brave,
    None but the brave deserves the fair.   15

[1] **royal feast:** in celebration of Alexander's victory at Arbela, 331 B.C.
[2] **Philip:** of Macedonia, father of Alexander
[3] **Thais:** Greek woman who accompanied Alexander back to Asia

CHORUS

Happy, happy, happy pair!
  None but the brave,
  None but the brave,
None but the brave deserves the fair.

Timotheus [4] placed on high   20
  Amid the tuneful choir,
With flying fingers touched the lyre:
  The trembling notes ascend the sky,
    And heavenly joys inspire.
The song began from Jove,[5]   25
Who left his blissful seats above,
(Such is the power of mighty love).
A dragon's fiery form [6] belied [7] the god:
Sublime on radiant spires [8] he rode
When he to fair Olympia [9] pressed;   30
And while he sought her snowy breast,
Then round her slender waist he curled,
And stamped an image of himself, a sovereign of the world.
The listening crowd admire the lofty sound.
"A present deity," they shout around;   35
"A present deity," the valted roofs rebound:
     With ravished ears
     The monarch hears,
     Assumes the god,
     Affects to nod,   40
And seems to shake the spheres.

CHORUS

With ravished ears
The monarch hears,

[4] **Timotheus:** Alexander's favorite musician
[5] **began from Jove:** comes from the story about Jupiter which immediately follows
[6] **fiery form:** Jove wooed Olympia in the form of a dragon
[7] **belied:** disguised
[8] **sublime on radiant spires:** aloft on shining coils
[9] **Olympia:** mother of Alexander

        Assumes the god,
        Affects to nod,   **45**
And seems to shake the spheres.

The praise of Bacchus [10] then the sweet musician sung,
    Of Bacchus ever fair and ever young:
        The jolly god in triumph comes;
        Sound the trumpets, beat the drums;   **50**
            Flushed with a purple grace
            He shows his honest [11] face:
Now give the hautboys [12] breath; he comes, he comes.
        Bacchus, ever fair and young,
           Drinking joys did first ordain;   **55**
        Bacchus' blessings are a treasure,
        Drinking is the soldier's pleasure;
           Rich the treasure,
           Sweet the pleasure,
        Sweet is pleasure after pain.   **60**

CHORUS

    Bacchus' blessings are a treasure,
    Drinking is the soldier's pleasure;
        Rich the treasure,
        Sweet the pleasure,
        Sweet is pleasure after pain.   **65**

Soothed with the sound, the king grew vain;
    Fought all his battles o'er again;
And thrice he routed all his foes, and thrice he slew the slain.
    The master saw the madness rise,
    His glowing cheeks, his ardent eyes;   **70**
    And while he heaven and earth defied,
    Changed his hand, and checked his pride.[13]
        He chose a mournful Muse,
        Soft pity to infuse;

[10] **Bacchus:** god of mirth and wine
[11] **honest:** handsome
[12] **hautboys:** oboes
[13] **his pride:** Alexander's pride

He sung Darius [14] great and good,   75
   By too severe a fate,
Fallen, fallen, fallen, fallen,
   Fallen from his high estate,
And weltering in his blood;
Deserted at his utmost need   80
By those his former bounty fed;
On the bare earth exposed he lies,
With not a friend to close his eyes.

With downcast looks the joyless victor sate,
   Revolving in his altered soul   85
      The various turns of Chance below;
   And now and then a sigh he stole,
      And tears began to flow.

CHORUS

   Revolving in his altered soul
      The various turns of Chance below;   90
   And now and then a sigh he stole,
      And tears began to flow.

The mighty master smiled to see
That love was in the next degree;
'Twas but a kindred sound to move,   95
For pity melts the mind to love.
   Softly sweet, in Lydian measures [15]
   Soon he soothed his soul to pleasures.
"War," he sung, "is toil and trouble;
Honor but an empty bubble;   100
   Never ending, still beginning,
Fighting still, and still destroying:
   If the world be worth thy winning,
Think, O think it worth enjoying:
   Lovely Thais sits beside thee,   105
   Take the good the gods provide thee."

[14] **Darius:** king of Persia who was stabbed to death by one of his companions
[15] **Lydian measures:** Lydian music

The many rend the skies with loud applause;
So Love was crowned, but Music won the cause.
    The prince, unable to conceal his pain,
        Gazed on the fair   110
        Who caused his care,
  And sighed and looked, sighed and looked,
  Sighed and looked, and sighed again;
At length, with love and wine at once oppressed,
The vanquished victor sunk upon her breast.   115

CHORUS

    The prince, unable to conceal his pain,
        Gazed on the fair
        Who caused his care,
  And sighed and looked, sighed and looked,
  Sighed and looked, and sighed again;   120
At length, with love and wine at once oppressed,
The vanquished victor sunk upon her breast.

    Now strike the golden lyre again:
    A louder yet, and yet a louder strain.
    Break his bands of sleep asunder   125
    And rouse him like a rattling peal of thunder.
      Hark, hark, the horrid sound
        Has raised up his head;
        As awaked from the dead,
    And, amazed, he stares around.   130
"Revenge, revenge!" Timotheus cries:
    "See the Furies [16] arise!
    See the snakes that they rear,
    How they hiss in their hair,
And the sparkles that flash from their eyes!   135
    Behold a ghastly band,
    Each a torch in his hand!
Those are Grecian ghosts, that in battle were slain,
      And unburied remain
      Inglorious on the plain: 140

[16] **Furies:** messengers of vengeance

Give the vengeance due
To the valiant crew.
Behold how they toss their torches on high,
How they point to the Persian abodes
And glittering temples of their hostile gods!"   145
The princes applaud with a furious joy;
And the King seized a flambeau [17] with zeal to destroy;
Thais led the way,[18]
To light him to his prey,
And, like another Helen,[19] fired another Troy.   150

CHORUS

And the king seized a flambeau with zeal to destroy;
Thais led the way,
To light him to his prey,
And, like another Helen, fired another Troy.

Thus, long ago,   155
Ere heaving bellows learned to blow,
While organs yet were mute,
Timotheus, to his breathing flute
And sounding lyre,
Could swell the soul to rage, or kindle soft desire.   160
At last, divine Cecilia came,
Inventress of the vocal frame; [20]
The sweet enthusiast,[21] from her sacred store,
Enlarged the former narrow bounds,
And added length to solemn sounds,   165
With Nature's mother wit, and arts unknown before.
Let old Timotheus yield the prize,
Or both divide the crown;
He raised a mortal to the skies;
She drew an angel down.   170

[17] flambeau: flaming torch
[18] Thais . . . way: According to legend Thais persuaded Alexander to burn Persepolis after he had captured it.
[19] Helen: wife of Menelaus over whom the Trojan War was fought
[20] vocal frame: organ; Cecilia has been the patron of music and art since early Christian times.
[21] enthusiast: inspired by God

GRAND CHORUS

At last, divine Cecilia came,
Inventress of the vocal frame;
The sweet enthusiast, from her sacred store,
Enlarged the former narrow bounds,
And added length to solemn sounds,   175
With Nature's mother wit, and arts unknown before.
Let old Timotheus yield the prize,
Or both divide the crown;
He raised a mortal to the skies;
She drew an angel down.   180

For Discussion

"A Song for Saint Cecilia's Day"

1. Read the first stanza aloud. What makes it sound so solemn and rich in tone? In what way is creation a harmonious composition?
2. What civilization is represented by Jubal, by Orpheus, and by St. Cecilia?
3. How does the change in meter suggest the musical instruments mentioned? What is this poetic device called?
4. Read the Grand Chorus aloud. This poem was set to music. What do you think the Grand Chorus would require as musical accompaniment?

"Alexander's Feast"

1. What effect does the chorus add at the end of each stanza? In 1736, Handel set this ode to music. Although the poem does not depend on its musical setting, what effects do you think such a musical setting could produce?
2. Briefly criticize the story in this ode. Is it too "clever" or "theatrical"? Why?
3. This is Dryden's most popular poem. What factors might explain its popularity?
4. Explain the classical references in the poem. How do they give "tone" to the ode?
5. Compare this ode with Dryden's previous one on the same occasion. Which do you prefer? Why?

from An Essay of Dramatic Poesy

(*An Essay of Dramatic Poesy* is cast in the form of a dialogue. The four speakers present different points of view. The first speaker, Crites, defends the classical authors for whom Dryden had great esteem. Eugenius, the second speaker, believes in the superiority of contemporary literature. The third speaker, Lisideius, shows a preference for French drama over English. The final speaker, Neander, is most like Dryden himself among the speakers. He defends the English drama as opposed to the French, and praises Shakespeare, Jonson, Beaumont and Fletcher. It is Neander's discourse that follows.)

To begin, then, with Shakespeare. He was the man who of all modern, and perhaps ancient poets, had the largest and most comprehensive soul. All the images of Nature were still present in him, and he drew them, not laboriously, but luckily; when he describes anything, you more than see it, you feel it too. Those who accuse him to have wanted [1] learning give him the greater commendation: he was naturally learned. He needed not the spectacles of books to read Nature; he looked inwards, and found her there. I cannot say he is everywhere alike; were he so, I should do him injury to compare him with the greatest of mankind. He is many times flat, insipid; his comic wit degenerating into clenches,[2] his serious swelling into bombast. But he is always great when some great occasion is presented to him; no man can say he ever had a fit subject for his wit[3] and did not raise himself as high above the rest of poets,

Quantum lenta solent inter viburna cupressi.[4]

The consideration of this made Mr. Hales of Eton say, that there is no subject of which any poet ever writ, but he would produce it much better done in Shakespeare; and however others are now more generally preferred before him, yet the age wherein he lived, which had contemporaries with him Fletcher and Jonson, never equalled them to him in their esteem: and in the last King's court,

[1] wanted: lacked
[2] clenches: puns
[3] wit: genius
[4] **Quantum . . . cupressi:** "As cypresses rise above low shrubs."

when Ben's reputation was at highest, Sir John Suckling, and with him the greater part of the courtiers, set our Shakespeare far above him. . . .

As for Jonson, to whose character I am now arrived, if we look upon him while he was himself (for his last plays were but his dotages [5]), I think him the most learned and judicious writer which any theater ever had. He was a most severe judge of himself, as well as others. One cannot say he wanted wit, but rather that he was frugal of it. In his works you find little to retrench or alter. Wit, and language, and humor also in some measure we had before him; but something of art was wanting to the drama till he came. He managed his strength to more advantage than any who preceded him. You seldom find him making love in any of his scenes, or endeavoring to move the passions; his genius was too sullen and saturnine [6] to do it gracefully, especially when he knew he came after those who had performed both to such a height. Humor was his proper sphere; and in that he delighted most to represent mechanic people.[7] He was deeply conversant in the ancients, both Greek and Latin, and he borrowed boldly from them: there is scarcely a poet or historian among the Roman authors of those times whom he has not translated in *Sejanus* and *Catiline*.[8] But he has done his robberies so openly, that one may see he fears not to be taxed [9] by any law. He invades authors like a monarch; and what would be theft in other poets is only victory in him. With the spoils of these writers he so represents old Rome to us, in its rites, ceremonies, and customs, that if one of their poets had written either of his tragedies, we had seen less of it than in him. If there was any fault in his language, 'twas that he weaved it too closely and laboriously, in his comedies especially: perhaps, too, he did a little too much to Romanize our tongue, leaving the words which he translated almost as much Latin as when he found them: wherein, though he learnedly followed their language, he did not enough comply with the idiom of ours. If I would compare him with Shakespeare, I must acknowledge him the more correct [10] poet, but Shakespeare the greater wit. Shakespeare was the Homer, or father

[5] **dotages:** products of feeble old age
[6] **saturnine:** gloomy
[7] **mechanic people:** tradesmen and artisans
[8] *Sejanus* **and** *Catiline*: tragedies by Ben Jonson
[9] **taxed:** accused
[10] **correct:** following literary rules more closely

of our dramatic poets; Jonson was the Virgil, the pattern of elaborate writing; I admire him, but I love Shakespeare. To conclude of him; as he has given us the most correct plays, so in the precepts which he has laid down in his *Discoveries*, we have as many and profitable rules for perfecting the stage, as any wherewith the French can furnish us. . . .

from *Preface to the Fables*

. . . It remains that I say somewhat of Chaucer in particular.

In the first place, as he is the father of English poetry, so I hold him in the same degree of veneration as the Grecians held Homer, or the Romans Virgil. He is a perpetual fountain of good sense; learn'd in all sciences; and, therefore, speaks properly on all subjects. As he knew what to say, so he knows also when to leave off; a continence [1] which is practised by few writers, and scarcely by any of the ancients, excepting Virgil and Horace. One of our late great poets [2] is sunk in his reputation, because he could never forgive any conceit which came in his way; but swept like a drag-net, great and small. There was plenty enough, but the dishes were ill sorted; whole pyramids of sweetmeats for boys and women but little of solid meat for men. All this proceeded not from any want of knowledge, but of judgment. Neither did he want that in discerning the beauties and faults of other poets, but only indulged himself in the luxury of writing; and perhaps knew it was a fault, but hoped the reader would not find it. For this reason, though he must always be thought a great poet, he is no longer esteemed a good writer; and for ten impressions, which his works have had in so many successive years, yet at present a hundred books are scarcely purchased once a twelvemonth; for, as my last Lord Rochester said, though somewhat profanely, *Not being of God, he could not stand.*

Chaucer followed Nature everywhere, but was never so bold to go beyond her; and there is a great difference of being *poeta* and *nimis poeta*,[3] if we may believe Catullus,[4] as much as betwixt a modest be-

[1] continence: control
[2] one . . . poets: Abraham Cowley
[3] poeta . . . nimis poeta: "a poet and too much of a poet"
[4] Catullus: Roman lyric poet

haviour and affectation. The verse of Chaucer, I confess, is not harmonious to us; but 'tis like the eloquence of one whom Tacitus [5] commends, it was *auribus istius temporis accommodata:* [6] they who lived
with him, and some time after him, thought it musical; and it continues so, even in our judgment, if compared with the numbers of
Lidgate and Gower,[7] his contemporaries: there is the rude sweetness
of a Scotch tune in it, which is natural and pleasing, though not perfect. 'Tis true, I cannot go so far as he who published the last edition
of him; for he would make us believe the fault is in our ears, and
that there were really ten syllables in a verse where we find but nine:
but this opinion is not worth confuting; 'tis so gross and obvious an
error, that common sense (which is a rule in everything but matters
of Faith and Revelation) must convince the reader that equality of
numbers, in every verse which we call *heroic*,[8] was either not known,
or not always practised, in Chaucer's age. It were an easy matter to
produce some thousands of his verses, which are lame for want of half
a foot, and sometimes a whole one, and which no pronunciation can
make otherwise. We can only say, that he lived in the infancy of our
poetry, and that nothing is brought to perfection at the first. We
must be children before we grow men. There was an Ennius, and in
process of time a Lucilius, and a Lucretius, before Virgil and Horace;
even after Chaucer there was a Spenser, a Harrington, a Fairfax, before
Waller and Denham were in being; and our numbers were in their
nonage [9] till these last appeared. I need say little of his parentage, life,
and fortunes; they are to be found at large in all the editions of his
works. He was employed abroad, and favoured, by Edward the Third,
Richard the Second, and Henry the Fourth, and was poet, as I suppose, to all three of them. In Richard's time, I doubt,[10] he was a
little dipt in the rebellion of the Commons; and being brother-in-law
to John of Ghant, it was no wonder if he followed the fortunes of
that family; and was well with Henry the Fourth when he had deposed his predecessor. Neither is it to be admired, that Henry, who was
a wise as well as a valiant prince, who claimed by succession, and was
sensible that his title was not sound, but was rightfully in Mortimer,

[5] **Tacitus**: Roman historian
[6] **auribus . . . accommodata**: suited to the ears of that time
[7] **Lidgate and Gower**: poets and friends of Chaucer
[8] **heroic**: form of verse highly praised in Dryden's day
[9] **nonage**: the period in which one is legally a minor
[10] **doubt**: suspect

who had married the heir of York; it was not to be admired, I say, if that great politician should be pleased to have the greatest wit of those times in his interests, and to be the trumpet of his praises. Augustus had given him the example, by the advice of Maecenas,[11] who recommended Virgil and Horace to him; whose praises helped to make him popular while he was alive, and after his death have made him precious to posterity. . . . In the meanwhile, I take up Chaucer where I left him.

He must have been a man of a most wonderful comprehensive nature, because, as it has been truly observed of him, he has taken into the compass of his *Canterbury Tales* the various manners and humours [12] (as we now call them) of the whole English nation in his age. Not a single character has escaped him. All his pilgrims are severally distinguished from each other; and not only in their inclinations, but in their very physiognomies [13] and persons. Baptista Porta [14] could not have described their natures better, than by the marks which the poet gives them. The matter and manner of their tales, and of their telling, are so suited to their different educations, humours, and callings, that each of them would be improper in any other mouth. Even the grave and serious characters are distinguished by their several sorts of gravity: their discourses are such as belong to their age, their calling, and their breeding; such as are becoming of them, and of them only. Some of his persons are vicious, and some virtuous; some are unlearn'd, or (as Chaucer calls them) lewd, and some are learn'd. Even the ribaldry of the low characters is different: the Reeve, the Miller, and the Cook, are several men, and distinguished from each other as much as the mincing Lady-Prioress and the broad-speaking, gap-toothed Wife of Bath. But enough of this; there is such a variety of game springing up before me that I am distracted in my choice, and know not which to follow. 'Tis sufficient to say, according to the proverb, that *here is God's plenty*. We have our forefathers and great-granddames all before us, as they were in Chaucer's days: their general characters are still remaining in mankind, and even in England, though they are called by other names than those of Monks, and Friars, and Canons, and Lady Abbesses,

[11] **Maecenas:** Roman statesman and wealthy patron of the arts during the reign of Augustus
[12] **humours:** temperaments
[13] **physiognomies:** facial features
[14] **Baptista Porta:** noted Italian physiognomist

and Nuns; for mankind is ever the same, and nothing lost out of Nature, though everything is altered. . . .

I have almost done with Chaucer, when I have answered some objections relating to my present work. I find some people are offended that I have turned these tales into modern English; because they think them unworthy of my pains, and look on Chaucer as a dry, old-fashioned wit, not worth reviving. I have often heard the late Earl of Leicester say that Mr. Cowley himself was of that opinion; who, having read him over at my Lord's request, declared he had no taste of him. I dare not advance my opinion against the judgment of so great an author; but I think it fair, however, to leave the decision to the public. Mr. Cowley was too modest to set up for a dictator; and being shocked perhaps with his old style, never examined into the depth of his good sense. Chaucer, I confess, is a rough diamond, and must first be polished ere he shines. I deny not likewise, that, living in our early days of poetry, he writes not always of a piece; but sometimes mingles trivial things with those of greater moment. Sometimes also, though not often, he runs riot, like Ovid, and knows not when he has said enough. But there are more great wits besides Chaucer, whose fault is their excess of conceits, and those ill sorted. An author is not to write all he can, but only all he ought. Having observed this redundancy in Chaucer (as it is an easy matter for a man of ordinary parts to find a fault in one of greater), I have not tied myself to a literal translation; but have often omitted what I judged unnecessary, or not of dignity enough to appear in the company of better thoughts. I have presumed further, in some places, and added somewhat of my own where I thought my author was deficient, and had not given his thoughts their true lustre, for want of words in the beginning of our language. And to this I was the more emboldened, because (if I may be permitted to say it of myself) I found I had a soul congenial to his, and that I had been conversant in the same studies. Another poet, in another age, may take the same liberty with my writings; if at least they live long enough to deserve correction. It was also necessary sometimes to restore the sense of Chaucer, which was lost or mangled in the errors of the press. . . .

But there are other judges who think I ought not to have translated Chaucer into English, out of a quite contrary notion: they suppose there is a certain veneration due to his old language, and that it is little less than profanation and sacrilege to alter it. They are farther of opinion, that somewhat of his good sense will suffer in this transfusion, and much of the beauty of his thoughts will infallibly be lost, which appear with more grace in their old habit. Of this opinion was that excellent person, whom I mentioned, the late Earl of Leicester, who valued Chaucer as much as Mr. Cowley despised him. My Lord dissuaded me from this attempt (for I was thinking of it some years before his death) and his authority prevailed so far with me, as to defer my undertaking while he lived, in deference to him: yet my reason was not convinced with what he urged against it. If the first end of a writer be to be understood, then, as his language grows obsolete, his thoughts must grow obscure—

Many words will be revived that are now obsolete; many will be become obsolete that are now honored; if it is so willed by usage, on which depend the judgment and the law and the rules of our speech.

When an ancient word, for its sound and significancy, deserves to be revived, I have that reasonable veneration for antiquity to restore it. All beyond this is superstition. Words are not like landmarks, so sacred as never to be removed; customs are changed, and even statutes are silently repealed, when the reason ceases for which they were enacted. As for the other part of the argument, that his thoughts will lose of their original beauty by the innovation of words; in the first place, not only their beauty, but their being is lost, where they are no longer understood, which is the present case. I grant that something must be lost in all transfusion, that is, in all translations; but the sense will remain, which would otherwise be lost, or at least be maimed, when it is scarce intelligible, and that but to a few. How few are there who can read Chaucer so as to understand him perfectly? And if imperfectly, then with less profit, and no pleasure. It is not for the use of some old Saxon friends that I have taken these pains with him: let them neglect my version, because they have no need of it. I made it for their sakes, who understand sense and poetry as well as they, when that poetry and sense is put into words which they understand. I will go farther, and dare to add, that what beauties I lose in some places, I give to others which had them not originally; but in this I may be partial to myself; let the reader judge, and I submit to his decision. Yet I think I have just occasion to complain of them, who because they understand Chaucer, would deprive the greater part of their countrymen of the same advantage, and hoard him up, as misers do their grandam gold, only to look on it themselves, and hinder others from making use of it. In sum, I seriously protest, that no man ever had, or can have, a greater veneration for Chaucer than myself. I have translated some part of his works, only that I might perpetuate his memory, or at least refresh it, amongst my countrymen. If I have altered him anywhere for the better, I must at the same time acknowledge that I could have done nothing without him. *Facile est inventis addere* [15] is no great commendation; and I am not so vain to think I have deserved a greater. I will conclude what I have to say of him singly, with this one remark: A lady of my acquaintance, who keeps a kind of correspondence with some authors of the fair sex in France, has been informed by them that Mademoiselle de Scudery, who is as old as Sibyl, and inspired like her by the same God of Poetry, is at this time translating Chaucer into modern French. From which I gather that he has been formerly translated into the old Provençal; for how she should come to understand old English, I know not. But the matter of fact being true, it makes me think that there is something in it like fatality; that, after certain periods of time, the fame and memory of great Wits should be renewed, as Chaucer is both in France and England. If this be wholly chance, 'tis extraordinary; and I dare not call it more, for fear of being taxed with superstition.

For Discussion

"An Essay of Dramatic Poesy"

1. Apply Dryden's criticism of Shakespeare to *Macbeth*. Is what Dryden says true? Why?
2. What did Jonson lack according to Dryden? What does Dryden mean by his comparison of Shakespeare and Jonson to Homer and Virgil?

"Preface to the Fables"

1. What does Dryden mean when he says "Chaucer followed Nature everywhere"?
2. Dryden seems captivated by Chaucer's "comprehensive nature." What proofs does he give for his love of Chaucer?
3. Briefly outline Dryden's arguments for translating and "modernizing" the classics. Do you agree with this argument? Why?
4. Dryden's prose style is justly praised by modern critics. Choose three qualities of his style that appeal to you.

[15] Facile . . . addere: "It is easy to add things that have already been invented."

ALEXANDER POPE

(1688–1744)

Just as Dryden was the major literary figure of the second half of the seventeenth century, so Alexander Pope dominated the literary scene in the first half of the eighteenth century. Regarded as the prince of English poets in his day, he was the spokesman for the "age of reason" and Neo-Classical poetry.

Born a Roman Catholic, Pope was excluded from the ordinary schools and recreation of his equals. He studied under tutors and excelled in Latin, Greek, Italian, and French. He was taught that the only way for a poet to excel was to imitate "the correctness" of the classics.

Aristotle, the Greek philosopher, had analyzed and formulated the principles of poetry in his *Poetics*, and the poets of the Renaissance made Aristotle their guide. But in the age of Pope, Aristotle became the god of poets. The theory and rules of Aristotle, often misunderstood, were made the sacred canons of poetry. Classicism to Pope and his followers meant imitating the older works of the ancients and applying strictly their rules of writing, which emphasized balance and proportion.

In Neo-Classical poetry, reasonableness, good sense, and scrupulous fidelity to the established facts were emphasized. What was imaginative, emotional, and not immediately recognizable to the average, intelligent man was scorned. Poetry's function was to appeal to the mind rather than to the emotions. As a result, the end product was frequently a perfection of *form* without enough of the substance of poetry. The chief beliefs of the Neo-Classical school can be summarized as follows:

1. *Perfect expression* was most important. This was attained by a clear, concise and orderly presentation of ideas. Diction was an ornament of style. Therefore it was to be witty and epigrammatic if possible. The smooth, balanced meter of the heroic couplet was preferred.

2. *Thought* was universalized and, therefore, an intellectually realized experience was the important content of poetry.

3. *Emotion* was subordinate to exposition or argumentation. It was often irrelevant.

4. *Imagination* was not needed as a creative faculty. Social and philosophical themes needed imagination only as a source of power.

In such an era, lyric poetry could not flourish. Pope, the master of his age, excelled in satiric verse and philosophical poetry. His "Essay on Criticism" and "Essay on Man," both written in rhymed couplets, present his views on literary criticism and of man's place in the world.

"An Essay on Criticism" tells us (1) "first follow nature"; that is the conduct of man in highly civilized society; (2) model your writings on the ancient classical writers; (3) follow the rules carefully; cultivate classical restraint and taste. "An Essay on Man" is well summarized by Pope himself in the *Argument* which precedes the poem (page 209).

from AN ESSAY ON CRITICISM

In "The Design" to the poem, addressed to Lord Bolingbroke, Pope says: "This I might have done in prose, but I chose verse, and even rime, for two reasons. The one will appear obvious; that principles, maxims, or precepts so written, both strike the reader more strongly at first, and are more easily retained by him afterwards. The other may seem odd, but it is true; I found I could express them more *shortly* this way than in prose itself; and nothing is more certain than that much of the force as well as grace of arguments or instructions depends on their conciseness. I was unable to treat this part of my subject more in detail without becoming dry and tedious; or more poetically without sacrificing perspicuity to ornament, without wandering from the precision, or breaking the chain of reasoning. If any man can unite all these without diminution of any of them, I freely confess he will compass a thing above my capacity."

Part I

'Tis hard to say, if greater want of skill
Appear in writing or in judging ill;
But, of the two, less dangerous is the offense
To tire our patience, than mislead our sense.
Some few in that, but numbers err in this,   5
Ten censure [1] wrong for one who writes amiss;
A fool might once himself alone expose,
Now one in verse makes many more in prose.

'Tis with our judgments as our watches; none
Go just alike, yet each believes his own.   10
In poets as true genius is but rare,
True taste as seldom is the critic's share;

[1] censure: judge

Both must alike from Heaven derive their light,
These born to judge, as well as those to write.
Let such teach others who themselves excel,   15
And censure freely who have written well.
Authors are partial to their wit, 'tis true,
But are not critics to their judgment too?

   Yet if we look more closely, we shall find
Most have the seeds of judgment in their mind: 20
Nature affords at least a glimmering light;
The lines, though touched but faintly, are drawn right.
But as the slightest sketch, if justly traced,
Is by ill-coloring but the more disgraced,
So by false learning is good sense defaced;   25
Some are bewildered in the maze of schools,
And some made coxcombs nature meant but fools.
In search of wit these lose their common sense,
And then turn critics in their own defense;
Each burns alike, who can, or cannot write,   30
Or with a rival's or an eunuch's spite.
All fools have still an itching to deride,
And fain would be upon the laughing side.
If Maevius [2] scribble in Apollo's [3] spite,
There are who judge still worse than he can write.   35

   Some have at first for wits, then poets passed,
Turned critics next, and proved plain fools at last.
Some neither can for wits nor critics pass,
As heavy mules are neither horse nor ass.
Those half-learned witlings, numerous in our isle,   40
As half-formed insects on the banks of Nile;
Unfinished things, one knows not what to call,
Their generation's so equivocal;
To tell [4] 'em, would a hundred tongues require,
Or one vain wit's, that might a hundred tire.   45

[2] Maevius: contemporary of Virgil; considered to be a classic example of the bad poet
[3] Apollo: god of poetry
[4] tell: count

But you who seek to give and merit fame,
And justly bear a critic's noble name,
Be sure yourself and your own reach to know,
How far your genius, taste, and learning go;
Launch not beyond your depth, but be discreet,   50
And mark that point where sense and dullness meet.

Nature to all things fixed the limits fit,
And wisely curbed proud man's pretending wit.[5]
As on the land while here the ocean gains,
In other parts it leaves wide sandy plains;   55
Thus in the soul while memory prevails,
The solid power of understanding fails;
Where beams of warm imagination play,
The memory's soft figures melt away.
One science only will one genius fit;   60
So vast is art, so narrow human wit:
Not only bounded to peculiar arts,
But oft in those confined to single parts.
Like kings we lose the conquests gained before,
By vain ambition still to make them more;   65
Each might his several province well command,
Would all but stoop to what they understand.

First follow nature, and your judgment frame
By her just standard, which is still the same:
Unerring nature, still divinely bright,   70
One clear, unchanged, and universal light,
Life, force, and beauty, must to all impart,
At once the source, and end, and test of art.
Art from that fund each just supply provides,
Works without show, and without pomp presides: 75
In some fair body thus the informing soul
With spirits feeds, with vigor fills the whole,
Each motion guides, and every nerve sustains;
Itself unseen, but in the effects, remains.
Some, to whom Heaven in wit has been profuse,   80
Want as much more, to turn it to its use;

[5] **wit:** intellect

For wit and judgment often are at strife,
Though meant each other's aid, like man and wife.
'Tis more to guide than spur the Muse's steed;
Restrain his fury, than provoke his speed;   85
The wingéd courser, like a generous horse,
Shows most true mettle when you check his course.

Those rules of old discovered,[6] not devised,
Are nature still, but nature methodized;
Nature, like liberty, is but restrained   90
By the same laws which first herself ordained.

Hear how learned Greece her useful rules indites,
When to repress, and when indulge our flights:
High on Parnassus'[7] top her sons she showed,
And pointed out those arduous paths they trod;   95
Held from afar, aloft, the immortal prize,
And urged the rest by equal steps to rise.
Just precepts thus from great examples given,
She drew from them what they derived from Heaven.
The generous critic fanned the poet's fire,   100
And taught the world with reason to admire.
Then criticism the Muse's handmaid proved,
To dress her charms, and make her more beloved:
But following wits from that intention strayed,
Who could not win the mistress, wooed the maid;   105
Against the poets their own arms they turned,
Sure to hate most the men from whom they learned.
So modern 'pothecaries, taught the art
By doctor's bills to play the doctor's part,
Bold in the practice of mistaken rules,   110
Prescribe, apply, and call their masters fools.
Some on the leaves of ancient authors prey,
Nor time nor moths e'er spoiled so much as they.
Some dryly plain, without invention's aid,
Write dull receipts,[8] how poems may be made.   115

[6] discovered: by Aristotle
[7] Parnassus: mythological mountain sacred to the Muses
[8] receipts: recipes

These leave the sense, their learning to display,
And those explain the meaning quite away.

You, then, whose judgment the right course would steer,
Know well each ancient's proper character;
His fable, subject, scope in every page;   120
Religion, country, genius of his age:
Without all these at once before your eyes,
Cavil you may, but never criticise.
Be Homer's works your study and delight,
Read them by day, and meditate by night;   125
Thence form your judgment, thence your maxims bring,
And trace the Muses upward to their spring.
Still with itself compared, his text peruse;
And let your comment be the Mantuan Muse.

When first young Maro [9] in his boundless mind   130
A work to outlast immortal Rome designed,
Perhaps he seemed above the critic's law,
And but from nature's fountains scorned to draw:
But when to examine every part he came,
Nature and Homer were, he found, the same.   135
Convinced, amazed, he checks the bold design;
And rules as strict his labored work confine,
As if the Stagirite [10] o'erlooked each line;
Learn hence for ancient rules a just esteem;
To copy nature is to copy them.   140

Some beauties yet no precepts can declare,
For there's a happiness as well as care.
Music resembles poetry; in each
Are nameless graces which no methods teach,
And which a master-hand alone can reach.   145
If, where the rules not far enough extend,
(Since rules were made but to promote their end)
Some lucky license answer to the full
The intent proposed, that license is a rule.

[9] **Maro:** Virgil
[10] **Stagirite:** Aristotle

Thus Pegasus,[11] a nearer way to take,   150
May boldly deviate from the common track;
From vulgar bounds with brave disorder part,
And snatch a grace beyond the reach of art,
Which without passing through the judgment, gains
The heart, and all its end at once attains.   155
In prospects thus, some objects please our eyes,
Which out of nature's common order rise,
The shapeless rock, or hanging precipice.
Great wits sometimes may gloriously offend,
And rise to faults true critics dare not mend.   160
But though the ancients thus their rules invade,
(As kings dispense with laws themselves have made)
Moderns, beware! or if you must offend
Against the precept, ne'er transgress its end; [12]
Let it be seldom and compelled by need;   165
And have, at least, their precedent to plead.
The critic else proceeds without remorse,
Seizes your fame, and puts his laws in force.

  I know there are, to whose presumptuous thoughts
Those freer beauties, even in them, seem faults.   170
Some figures monstrous and mis-shaped appear,
Considered singly, or beheld too near,
Which, but proportioned to their light or place,
Due distance reconciles to form and grace.
A prudent chief not always must display   175
His powers in equal ranks, and fair array,
But with the occasion and the place comply,
Conceal his force, nay, seem sometimes to fly.
Those oft are stratagems which errors seem,
Nor is it Homer nods, but we that dream.   180

  Still green with bays each ancient altar stands,
Above the reach of sacrilegious hands;
Secure from flames, from envy's fiercer rage,
Destructive war, and all-involving age.
See, from each clime the learned their incense bring!   185

[11] **Pegasus:** winged horse of mythology, here identified with poetic inspiration
[12] **end:** purpose

Hear, in all tongues, consenting paeans ring!
In praise so just let every voice be joined,
And fill the general chorus of mankind.
Hail, bards triumphant! born in happier days;
Immortal heirs of universal praise!   190
Whose honors with increase of ages grow,
As streams roll down, enlarging as they flow;
Nations unborn your mighty names shall sound,
And worlds applaud that must not yet be found!
Oh, may some spark of your celestial fire,   195
The last, the meanest of your sons inspire,
(That on weak wings, from far, pursues your flights;
Glows while he reads, but trembles as he writes)
To teach vain wits a science little known,
To admire superior sense, and doubt their own!   200

from AN ESSAY ON MAN

Epistle I. *Of the nature and state of man, with respect to the universe*

ARGUMENT: Of Man in the abstract. I. That we can judge only with regard to our own system, being ignorant of the relations of systems and things, verse 17, etc. II. That Man is not to be deemed imperfect, but a being suited to his place and rank in the creation, agreeable to the general order of things, and conformable to ends and relations to him unknown, verse 35, etc. III. That it is partly upon his ignorance of future events, and partly upon the hope of a future state, that all his happiness in the present depends, verse 77, etc. IV. The pride of aiming at more knowledge, and pretending to more perfection, the cause of Man's error and misery. The impiety of putting himself in the place of God, and judging of the fitness or unfitness, perfection or imperfection, justice or injustice, of his dispensations, verse 113, etc. V. The absurdity of conceiting himself the final cause of the creation, or expecting that perfection in the moral world which is not in the natural, verse 131, etc. VI. The unreasonableness of his complaints against Providence, while, on the one hand, he demands the perfections of the angels, and, on the other, the bodily qualifications of the brutes; though to possess any of the sensitive faculties in a higher degree would render him miserable, verse 173, etc. VII. That throughout the whole visible world a universal order and gradation in the sensual and mental faculties is observed, which causes a subordination of creature to creature, and of all creatures to man. The gradations of Sense, Instinct, Thought, Reflection, Reason: that Reason alone countervails all the other faculties, verse 207, etc. VIII. How much further this order and subordination of living creatures may extend above and below us; were any part of which broken, not that part only, but the whole connected creation must be destroyed, verse 233, etc. IX. The extravagance, madness, and pride of such a desire, verse 259, etc. X. The consequence of all, the absolute submission due to Providence, both as to our present and future state, verse 281, etc., to the end.

Awake, my St. John! [1] leave all meaner things
To low ambition and the pride of Kings.
Let us, since life can little more supply
Than just to look about us and to die,
Expatiate free o'er all this scene of man;   5
A mighty maze! but not without a plan;
A wild, where weeds and flowers promiscuous shoot,
Or garden, tempting with forbidden fruit.
Together let us beat this ample field,
Try what the open, what the covert yield;   10
The latent tracts, the giddy heights, explore
Of all who blindly creep or sightless soar;
Eye Nature's walks, shoot folly as it flies,
And catch the manners living as they rise.
Laugh where we must, be candid where we can,   15
But vindicate the ways of God to man.

    I. Say first, of God above or Man below
What can we reason but from what we know?
Of man what see we but his station here,
From which to reason, or to which refer?   20
Thro' worlds unnumbered tho' the God be known,
'Tis ours to trace him only in our own.
He who thro' vast immensity can pierce,
    See worlds on worlds compose one universe,
Observe how system into system runs,   25

[1] St. John: Henry St. John, Viscount Bolingbroke

What other planets circle other suns,
What varied being peoples every star,
May tell why Heaven has made us as we are:
But of this frame, the bearings and the ties,
The strong connexions, nice dependencies,[2]   30
Gradations just, has thy pervading soul
Looked thro'; or can a part contain the whole?
    Is the great chain that draws all to agree,
And drawn supports, upheld by God or thee?

    II. Presumptuous man! the reason wouldst thou find,   35
Why formed so weak, so little, and so blind?
First, if thou canst, the harder reason guess
Why formed no weaker, blinder, and no less!
Ask of thy mother earth why oaks are made
Taller or stronger than the weeds they shade!   40
Or ask of yonder argent fields above
Why Jove's satellites [3] are less than Jove!
    Of systems possible, if 'tis confest
That wisdom infinite must form the best,
Where all must fall or not coherent be,   45
And all that rises rise in due degree;
Then in the scale of reasoning life 'tis plain
There must be, somewhere, such a rank as Man:
And all the question (wrangle e'er so long)
Is only this,—if God has placed him wrong?   50
    Respecting man, whatever wrong we call,
May, must be right, as relative to all.
In human works, tho' labored on with pain,
A thousand movements scarce one purpose gain;
In God's, one single can its end produce,   55
Yet serve to second too some other use:
So man, who here seems principal alone,
Perhaps acts second to some sphere unknown,
Touches some wheel, or verges to some goal:
'Tis but a part we see, and not a whole.   60
    When the proud steed shall know why man restrains
His fiery course, or drives him o'er the plains;

[2] **nice dependencies:** harmony of the body's different parts
[3] **Jove's satellites:** planet Jupiter

When the dull ox, why now he breaks the clod,
Is now a victim, and now Egypt's god;
Then shall man's pride and dulness comprehend   65
His actions', passions', being's, use and end;
Why doing, suffering, checked, impelled; and why
This hour a slave, the next a deity.
    Then say not man's imperfect, Heaven in fault;
Say rather man's as perfect as he ought;   70
His knowledge measured to his state and place,
His time a moment, and a point his space.
If to be perfect in a certain sphere,
What matter soon or late, or here or there?
The blest to-day is as completely so   75
As who began a thousand years ago.

    III. Heaven from all creatures hides the book of Fate,
All but the page prescribed, their present state;
From brutes what men, from men what spirits know;
Or who could suffer being here below?   80
The lamb thy riot dooms to bleed to-day,
Had he thy reason would he skip and play?
Pleased to the last he crops the flowery food,
And licks the hand just raised to shed his blood.
O blindness to the future! kindly given,   85
That each may fill the circle marked by Heaven;
Who sees with equal eye, as God of all,
A hero perish or a sparrow fall,
Atoms or systems into ruin hurled,
And now a bubble burst, and now a world.   90
    Hope humbly then; with trembling pinions soar;
Wait the great teacher Death, and God adore.
What future bliss He gives not thee to know,
But gives that hope to be thy blessing now.
Hope springs eternal in the human breast: 95
Man never is, but always to be, blest.
The soul, uneasy and confined from home,
Rests and expatiates in a life to come.
    Lo, the poor Indian! whose untutored mind
Sees God in clouds, or hears him in the wind;   100
His soul proud Science never taught to stray

Far as the solar walk [4] or milky way;
Yet simple nature to his hope has given,
Behind the cloud-topt hill, and humbler Heaven,
Some safer world in depth of woods embraced,   105
Some happier island in the watery waste,
Where slaves once more their native land behold,
No fiends torment, no Christians thirst for gold.
To be, contents his natural desire;
He asks no Angel's wing, no Seraph's fire;   110
But thinks, admitted to that equal sky,
His faithful dog shall bear him company.

    IV. Go, wiser thou! and in thy scale of sense
Weigh thy opinion against Providence;
Call imperfection what thou fanciest such;   115
Say, here he gives too little, there too much;
Destroy all creatures for thy sport or gust,[5]
Yet cry, if man's unhappy, God's unjust;
If man alone engross not Heaven's high care,
Alone made perfect here, immortal there,   120
Snatch from his hand the balance and the rod,
Rejudge his justice, be the god of God.
In pride, in reasoning pride, our error lies;
All quit their sphere, and rush into the skies!
Pride still is aiming at the blessed abodes,   125
Men would be angels, angels would be gods.
Aspiring to be gods if angels fell,
Aspiring to be angels men rebel:
And who but wishes to invert the laws
Of order, sins against th' Eternal Cause.   130

    V. Ask for what end the heav'nly bodies shine,
Earth for whose use,—Pride answers, " 'Tis for mine:
For me kind Nature wakes her genial power,
Suckles each herb, and spreads out every flower:
Annual for me the grape, the rose, renew   135
The juice nectareous and the balmy dew;
For me the mine a thousand treasures brings;

---

[4] **solar walk:** path of the sun
[5] **gust:** appetite

For me health gushes from a thousand springs;
Seas roll to waft me, suns to light me rise;
My footstool earth, my canopy the skies."   140
    But errs not Nature from this gracious end,
From burning suns when livid deaths descend,
When earthquakes swallow, or when tempests sweep
Towns to one grave, whole nations to the deep?
"No," 'tis replied, "the first Almighty Cause   145
Acts not by partial but by general laws;
Th' exceptions few; some change since all began;
And what created perfect?"—Why then man?
If the great end be human happiness,
Then Nature deviates; and can man do less?   150
As much that end a constant course requires
Of showers and sunshine, as of man's desires;
As much eternal springs and cloudless skies,
As men for ever temperate, calm, and wise.
If plagues or earthquakes break not Heaven's design,   155
Why then a Borgia [6] or a Catiline? [7]
Who knows but He, whose hand the lightning forms,
Who heaves old ocean, and who wings the storms;
Pours fierce ambition in a Cæsar's mind,
Or turns young Ammon [8] loose to scourge mankind?   160
From pride, from pride, our very reasoning springs;
Account for moral as for natural things:
Why charge we Heaven in those, in these acquit?
In both, to reason right is to submit.
    Better for us, perhaps, it might appear,   165
Were there all harmony, all virtue here;
That never air or ocean felt the wind,
That never passion discomposed the mind:
But all subsists by elemental strife;
And passions are the elements of life.   170
The general order, since the whole began,
Is kept in Nature, and is kept in Man.

---

[6] **Borgia**: famous Italian family of the Renaissance known for their trickery and deceit
[7] **Catiline**: famous Roman conspirator
[8] **Ammon**: Alexander the Great

VI. What would this Man? Now upward will he soar,
And little less than Angel, would be more;
Now looking downwards, just as grieved appears   175
To want the strength of bulls, the fur of bears.
Made for his use all creatures if he call,
Say what their use, had he the powers of all?
Nature to these without profusion kind,
The proper organs, proper powers assigned;   180
Each seeming want compensated of course,
Here with degrees of swiftness, there of force;
All in exact proportion to the state;
Nothing to add, and nothing to abate;
Each beast, each insect, happy in its own: 185
Is Heaven unkind to man, and man alone?
Shall he alone, whom rational we call,
Be pleased with nothing if not blessed with all?
    The bliss of man (could pride that blessing find)
Is not to act or think beyond mankind;   190
No powers of body or of soul to share,
But what his nature and his state can bear.
Why has not man a microscopic eye?
For this plain reason, man is not a fly.
Say, what the use, were finer optics given,   195
To inspect a mite, not comprehend the Heaven?
Or touch, if tremblingly alive all o'er,
To smart and agonize at every pore?
Or quick effluvia darting thro' the brain,
Die of a rose in aromatic pain?   200
If Nature thundered in his opening ears,
And stunned him with the music of the spheres,[9]
How would he wish that Heaven had left him still
The whispering zephyr and the purling rill?
Who finds not Providence all good and wise,   205
Alike in what it gives and what it denies?

    VII. Far as creation's ample range extends,
The scale of sensual, mental powers ascends.
Mark how it mounts to man's imperial race

---

[9] **music . . . spheres:** a common belief in ancient times that the revolution of the planets in the heavens gave rise to music

From the green myriads in the peopled grass: 210
What modes of sight betwixt each wide extreme,
The mole's dim curtain and the lynx's beam:
Of smell, the headlong lioness between
And hound sagacious on the tainted green:
Of hearing, from the life that fills the flood   215
To that which warbles thro' the vernal wood.
The spider's touch, how exquisitely fine,
Feels at each thread, and lives along the line:
In the nice [10] bee, what sense so subtly true
From poisonous herbs extracts the healing dew!   220
How instinct varies in the grovelling swine,
Compared, half-reasoning elephant, with thine!
'Twixt that and reason what a nice [11] barrier!
For ever separate, yet for ever near!
Remembrance and reflection how allied!   225
What thin partitions sense from thought divide!
And middle natures how they long to join,
Yet never pass th' insuperable line!
Without this just gradation could they be
Subjected these to those, or all to thee!   230
The powers of all subdued by thee alone,
Is not thy reason all these powers in one?

   VIII. See thro' this air, this ocean, and this earth
All matter quick,[12] and bursting into birth:
Above, how high progressive life may go!   235
Around, how wide! how deep extend below!
Vast chain of being! which from God began;
Natures ethereal, human, angel, man,
Beast, bird, fish, insect, what no eye can see,
No glass can reach; from infinite to thee;   240
From thee to nothing.—On superior powers
Were we to press, inferior might on ours;
Or in the full creation leave a void,
Where, one step broken, the great scale's destroyed:
From Nature's chain whatever link you like,   245

[10] nice: wise
[11] nice: thin
[12] quick: alive

Tenth, or ten thousandth, breaks the chain alike.
    And if each system in gradation roll,
Alike essential to th' amazing whole,
The least confusion but in one, not all
That system only, but the whole must fall.   250
Let earth unbalanced from her orbit fly,
Planets and stars run lawless thro' the sky;
Let ruling angels from their spheres be hurled,
Being on being wrecked, and world on world;
Heaven's whole foundations to their center nod,   255
And Nature tremble to the throne of God!
All this dread order break—for whom? for thee?
Vile worm!—O madness! pride! impiety!

    IX. What if the foot, ordained the dust to tread
Or hand to toil, aspired to be the head?   260
What if the head, the eye, or ear repined
To serve mere engines to the ruling mind?
Just as absurd for any part to claim
To be another in this general frame;
Just as absurd to mourn the tasks or pains   265
The great directing mind of all ordains.
    All are but parts of one stupendous whole,
Whose body nature is, and God the soul;
That changed thro' all, and yet in all the same,
Great in the earth as in th' ethereal frame,   270
Warms in the sun, refreshes in the breeze,
Glows in the stars, and blossoms in the trees;
Lives thro' all life, extends thro' all extent,
Spreads undivided, operates unspent;
Breathes in our soul, informs our mortal part,   275
As full, as perfect, in a hair as heart;
As full, as perfect, in vile man that mourns,
As the rapt seraph that adores and burns.
To him no high, no low, no great, no small;
He fills, he bounds, connects, and equals all!   280

    X. Cease, then, nor Order imperfection name;
Our proper bliss depends on what we blame.
Know thy own point: this kind, this due degree

Of blindness, weakness, Heaven bestows on thee.
Submit: in this or any other sphere,   285
Secure to be as blessed as thou canst bear;
Safe in the hand of one disposing Power,
Or in the natal or the mortal hour.
All nature is but art unknown to thee;
All chance, direction, which thou canst not see;   290
All discord, harmony not understood;
All partial evil, universal good:
And spite of pride, in erring reason's spite,
One truth is clear, *Whatever is, is right.*

For Discussion

"An Essay on Criticism"

1. What gives a critic "taste"? What should a critic know about himself? What qualities are essential to a critic? Do you agree? Why or why not?
2. Find examples of the Neo-Classical style in Pope's poem.
3. Why does "music resemble poetry"? How does this apply to Dryden's odes?
4. Why should "Moderns, beware" (lines 163–168)? Who are "the Moderns"?
5. Explain what Pope means when he says "Nor is it Homer nods" (line 180).
6. List and explain the classical allusions in the poem. Are they part of Neo-Classical rules? Explain.

"An Essay on Man"

1. What is the relation of man to God as Pope sees it? Why is the universe perfect?
2. Compare line 16 with Milton's "and justify the ways of God to men" (line 26 of *Paradise Lost*). What different methods are used by these poets for the same purpose?
3. What is man's place in the universe? Do you agree with Pope's ideas? Why or why not?
4. Explain the final truth of the poem. Does Pope seem to deny the existence of evil or does he say that evil works God's will? Explain.
5. In this poem, Pope seems to be trying to build a system of moral science and natural theology without a real religion. Is this possible? Discuss.
6. Choose three couplets that are striking and can be used as epigrams.

JONATHAN SWIFT

(1667–1745)

Swift's personal life is closely related to his writings. Born and bred in Ireland, he never really liked the country. His years as a youth were spent in poverty. Even as a secretary to Sir William Temple he was dependent on the charity of his employer. Finally, he became an Anglican clergyman, less from religious motives than in a hope of gaining "a preferment." In his later years, he was given a post in the Irish Church and, for all practical purposes, banished from the world and society he loved. One of his contemporaries called him "the unhappiest man that ever lived."

Swift excelled in the field of prose satire. He satirized learning, religion, politics, and human nature in general. In a letter to Alexander Pope he said, "I have ever hated all nations, professions, and communities, all my love is toward individuals." With such a creed, he turned his attack on the institutions, fashions, and follies of his day.

Swift was a learned man with an insatiable thirst for knowledge. He could never be satisfied with external appearances when he saw corruption in so many human beings and institutions. He once wrote that "to expose vice and to make people laugh with innocence does more public service than all the Ministers of State. . . ."

He was no intellectual snob, however, for his personality was rich and had many facets. For all his apparent haughtiness, he was capable of the deepest tenderness and affection. His charity was well known and was usually performed in secret. The few friends he had respected and loved him.

Gulliver's Travels is Swift's masterpiece and gives him a place with the great satirists of literature. Although he claimed that he wrote this work to vex the world rather than amuse it, posterity, especially children, has been entertained by the adventures and observations of Gulliver.

The first adventure takes place in Lilliput, the land of little people, where the tallest men are six inches high. Lilliput is an imaginary land in which the author finds that the greatness of his nation appears ridiculous when compared to a race of pygmies. Gulliver's fourth voyage takes him to the country of the Houyhnhnms, an ideal land ruled by a race of wonderful horses who possess all the qualities that should be man's. The slaves of the Houyhnhnms, called Yahoos, are degraded humans without moral or social control.

Gulliver's Travels

from A VOYAGE TO LILLIPUT

CHAPTER FIVE: *The Author by an extraordinary stratagem prevents an invasion. A high title of honour is conferred upon him. Ambassadors arrive from the Emperor of Blefuscu, and sue for peace. The Empress's apartment on fire by an accident. The Author instrumental in saving the rest of the palace.*

The Empire of Blefuscu is an island situated to the north-north-east side of Lilliput, from whence it is parted only by a channel of eight hundred yards wide. I had not yet seen it, and upon this notice of an intended invasion, I avoided appearing on that side of the coast, for fear of being discovered by some of the enemy's ships, who had received no intelligence of me, all intercourse between the two empires having been strictly forbidden during the war, upon pain of death, and an embargo laid by our Emperor upon all vessels whatsoever. I communicated to his Majesty a project I had formed of seizing the enemy's whole fleet: which, as our scouts assured us, lay at anchor in the harbour ready to sail with the first fair wind. I consulted the most experienced seamen, upon the depth of the channel, which they had often plumbed; who told me that in the middle at high water it was seventy *glumgluffs* deep, which is about six foot of European measure; and the rest of it fifty *glumgluffs* at most. I walked to the north-east coast over against Blefuscu; where, lying down behind a hillock, I took out my small pocket perspective-glass, and viewed the enemy's fleet at anchor, consisting of about fifty men of war, and a great number of transports: I then came back to my house, and gave order (for which I had a warrant) for a great quantity of the strongest cable and bars of iron. The cable was about as thick as packthread, and the bars of the length and size of a knitting-needle. I trebled the cable to make it stronger, and for the same reason I twisted three of the iron bars together, binding the extremities into a hook. Having thus fixed fifty hooks to as many cables, I went back to the north-east coast, and putting off my coat, shoes, and stockings, walked into the sea in my leathern jerkin, about half an hour before high water. I waded with what haste I could, and swam in the middle about thirty yards till I felt ground; I arrived at the fleet in less than half an hour. The enemy was so frighted when they saw me, that they leaped out of their ships, and swam to shore, where there could not be fewer than thirty thousand souls. I then took my tackling, and fastening a hook to the hole at the prow of each, I tied all the cords together at the end. While I was thus employed, the enemy discharged several thousand arrows, many of which stuck in my hands and face; and besides the excessive smart, gave me much disturbance in my work. My greatest apprehension was for mine eyes, which I should have infallibly lost, if I had not suddenly thought of an expedient. I kept among other little necessaries a pair of spectacles in a private pocket, which, as I observed before, had escaped the Emperor's searchers. These I took out and fastened as strongly as I could upon my nose, and thus armed went on boldly with my work in spite of the enemy's arrows, many of which struck against the glasses of my spectacles, but without any other effect, further than a little to discompose them. I had now fastened all the hooks, and taking the knot in my hand, began to pull; but not a ship would stir, for they were all too fast held by their anchors, so that the boldest part of my enterprise remained. I therefore let go the cord, and leaving the hooks fixed to the ships, I resolutely cut with my knife the cables that fastened the anchors, receiving above two hundred shots in my face and hands; then I took up the knotted end of the cables to which my hooks were tied, and with great ease drew fifty of the enemy's largest men-of-war after me.

The Blefuscudians, who had not the least imagination of what I intended, were at first confounded with astonishment. They had seen me cut the cables, and thought my design was only to let the ships run a-drift, or fall foul on each other: but when they perceived the whole fleet moving in order, and saw me pulling at the end, they set up such a scream of grief and despair, that it is almost impossible to describe or conceive. When I had got out of danger, I stopt awhile to pick out the arrows that stuck in my hands and face, and rubbed on some of the same ointment that was given me at my first arrival, as I have formerly mentioned. I then took off my spectacles, and waiting about an hour, till the tide was a little fallen, I waded through the middle with my cargo, and arrived safe at the royal port of Lilliput.

The Emperor and his whole court stood on the shore expecting the issue of this great adventure. They saw the ships move forward in a large half-moon, but could not discern me, who was up to my breast in water. When I advanced to the middle of the channel, they were yet in more pain, because I was under water to my neck. The Emperor concluded me to be drowned, and that the enemy's fleet was approaching in a hostile manner: but he was soon eased of his fears, for the channel growing shallower every step I made, I came in a short time within hearing, and holding up the end of the cable by which the fleet was fastened, I cried in a loud voice, *Long live the most puissant Emperor of Lilliput!* This great prince received me at my landing with all possible encomiums, and created me a *Nardac* upon the spot, which is the highest title of honour among them.

His Majesty desired I would take some other opportunity of bringing all the rest of his enemy's ships into his ports. And so unmeasurable is the ambition of princes, that he seemed to think of nothing less than reducing the whole empire of Blefuscu into a province, and governing it by a Viceroy; of destroying the Big-Endian exiles, and compelling that people to break the smaller end of their eggs, by which he would remain the sole monarch of the whole world. But I endeavoured to divert him from this design, by many arguments drawn from the topics of policy as well as justice; and I plainly protested, that I would never be an instrument of bringing a free and brave people into slavery. And when the matter was debated in council, the wisest part of the ministry were of my opinion.

This open bold declaration of mine was so opposite to the schemes and politics of his Imperial Majesty, that he could never forgive me: he mentioned it in a very artful manner at council, where, I was told, that some of the wisest appeared, at least by their silence, to be of my opinion; but others, who were my secret enemies, could not forbear some expressions, which by a side-wind reflected on me. And from this time began an intrigue between his Majesty and a junto of ministers maliciously bent against me, which broke out in less than two months, and had like to have ended in my utter destruction. Of so little weight are the greatest services to princes, when put into the balance with a refusal to gratify their passions.

About three weeks after this exploit, there arrived a solemn embassy from Blefuscu, with humble offers of a peace; which was soon concluded upon conditions very advantageous to our Emperor, wherewith I shall not trouble the reader. There were six ambassadors, with a train of about five hundred persons; and their entry was very magnificent, suitable to the grandeur of their master, and the importance of their business. When their treaty was finished, wherein I did them several good offices by the credit I now had, or at least appeared to have at court, their Excellencies, who were privately told how much I had been their friend, made me a visit in form. They began with many compliments upon my valour and generosity, invited me to that kingdom in the Emperor their master's name, and desired me to show them some proofs of my prodigious strength, of which they had heard so many wonders; wherein I readily obliged them, but shall not trouble the reader with the particulars.

When I had for some time entertained their Excellencies, to their infinite satisfaction and surprise, I desired they would do me the honour to present my most humble respects to the Emperor their master, the renown of whose virtues had so justly filled the whole world with admiration, and whose royal person I resolved to attend before I returned to my own country. Accordingly, the next time I had the honour to see our Emperor, I desired his general license to wait on the Blefuscudian monarch, which he was pleased to grant me, as I could plainly perceive, in a very cold manner; but could not guess the reason, till I had a whisper from a certain person, that Flimnap and Bolgolam had represented my intercourse with those ambassadors as a mark of disaffection, from which I am sure my heart was wholly free. And this was the first time I began to conceive some imperfect idea of courts and ministers.

It is to be observed, that these ambassadors spoke to me by an interpreter; the languages of both empires differing as much from each other as any two in Europe, and each nation priding itself upon the antiquity, beauty, and energy of their own tongues, with an avowed contempt for that of their neighbour; yet our Emperor, standing upon the advantage he had got by the seizure of their fleet, obliged them to deliver their credentials, and make their speech in the Lilliputian tongue. And it must be confessed, that from the great intercourse of trade and commerce between both realms, from the continual reception of exiles, which is mutual among them, and from the custom in each empire to send their young nobility and richer gentry to the other, in order to polish themselves by seeing the world and understanding men and manners; there are few persons of distinction, or merchants, or seamen, who dwell in the maritime parts, but what can hold conversation in both tongues; as I found some weeks after, when I went to pay my respects to the Emperor of Blefuscu, which in the midst of great misfortunes, through the malice of my enemies, proved a very happy adventure to me, as I shall relate in its proper place.

The reader may remember, that when I signed those articles upon which I recovered my liberty, there were some which I disliked upon account of their being too servile, neither could anything but an extreme necessity have forced me to submit. But being now a Nardac, of the highest rank in that empire, such offices were looked upon as below my dignity, and the Emperor (to do him justice) never once mentioned them to me. However, it was not long before I had an opportunity of doing his Majesty, at least, as I then thought, a most signal service. I was alarmed at midnight with the cries of many hundred people at my door; by which being suddenly awaked, I was in some kind of terror. I heard the word *burglum* repeated incessantly; several of the Emperor's court, making their way through the crowd, entreated me to come immediately to the palace, where her Imperial Majesty's apartment was on fire, by the carelessness of a maid of honour, who fell asleep while she was reading a romance. I got up in an instant; and orders being given to clear the way before me, and it being likewise a moonshine night, I made a shift to get to the palace without trampling on any of the people. I found they had already applied ladders to the walls of the apartment, and were well provided with buckets, but the water was at some distance. These buckets were about the size of a large thimble, and the poor people supplied me with them as fast as they could; but the flame was so violent that they did little good. I might easily have stifled it with my coat, which I unfortunately left behind me for haste, and came away only in my leathern jerkin. The case seemed wholly desperate and deplorable; and this magnificent palace would have infallibly been burnt down to the ground, if, by a presence of mind, unusual to me, I had not suddenly thought of an expedient. I had the evening before drank plentifully of a most delicious wine, called *glimigrim*, (the Blefuscudians call it *flunec*, but ours is esteemed the better sort) which is very diuretic. By the luckiest chance in the world, I had not discharged myself of any part of it. The heat I had contracted by coming very near the flames, and by my labouring to quench them, made the wine begin to operate by urine; which I voided in such a quantity, and applied so well to the proper places, that in three minutes the fire was wholly extinguished, and the rest of that noble pile, which had cost so many ages in erecting, preserved from destruction.

It was now daylight, and I returned to my house, without waiting to congratulate with the Emperor; because, although I had done a very eminent piece of service, yet I could not tell how his Majesty might resent the manner by which I had performed it: for, by the fundamental laws of the realm, it is capital in any person, of what quality soever, to make water within the precincts of the palace. But I was a little comforted by a message from his Majesty, that he would give orders to the Grand Judiciary for passing my pardon in form; which, however, I could not obtain. And I was privately assured, that the Empress, conceiving the greatest abhorrence of what I had done, removed to the most distant side of the court, firmly resolved that those buildings should never be repaired for her use; and, in the presence of her chief confidents, could not forbear vowing revenge.

For Discussion

1. Note the careful way in which Swift describes the land of Lilliput. What does this add to his narrative? Choose four words which Swift created for his Lilliputian vocabulary. Are they meant to be humorous? What effect do such words produce?
2. What is the author's point in relating the revolt of the Big-Endians? Why is this satirical?
3. J. B. Priestley has defined humor as "thinking in fun while feeling in earnest." Using his definition as a guide, point out what Swift *felt in earnest* in this episode.
4. Would you say that Swift emphasizes plot construction or characterization? Why?
5. Swift is one of the great masters of English prose. Select five examples of his use of the proper word in the proper place.

from A VOYAGE TO THE COUNTRY OF THE HOUYHNHNMS

CHAPTER FIVE: *The Author, at his master's command, informs him of the state of England. The causes of war among the princes of Europe. The Author begins to explain the English constitution.*

The reader may please to observe, that the following extract of many conversations I had with my master, contains a summary of the most material points which were discoursed at several times for above two years; his Honour often desiring fuller satisfaction as I farther improved in the Houyhnhnm tongue. I laid before him, as well as I could, the whole state of Europe; I discoursed of trade and manufactures, of arts and sciences; and the answers I gave to all the questions he made, as they arose upon several subjects, were a fund of conversation not to be exhausted. But I shall here only set down the substance of what passed between us concerning my own country, reducing it into order as well as I can, without any regard to time or other circumstances, while I strictly adhere to truth. My only concern is that I shall hardly be able to do justice to my master's arguments and expressions, which must needs suffer by my want of capacity, as well as by a translation into our barbarous English.

In obedience therefore to his Honour's commands, I related to him the Revolution under the Prince of Orange; the long war with France entered into by the said prince, and renewed by his successor the present Queen; wherein the greatest powers of Christendom were engaged, and which still continued: I computed at his request that about a million of Yahoos might have been killed in the whole progress of it, and perhaps a hundred or more cities taken, and five times as many ships burnt or sunk.

He asked me what were the usual causes or motives that made one country go to war with another. I answered they were innumerable, but I should only mention a few of the chief. Sometimes the ambition of princes, who never think they have land or people enough to govern; sometimes the corruption of ministers, who engage their master in a war in order to stifle or divert the clamour of the subjects against their evil administration. Difference in opinions hath cost many millions of lives: for instance, whether *flesh* be *bread*, or *bread* be *flesh*; whether the juice of a certain *berry* be *blood* or *wine*; whether *whistling* be a vice or a *virtue*; whether it be better to *kiss a post*, or throw it into the fire; what is the best colour for a *coat*, whether *black*, *white*, *red* or *gray*; and whether it should be *long* or *short*, *narrow* or *wide*, *dirty* or *clean*; with many more. Neither are any wars so furious and bloody, or of so long continuance, as those occasioned by difference in opinion, especially if it be in things indifferent.

Sometimes the quarrel between two princes is to decide which of them shall dispossess a third of his dominions, where neither of them pretend to any right. Sometimes one prince quarrelleth with another, for fear the other should quarrel with him. Sometimes a war is entered upon, because the enemy is too *strong*, and sometimes because he is too *weak*. Sometimes our neighbours *want* the *things* which we *have*, or *have* the things which we *want*; and we both fight, till they take ours or give us theirs. It is a very justifiable cause of war to invade a country after the people have been wasted by famine, destroyed by pestilence, or embroiled by factions among themselves. It is justifiable to enter into war against our nearest ally, when one of his towns lies convenient for us, or a territory of land, that would render our dominions round and complete. If a prince sends forces into a nation where the people are poor and ignorant, he may lawfully put half of them to death, and make slaves of the rest, in order to civilize and reduce them from their barbarous way of living. It is a very kingly, honourable, and frequent practice, when one prince desires the assistance of another to secure him against an invasion, that the assistant, when he hath driven out the invader, should seize on the dominions himself, and kill, imprison or banish the prince he came to relieve. Alliance by blood or marriage is a frequent cause of war between princes; and the nearer the kindred is, the greater is their disposition to quarrel: *poor* nations are *hungry*, and *rich* nations are *proud*; and pride and hunger will ever be at variance. For these reasons, the trade of a *soldier* is held the most honourable of all others; because a *soldier* is a Yahoo hired to kill in cold blood as many of his own species, who have never offended him, as possibly he can.

There is likewise a kind of beggarly princes in Europe, not able to make war by themselves, who hire out their troops to richer nations, for so much a day to each man; of which they keep three fourths to themselves, and it is the best part of their maintenance; such are those in Germany and other northern parts of Europe.

What you have told me, (said my master) upon the subject of war, does indeed discover most admirably the effects of that reason you prentend to: however, it is happy that the shame is greater than the danger; and that nature hath left you utterly uncapable of doing much mischief: for your mouths lying flat with your faces, you can hardly bite each other to any purpose, unless by consent. Then as to the claws upon your feet before and behind, they are so short and tender, that one of our Yahoos would drive a dozen of yours before him. And therefore in recounting the numbers of those who have been killed in battle, I cannot but think that you have *said the thing which is not*.

I could not forbear shaking my head and smiling a little at his ignorance. And being no stranger to the art of war, I gave him a description of cannons, culverins, muskets, carabines, pistols, bullets, powder, swords, bayonets, battles, sieges, retreats, attacks, undermines, countermines, bombardments, sea fights; ships sunk with a thousand men, twenty thousand killed on each side; dying groans, limbs flying in the air; smoke, noise, confusion, trampling to death under horses' feet; flight, pursuit, victory; fields strewed with carcasses left for food to dogs, and wolves, and birds of prey; plundering, stripping, ravishing, burning, and destroying. And to set forth the valour of my own dear countrymen, I assured him that I had seen them blow up a hundred enemies at once in a siege, and as many in a ship, and beheld the dead bodies come down in pieces from the clouds, to the great diversion of the spectators.

I was going on to more particulars, when my master commanded me silence. He said whoever understood the nature of Yahoos might easily believe it possible for so vile an animal to be capable of every action I had named, if their strength and cunning equalled their malice. But as my discourse had increased his abhorrence of the whole species, so he found it gave him a disturbance in his mind, to which he was wholly a stranger before. He thought his ears being used to such abominable words, might by degrees admit them with less detestation. That although he hated the Yahoos of this country, yet he no more blamed them for their odious qualities, than he did a *gnnayh* (a bird of prey) for its cruelty, or a sharp stone for cutting his hoof. But when a creature pretending to reason could be capable of such enormities, he dreaded lest the corruption of that faculty might be worse than brutality itself. He seemed therefore confident, that instead of reason, we were only possessed of some quality fitted to increase our natural vices; as the reflection from a troubled stream returns the image of an ill-shapen body, not only larger, but more distorted.

He added, that he had heard too much upon the subject of war, both in this and some former discourses. There was another point which a little perplexed him at present. I had informed him, that some of our crew left their country on account of being ruined by *Law*; that I had already explained the meaning of the word; but he was at a loss how it should come to pass, that the law which was intended for every man's preservation, should be any man's ruin. Therefore he desired to be farther satisfied what I meant by *Law*, and the dispensers thereof, according to the present practice in my own country; because he thought nature and reason were sufficient guides for a reasonable animal, as we pretended to be, in showing us what we ought to do, and what to avoid.

I assured his Honour that law was a science wherein I had not much conversed, further than by employing advocates, in vain, upon some injustices that had been done me: however, I would give him all the satisfaction I was able.

I said there was a society of men among us, bred up from their youth in the art of proving by words multiplied for the purpose, that *white* is *black*, and *black* is *white*, according as they are paid. To this society all the rest of the people are slaves.

For example, if my neighbour hath a mind to my cow, he hires a lawyer to prove that he ought to have my cow from me. I must then hire another to defend my right, it being against all rules of law that any man should be allowed to speak for himself. Now in this case I who am the right owner lie under two great disadvantages. First, my lawyer, being practised almost from his cradle in defending falsehood, is quite out of his element when he would be an advocate for justice, which as an office unnatural, he always attempts with great awkwardness, if not with ill-will. The second disadvantage is that my lawyer must proceed with great caution, or else he will be reprimanded by the judges, and abhorred by his brethren, as one that would lessen the practice of the law. And therefore I have but two methods to preserve my cow. The first is to gain over my adversary's lawyer with a double fee, who will then betray his client by insinuating that he hath justice on his side. The second way is for my lawyer to make my cause appear as unjust as he can, by allowing the cow to belong to my adversary; and this, if it be skilfully done, will certainly bespeak the favour of the bench.

Now, your Honour is to know that these judges are persons appointed to decide all controversies of property, as well as for the trial of criminals; and picked out from the most dexterous lawyers, who are grown old or lazy; and having been biassed all their lives against truth and equity, are under such a fatal necessity of favouring fraud, perjury, and oppression, that I have known several of them refuse a large bribe from the side where justice lay, rather than injure the faculty, by doing any thing unbecoming their nature or their office.

It is a maxim among these lawyers, that whatever hath been done before may legally be done again: and therefore they take special care to record all the decisions formerly made against common justice and the general reason of mankind. These, under the name of *precedents*, they produce as authorities, to justify the most iniquitous opinions; and the judges never fail of directing accordingly.

In pleading they studiously avoid entering into the merits of the cause, but are loud, violent, and tedious in dwelling upon all *circumstances* which are not to the purpose. For instance, in the case already mentioned, they never desire to know what claim or title my adversary hath to my cow; but whether the said cow were red or black, her horns long or short; whether the field I graze her in be round or square; whether she was milked at home or abroad; what diseases she is subject to, and the like. After which they consult *precedents*, adjourn the cause from time to time, and in ten, twenty, or thirty years, come to an issue.

It is likewise to be observed, that this society hath a peculiar cant and jargon of their own, that no other mortal can understand, and wherein all their laws are written, which they take special care to multiply; whereby they have wholly confounded the very essence of truth and falsehood, of right and wrong; so that it will take thirty years to decide whether the field left me by my ancestors for six generations belongs to me, or to a stranger three hundred miles off.

In the trial of persons accused for crimes against the state the method is more short and commendable: the judge first sends to sound the disposition of those in power, after which he can easily hang or save the criminal, strictly preserving all the forms of law.

Here my master interposing, said it was a pity that creatures endowed with such prodigious abilities of mind as these lawyers, by the description I gave of them, must certainly be, were not rather encouraged to be instructors of others in wisdom and knowledge. In answer to which I assured his Honour that in all points out of their own trade, they were usually the most ignorant and stupid generation among us, the most despicable in common conversation, avowed enemies to all knowledge and learning; and equally disposed to pervert the general reason of mankind in every other subject of discourse, as in that of their own profession.

For Discussion

1. What is the tone of Gulliver's own description of the causes of war? What is the reaction of his Houyhnhnm Master to this description? What is Swift satirizing in this episode? Explain.
2. What is Gulliver's view of lawyers? What wish does his Master express?
3. Under the powder, patches, wigs, and silken finery of the eighteenth century, Swift saw the stupidity, self-seeking, and savageness of mankind. Are such faults prevalent today? Why? Point out examples.
4. Does a satirist need courage to look at the facts? Explan. Point out how exaggeration is used by Swift. Is it a part of good satire? Why?
5. Which of these two selections from *Gulliver's Travels* shows more clearly that Swift was a satirist and not a writer of children's stories? Explain.
6. What modern authors are satirists in the Swift vein? Name one of the works of each.

JOSEPH ADDISON

(1672–1719)

When he was a student at the Charterhouse and at Oxford, Joseph Addison had a friend named Richard Steele. These two young men ventured on a literary project that was to entertain the English reading public for a decade.

One of the social centers of the London of their day was the coffee-house. The first coffee-house was opened in 1652, and by 1700 there were almost 3,000 of them. Every Londoner, no matter what his social and financial position, had his favorite coffee-house where he spent his leisure hours looking over the newspapers of the day, smoking his pipe, sipping his coffee, and exchanging information and gossip with his friends.

Steele, who knew his London, saw an ideal chance for a writer who could capture the attention of this vast organized public by a periodical of instruction and entertainment. Under the pen-name of Isaac Bickerstaff, he published *The Tatler*, a periodical published three times a week, which drew more patrons to the coffee-houses than any other paper of its day.

Addison, who was Secretary to the Lord Lieutenant of Ireland at this time, recognized his friend Steele in Isaac Bickerstaff and decided to submit some of his own essays to the paper. *The Tatler* was a most fortunate occurrence for Addison because it showed him where his real talent lay.

On March 1, 1711, a superior periodical, *The Spectator*, replaced *The Tatler*. It appeared every day except Sunday. Under the combined genius of Addison and Steele, *The Spectator* was even more popular than its predecessor. Carefully avoiding any party politics, it humorously and sensibly criticized the manners, customs, and petty vanities of everyday life in early eighteenth-century England.

The Spectator became a powerful force in instructing English society. Through witty and conversational essays, good breeding, manners, and morality were taught. London readers were surprised to see that charm, elegance, and wit, all of which had been considered the exclusive possession of cultivated gentlemen, were now of the essence of good morals.

Addison and Steele laughed their readers into better manners and ethics with their light satire.

What Addison and Steele had actually done was to introduce the *informal essay* to the English literary world. They had taken the form introduced by Francis Bacon and added their own personalities and personal impressions, thereby bringing a new freedom and dimension to the essay.

Of the two editors, Addison was the better literary critic and writer. The charm of his essays is in the gracious, kindly, and cultivated observations of everyday life expressed in a polished style. The beauty and power this style could achieve can be seen in the famous final sentences of "Westminster Abbey" beginning "When I look upon the tombs of the great . . ." (page 235).

Westminster Abbey

The Spectator, No. 26: Friday, March 30, 1711.

When I am in a serious humor, I very often walk by myself in Westminster Abbey; where the gloominess of the place, and the use to which it is applied, with the solemnity of the building, and the condition of the people who lie in it, are apt to fill the mind with a kind of melancholy, or rather thoughtfulness, that is not disagreeable. I yesterday passed a whole afternoon in the churchyard, the cloisters, and the church, amusing myself with the tombstones and inscriptions that I met with in those several regions of the dead. Most of them recorded nothing else of the buried person, but that he was born upon one day and died upon another: the whole history of his life being comprehended in those two circumstances, that are common to all mankind. I could not but look upon these registers of existence, whether of brass or marble, as a kind of satire upon the departed persons; who had left no other memorial of them, but that they were born and that they died. They put me in mind of several persons mentioned in the battles of heroic poems, who have sounding names given them, for no other reason but that they may be killed, and are celebrated for nothing but being knocked on the head. The life of these men is finely described in holy writ by "the path of an arrow," which is immediately closed up and lost.

Upon my going into the church, I entertained myself with the digging of a grave, and saw in every shovelful of it that was thrown up, the fragment of a bone or skull intermixt with a kind of fresh moldering earth that some time or other had a place in the composition of a human body. Upon this I began to consider with myself what innumerable multitudes of people lay confused together under the pavement of that ancient cathedral; how men and women, friends and enemies, priests and soldiers, monks and prebendaries,[1] were crumbled amongst one another and blended together in the same common mass; how beauty, strength, and youth, with old age, weakness, and deformity, lay undistinguished in the same promiscuous heap of matter.

After having thus surveyed this great magazine of mortality, as it were, in the lump, I examined it more particularly by the accounts which I found on several of the monuments which are raised in every quarter of that ancient fabric. Some of them were covered with such extravagant epitaphs that, if it were possible for the dead person to be acquainted with them, he would blush at the praises which his friends have bestowed upon him. There are others so excessively modest that they deliver the character of the person departed in Greek or Hebrew, and by that means are not understood once in a twelvemonth. In the poetical quarter, I found there were poets who had no monuments, and monuments which had no poets. I observed, indeed, that the present war[2] had filled the church with many of these uninhabited monuments, which had been erected to the memory of persons whose bodies were perhaps buried in the plains of Blenheim, or in the bosom of the ocean.

I could not but be very much delighted with several modern epitaphs, which are written with great elegance of expression and justness of thought, and therefore do honor to the living as well as to the dead. As a foreigner is very apt to conceive an idea of the ignorance or politeness of a nation from the turn of their public monuments and inscriptions, they should be submitted to the perusal of men of learning and genius before they are put in execution. Sir Cloudesly Shovel's[3] monument has very often given me great offense: instead of the brave rough English Admiral, which was the distin-

---

[1] **prebendaries**: clergymen who receive salaries from the revenues of a cathedral
[2] **the present war**: the War of the Spanish Succession
[3] **Sir Cloudesly Shovel**: prominent British naval figure of the 17th century

guishing character of that plain gallant man, he is represented on his tomb by the figure of a beau, dressed in a long periwig, and reposing himself upon velvet cushions under a canopy of state. The inscription is answerable to the monument; for instead of celebrating the many remarkable actions he had performed in the service of his country, it acquaints us only with the manner of his death, in which it was impossible for him to reap any honor. The Dutch, whom we are apt to despise for want of genius, show an infinitely greater taste of antiquity and politeness in their buildings and works of this nature than what we meet within those of our own country. The monuments of their admirals, which have been erected at the public expense, represent them like themselves; and are adorned with rostral crowns and naval ornaments, with beautiful festoons of seaweed, shells, and coral.

But to return to our subject. I have left the repository of our English kings for the contemplation of another day, when I shall find my mind disposed for so serious an amusement. I know that entertainments of this nature are apt to raise dark and dismal thoughts in timorous minds and gloomy imaginations; but for my own part, though I am always serious, I do not know what it is to be melancholy; and can therefore take a view of nature in her deep and solemn scenes, with the same pleasure as in her most gay and delightful ones. By this means I can improve myself with those objects which others consider with terror. When I look upon the tombs of the great, every emotion of envy dies in me; when I read the epitaphs of the beautiful, every inordinate desire goes out; when I meet with the grief of parents upon a tombstone, my heart melts with compassion; when I see the tomb of the parents themselves, I consider the vanity of grieving for those whom we must quickly follow: when I see kings lying by those who deposed them, when I consider rival wits placed side by side, or the holy men that divided the world with their contests and disputes, I reflect with sorrow and astonishment on the little competitions, factions, and debates of mankind. When I read the several dates of the tombs, of some that died yesterday, and some six hundred years ago, I consider that great day when we shall all of us be contemporaries, and make our appearance together.

A Consideration of Milton's
Paradise Lost

The Spectator, No. 267: Saturday, January 5, 1712.

There is nothing in nature so irksome as general discourses, especially when they turn chiefly upon words. For this reason I shall waive the discussion of that point which was started some years since, whether Milton's *Paradise Lost* may be called an heroic poem. Those who will not give it that title, may call it (if they please) a divine poem. It will be sufficient to its perfection, if it has in it all the beauties of the highest kind of poetry; and as for those who allege it is not an heroic poem, they advance no more to the diminution of it, than if they should say Adam is not Aeneas, nor Eve Helen.

I shall therefore examine it by the rules of epic poetry, and see whether it falls short of the *Iliad* or *Aeneid* in the beauties which are essential to that kind of writing. The first thing to be considered in an epic poem is the fable, which is perfect or imperfect according as the action which it relates is more or less so. This action should have three qualifications in it. First, it should be but one action. Secondly, it should be an entire action; and, thirdly, it should be a great action. To consider the action of the *Iliad, Aeneid*, and *Paradise Lost*, in these three several lights: Homer, to preserve the unity of his action, hastens into the midst of things, as Horace has observed. Had he gone up to Leda's egg,[1] or begun much later, even at the rape of Helen, or the investing of Troy, it is manifest that the story of the poem would have been a series of several actions. He therefore opens his poem with the discord of his princes and artfully interweaves, in the several succeeding parts of it, an account of everything material which relates to them and had passed before that fatal dissention. After the same manner Aeneas makes his first appearance in the Tyrrhene seas,[2] and within sight of Italy, because the action

[1] **Leda's egg:** Helen was supposedly born from an egg delivered by her mother, Leda.
[2] **Tyrrhene seas:** part of the Mediterranean off the western coast of Italy

proposed to be celebrated was that of his settling himself in Latium. But because it was necessary for the reader to know what had happened to him in the taking of Troy, and in the preceding parts of his voyage, Virgil makes his hero relate it by way of episode in the second and third books of the *Aeneid.* The contents of both which books came before those of the first book in the thread of the story, though for preserving this unity of action they follow them in the disposition of the poem. Milton, in imitation of these two great poets, opens his *Paradise Lost* with an infernal council plotting the fall of man, which is the action he proposed to celebrate; and as for those great actions, which preceded, in point of time, the battle of the angels, and the creation of the world, (which would have entirely destroyed the unity of the principal action, had he related them in the same order that they happened) he cast them into the fifth, sixth, and seventh books, by way of episode to this noble poem.

Aristotle himself allows that Homer has nothing to boast of as to the unity of his fable, though at the same time that great critic and philosopher endeavors to palliate [3] this imperfection in the Greek poet by imputing it in some measure to the very nature of an epic poem. Some have been of opinion that the *Aeneid* also labors in this particular, and has episodes which may be looked upon as excrescences [4] rather than as parts of the action. On the contrary, the poem which we have now under our consideration hath no other episodes than such as naturally arise from the subject, and yet is filled with such a multitude of astonishing incidents that it gives us at the same time a pleasure of the greatest variety and of the greatest simplicity; *uniform in its nature though diversified in the execution.*

I must observe also, that as Virgil, in the poem which was designed to celebrate the original of the Roman empire, has described the birth of its great rival, the Carthaginian commonwealth; Milton, with the like art, in his poem on the fall of man, has related the fall of those angels who are his professed enemies. Besides the many other beauties in such an episode, its running parallel with the great action of the poem hinders it from breaking the unity so much as another episode would have done, that had not so great an affinity with the principal subject. In short, this is the same kind of beauty which the critics admire in the Spanish Friar, or the Double Discovery, where

[3] **palliate:** hide, reduce
[4] **excrescences:** abnormal growths

the two different plots look like counterparts and copies of one another.

The second qualification required in the action of an epic poem is that it should be an entire action. An action is entire when it is complete in all its parts; or as Aristotle describes it, when it consists of a beginning, a middle, and an end. Nothing should go before it, be intermixed with it, or follow after it, that is not related to it. As, on the contrary, no single step should be omitted in that just and regular process which it must be supposed to take from its original to its consumation. Thus we see the anger of Achilles in its birth, its continuance, and effects; and Aeneas's settlement in Italy carried on through all the oppositions in his way to it both by sea and land. The action in Milton excels (I think) both the former in this particular; we see it contrived in hell, executed upon earth, and punished by heaven. The parts of it are told in the most distinct manner and grow out of one another in the most natural method.

The third qualification of an epic poem is its greatness. The anger of Achilles was of such consequence that it embroiled the kings of Greece, destroyed the heroes of Troy, and engaged all the gods in factions. Aeneas's settlement in Italy produced the Caesars and gave birth to the Roman empire. Milton's subject was still greater than either of the former; it does not determine the fate of single persons or nations; but of a whole species. The united powers of hell are joined together for the destruction of mankind, which they effected in part, and would have completed, had not Omnipotence itself interposed. The principal actors are man in his greatest perfection, and woman in her highest beauty. Their enemies are the fallen angels; the Messiah their friend, and the Almighty their Protector. In short, everything that is great in the whole circle of being, whether within the verge of nature, or out of it, has a proper part assigned it in this admirable poem.

In poetry, as in architecture, not only the whole, but the principal members, and every part of them, should be great. I will not presume to say, that the book of games in the *Aeneid*, or that in the *Iliad*, are not of this nature; nor to reprehend Virgil's simile of the top, and many other of the same kind in the *Iliad*, as liable to any censure in this particular; but I think we may say, without derogating [5] from those wonderful performances, that there is an unquestionable mag-

[5] **derogating:** detracting

nificence in every part of *Paradise Lost,* and indeed a much greater than could have been formed upon any pagan system.

But Aristotle, by the greatness of the action, does not only mean that it should be great in its nature, but also in its duration, or in other words, that it should have a due length in it, as well as what we properly call greatness. The just measure of this kind of magnitude he explains by the following similitude: An animal no bigger than a mite cannot appear perfect to the eye, because the sight takes it in at once and has only a confused idea of the whole, and not a distinct idea of all its parts; if on the contrary, you should suppose an animal of ten thousand furlongs [6] in length, the eye would be so filled with a single part of it that it could not give the mind an idea of the whole. What these animals are to the eye, a very short or a very long action would be to the memory. The first would be, as it were, lost and swallowed up by it, and the other difficult to be contained in it. Homer and Virgil have shown their principal art in this particular; the action of the *Iliad,* and that of the *Aeneid,* were in themselves exceeding short but are so beautifully extended and diversified by the invention of episodes, and the machinery of gods, with the like poetical ornaments, that they make up an agreeable story, sufficient to employ the memory without overcharging it. Milton's action is enriched with such a variety of circumstances that I have taken as much pleasure in reading the contents of his books as in the best invented story I ever met with. It is possible that the traditions on which the *Iliad* and the *Aeneid* were built had more circumstances in them than the history of the fall of man, as it is related in scripture. Besides, it was easier for Homer and Virgil to dash the truth with fiction, as they were in no danger of offending the religion of their country by it. But as for Milton, he had not only a very few circumstances upon which to raise his poem but was also obliged to proceed with the greatest caution in everything that he added out of his own invention. And indeed, notwithstanding all the restraint he was under, he has filled his story with so many surprising incidents, which bear so close an analogy with what is delivered in holy writ, that it is capable of pleasing the most delicate reader without giving offense to the most scrupulous.

The modern critics have collected from several hints in the *Iliad* and *Aeneid* the space of time which is taken up by the action of

[6] **furlong:** one-eighth of a mile

each of those poems; but as a great part of Milton's story was translated in regions that lie out of the reach of the sun and the sphere of day, it is impossible to gratify the reader with such a calculation, which indeed would be more curious than instructive, none of the critics, either ancient or modern, having laid down rules to circumscribe the action of an epic poem with any determined number of years, days, or hours.

This piece of criticism on Milton's *Paradise Lost* shall be carried on in the following Saturdays' papers.

For Discussion

"Westminster Abbey"

1. Why is this an informal essay? What qualities in this essay are not found in Bacon's *Of Studies* (page 98)?
2. Reread the last paragraph and explain its meaning.
3. How has Addison instructed his reading audience in an entertaining way?
4. Compare this essay with John Donne's meditation on death (page 126). Which appeals to you more? Why?

"On *Paradise Lost*"

1. Addison's ability as a literary critic is well known. Briefly outline this essay. Does it seem to be more formal than informal? Explain.
2. Do you agree with Addison's idea of "the heroic" in *Paradise Lost*? Discuss.
3. Addison manifests certain Neo-Classic traits in this essay. What are they?
4. Does Milton suffer by this comparison with Homer and Virgil? Discuss.

A Country Sunday

The Spectator, No. 112: Monday, July 9, 1711.

I am always very well pleased with a country Sunday, and think, if keeping holy the seventh day were only a human institution, it would be the best method that could have been thought of for the polishing and civilizing of mankind. It is certain the country people would soon degenerate into a kind of savages and barbarians were there not such frequent returns of a stated time in which the whole village meet together with their best faces, and in their cleanliest habits, to converse with one another upon indifferent subjects, hear their duties explained to them, and join together in adoration of the Supreme Being. Sunday clears away the rust of the whole week, not only as it refreshes in their minds the notions of religion, but as it puts both the sexes upon appearing in their most agreeable forms, and exerting all such qualities as are apt to give them a figure in the eye of the village. A country fellow distinguishes himself as much in the churchyard as a citizen does upon the 'Change,[1] the whole parish politics being generally discussed in that place either after sermon or before the bell rings.

My friend Sir Roger, being a good churchman, has beautified the inside of his church with several texts of his own choosing; he has likewise given a handsome pulpit-cloth, and railed in the communion-table at his own expense. He has often told me that, at his coming to his estate, he found his parishioners very irregular; and that, in order to make them kneel and join in the responses, he gave every one of them a hassock and a common-prayer book, and at the same time employed an itinerant singing-master, who goes about the country for that purpose, to instruct them rightly in the tunes of the Psalms; upon which they now very much value themselves, and indeed outdo most of the country churches that I have ever heard.

As Sir Roger is landlord to the whole congregation, he keeps them in very good order, and will suffer nobody to sleep in it besides himself; for, if by chance he has been surprised into a short nap at sermon, upon recovering out of it he stands up and looks about him, and if he sees anybody else nodding, either wakes them himself, or sends his servant to them. Several other of the old knight's particularities break out upon these occasions; sometimes he will be lengthening out a verse in the Singing-Psalms half a minute after the rest of the congregation have done with it; sometimes, when he is pleased with the matter of his devotion, he pronounces "Amen" three or four times to the same prayer; and sometimes stands up when everybody else is upon their knees, to count the congregation, or see if any of his tenants are missing.

I was yesterday very much surprised to hear my old friend, in the

[1] 'Change: London Stock Exchange

midst of the service, calling out to one John Matthews to mind what he was about, and not disturb the congregation. This John Matthews, it seems, is remarkable for being an idle fellow, and at that time was kicking his heels for his diversion. This authority of the knight, though exerted in that odd manner which accompanies him in all circumstances of life, has a very good effect upon the parish, who are not polite enough to see anything ridiculous in his behavior; besides that the general good sense and worthiness of his character makes his friends observe these little singularities as foils that rather set off than blemish his good qualities.

As soon as the sermon is finished, nobody presumes to stir till Sir Roger is gone out of the church. The knight walks down from his seat in the chancel between a double row of his tenants, that stand bowing to him on each side, and every now and then inquires how such an one's wife, or mother, or son, or father do, whom he does not see at church—which is understood as a secret reprimand to the person that is absent.

The chaplain has often told me that, upon a catechizing day, when Sir Roger had been pleased with a boy that answers well, he has ordered a Bible to be given him next day for his encouragement, and sometimes accompanies it with a flitch of bacon [2] to his mother. Sir Roger has likewise added five pounds a year to the clerk's place; and, that he may encourage the young fellows to make themselves perfect in the church service, has promised, upon the death of the present incumbent, who is very old, to bestow it according to merit.

The fair understanding between Sir Roger and his chaplain, and their mutual concurrence in doing good, is the more remarkable because the very next village is famous for the differences and contentions that rise between the parson and the squire, who live in a perpetual state of war. The parson is always preaching at the squire, and the squire, to be revenged on the parson, never comes to church. The squire has made all his tenants atheists and tithe-stealers, while the parson instructs them every Sunday in the dignity of his order, and insinuates to them in almost every sermon that he is a better man than his patron. In short, matters are come to such an extremity that the squire has not said his prayers either in public or in private this half year; and that the parson threatens him, if he does not mend his manners, to pray for him in the face of the whole congregation.

[2] flitch of bacon: a side of hog

Feuds of this nature, though too frequent in the country, are very fatal to the ordinary people, who are so used to be dazzled with riches that they pay as much deference to the understanding of a man of an estate as of a man of learning; and are very hardly brought to regard any truth, how important soever it may be, that is preached to them, when they know there are several men of five hundred [3] a year who do not believe it.

[3] **five hundred:** 500 pounds income

The Coquette's Heart

The Spectator, No. 281: Tuesday, January 22, 1712.

Having already given an account of the dissection of a beau's head, with the several discoveries made on that occasion, I shall here, according to my promise, enter upon the dissection of a coquette's [1] heart, and communicate to the public such particularities as we observed in that curious piece of anatomy.

I should perhaps have waived this undertaking, had not I been put in mind of my promise by several of my unknown correspondents, who are very importunate with me to make an example of the coquette, as I have already done of the beau. It is therefore in compliance with the request of friends that I have looked over the minutes of my former dream, in order to give the public an exact relation of it, which I shall enter upon without further preface.

Our operator, before he engaged in this visionary dissection, told us that there was nothing in his art more difficult than to lay open the heart of a coquette, by reason of the many labyrinths and recesses which are to be found in it, and which do not appear in the heart of any other animal.

He desired us first of all to observe the pericardium, or outward case of the heart, which we did very attentively; and by the help of our glasses discerned in it millions of little scars, which seemed to have been occasioned by the points of innumerable darts and arrows, that from time to time had glanced upon the outward coat; though we could not discover the smallest orifice by which any of them had entered and pierced the inward substance.

[1] **coquette:** flirt

Every smatterer [2] in anatomy knows that this pericardium, or case of the heart, contains in it a thin reddish liquor, supposed to be bred from the vapors which exhale out of the heart and, being stopped here, are condensed into this watery substance. Upon examining this liquor, we found that it had in it all the qualities of that spirit which is made use of in the thermometer to show the change of weather.

Nor must I here omit an experiment one of the company assured us he himself had made with this liquor, which he found in great quantity about the heart of a coquette whom he had formerly dissected. He affirmed to us that he had actually enclosed it in a small tube made after the manner of a weatherglass; but that, instead of acquainting him with the variations of the atmosphere, it showed him the qualities of those persons who entered the room where it stood. He affirmed also that it rose at the approach of a plume of feathers, an embroidered coat, or a pair of fringed gloves; and that it fell as soon as an ill-shaped periwig, a clumsy pair of shoes, or an unfashionable coat came into his house. Nay, he proceeded so far as to assure us that upon his laughing aloud when he stood by it, the liquor mounted very sensibly, and immediately sank again upon his looking serious. In short, he told us that he knew very well by this invention whenever he had a man of sense or a coxcomb [3] in his room.

Having cleared away the pericardium, or the case, and liquor above mentioned, we came to the heart itself. The outward surface of it was extremely slippery, and the mucro, or point, so very cold withal that upon endeavoring to take hold of it, it glided through the fingers like a smooth piece of ice.

The fibers were turned and twisted in a more intricate and perplexed manner than they are usually found in other hearts; insomuch that the whole heart was wound up together like a Gordian knot, [4] and must have had very irregular and unequal motions, while it was employed in its vital function.

One thing we thought very observable, namely, that upon examining the vessels which came into it, or issued out of it, we could not discover any communication that it had with the tongue.

We could not but take notice likewise that several of those little

[2] smatterer: dabbler
[3] coxcomb: conceited person, fool
[4] Gordian knot: The legend of this famous knot was that whoever could untie it would reign over the entire East.

nerves in the heart which are affected by the sentiments of love, hatred, and other passions, did not descend to this before us from the brain, but from the muscles which lie about the eye.

Upon weighing the heart in my hand, I found it to be extremely light, and consequently very hollow, which I did not wonder at, when, upon looking into the inside of it, I saw multitudes of cells and cavities running one within another, as our historians describe the apartments of Rosamond's bower.[5] Several of these little hollows were stuffed with innumerable sorts of trifles, which I shall forbear giving any particular account of, and shall, therefore, only take notice of what lay first and uppermost, which, upon our unfolding it, and applying our microscopes to it, appeared to be a flame-colored hood.

We are informed that the lady of this heart, when living, received the addresses of several who made love to her, and did not only give each of them encouragement, but made everyone she conversed with believe that she regarded him with an eye of kindness; for which reason we expected to have seen the impression of multitudes of faces among the several plaits and foldings of the heart; but to our great surprise not a single print of this nature discovered itself till we came into the very core and center of it. We there observed a little figure, which, upon applying our glasses to it, appeared dressed in a very fantastic manner. The more I looked upon it, the more I thought I had seen the face before, but could not possibly recollect either the place or time; when at length one of the company, who had examined this figure more nicely [6] than the rest, showed us plainly by the make of its face, and the several turns of its features, that the little idol which was thus lodged in the very middle of the heart was the deceased beau, whose head I gave some account of in my last Tuesday's paper.

As soon as we had finished our dissection, we resolved to make an experiment of the heart, not being able to determine among ourselves the nature of its substance, which differed in so many particulars from that in the heart of other females. Accordingly, we laid it into a pan of burning coals, when we observed in it a certain salamandrine [7] quality that made it capable of living in the midst of fire and flame, without being consumed or so much as singed.

[5] **Rosamond's bower:** maze built by Henry II for Rosamond in order to conceal her from his jealous wife
[6] **nicely:** closely
[7] **salamandrine:** salamander, a lizard that supposedly is able to live in fire

As we were admiring this strange phenomenon, and standing round the heart in a circle, it gave a most prodigious sigh, or rather crack, and dispersed all at once in smoke and vapor. This imaginary noise, which methought was louder than the burst of a cannon, produced such a violent shake in my brain, that it dissipated the fumes of sleep, and left me in an instant broad awake.

"A Country Sunday"

1. Sir Roger de Coverley is one of the famous creations of literature. Often described as an eccentric country squire, he, nevertheless, brings out the author's lesson quite well. What instruction does Addison present along with his humor?
2. With all his eccentricities, Sir Roger seems to achieve a great deal of good. Why?
3. What general principle of human behaviour is exemplified in this essay?

"The Coquette's Heart"

1. What is the author's purpose in this essay? Does he achieve it? Explain.
2. Make a list of the qualities which Addison finds in the coquette's heart. Are these flattering qualities? Why did he not offend those who read *The Spectator*?
3. What was the author trying to tell the young ladies of his day? Do you think he succeeded? Why or why not?

For Composition: Write your own description of a teen-age girl's or boy's heart. Use an informal style like that of Addison's.

JAMES BOSWELL

(1740–1795)

James Boswell was the son of Alexander Boswell of Auchinleck, a distinguished lawyer and judge. Under parental pressure, James studied law and was admitted to the bar in 1766. But from his early days, his heart was in something quite different from the dry profession of law. He had "a rage for knowing anybody that was ever talked of," as Horace Walpole said.

In 1760 he made his first trip to London, which made him more restless than ever. Life on his Scottish estate was dull by comparison with life in London, so he returned to London again in 1762. In his desire to know everybody who was anybody, he obtained interviews with Jean Jacques Rousseau, Voltaire, and other important figures, and recorded his talks with them.

In 1773 Boswell was admitted into the Literary Club in London, which had the leaders of English letters and politics among its members. In this same "memorable year" he met Samuel Johnson, the most important and colorful literary figure of the second half of the eighteenth century. A friendship was formed between Johnson and Boswell which lasted until Johnson's death in 1784. Boswell was more than just a good listener and note-taker; he prodded Johnson with questions, directed the conversation into the right channels, and surrounded him with stimulating company. After Johnson's death, Boswell proceeded to write *The Life of Samuel Johnson*, one of the great biographies in English literature, and the book that was to bring Boswell lasting fame.

One of the great adventure stories of the literary world is the gradual discovery over the years of Boswell's personal letters and papers. Among these papers was found a journal which showed a great deal about James Boswell himself, and made him a subject of serious studies by literary scholars. Such discoveries have revealed Boswell in a new dimension— not as the self-effacing author of *The Life of Samuel Johnson*—but as a real man who took himself very seriously, a man of great introspection with an incredible zest for life.

from *The Life of Samuel Johnson*

He was first taught to read English by Dame Oliver, a widow, who kept a school for young children in Lichfield. He told me she could read the black letter,[1] and asked him to borrow for her, from his father, a bible in that character. When he was going to Oxford, she came to take leave of him, brought him, in the simplicity of her kindness, a present of gingerbread, and said he was the best scholar she ever had. He delighted in mentioning this early compliment: adding, with smile, that "this was as high a proof of his merit as he could conceive." His next instructor in English was a master, whom, when he spoke of him to me, he familiarly called Tom Brown, who, said he, "published a spelling-book, and dedicated it to the UNIVERSE; but, I fear, no copy of it can now be had."

He began to learn Latin with Mr. Hawkins, usher, or undermaster of Lichfield school, "a man (said he) very skilful in his little way." With him he continued two years, and then rose to be under the care of Mr. Hunter, the headmaster, who, according to his account, "was very severe, and wrong-headedly severe. He used (said he) to beat us unmercifully; and he did not distinguish between ignorance and negligence; for he would beat a boy equally for not knowing a thing, as for neglecting to know it. He would ask a boy a question, and if he did not answer it, he would beat him, without considering whether he had an opportunity of knowing how to answer it. For instance, he would call up a boy and ask him Latin for a candlestick, which the boy could not expect to be asked. Now, Sir, if a boy could answer every question, there would be no need of a master to teach him."

It is, however, but justice to the memory of Mr. Hunter to mention, that though he might err in being too severe, the school of Lichfield was very respectable in his time. The late Dr. Taylor, Prebendary of Westminster, who was educated under him, told me, that "he was an excellent master, and that his ushers were most of them men of eminence; that Holbrook, one of the most ingenious men, best scholars, and best preachers of his age, was usher during the greatest part of the time that Johnson was at school. Then came

---

[1] **black letter:** form of Gothic type

Hague, of whom as much might be said, with the addition that he was an elegant poet. Hague was succeeded by Green, afterwards Bishop of Lincoln, whose character in the learned world is well known. In the same form with Johnson was Congreve, who afterwards became chaplain to Archbishop Boulter, and by that connection obtained good preferment in Ireland. He was a younger son of the ancient family of Congreve, in Staffordshire, of which the poet was a branch. His brother sold the estate. There was also Lowe, afterwards Canon of Windsor."

Indeed Johnson was very sensible how much he owed to Mr. Hunter. Mr. Langton one day asked him how he had acquired so accurate a knowledge of Latin, in which, I believe, he was exceeded by no man of his time; he said, "My master whipt me very well. Without that, Sir, I should have done nothing." He told Mr. Langton, that while Hunter was flogging his boys unmercifully, he used to say, "And this I do to save you from the gallows." Johnson, upon all occasions, expressed his approbation of enforcing instruction by means of the rod. "I would rather (said he) have the rod to be the general terror to all, to make them learn, than tell a child, if you do thus, or thus, you will be more esteemed than your brothers or sisters. The rod produces an effect which terminates in itself. A child is afraid of being whipped, and gets his task, and there's an end on't; whereas, by exciting emulation and comparisons of superiority, you lay the foundation of lasting mischief; you make brothers and sisters hate each other."

When Johnson saw some young ladies in Lincolnshire who were remarkably well behaved, owing to their mother's strict discipline and severe correction, he exclaimed, in one of Shakespeare's lines a little varied,

"*Rod*, I will honour thee for this thy duty." [2]

That superiority over his fellows, which he maintained with so much dignity in his march through life, was not assumed from vanity and ostentation, but was the natural and constant effect of those extraordinary powers of mind, of which he could not but be conscious by comparison; the intellectual difference, which in other cases of comparison of characters, is often a matter of undecided contest, being as clear in his case as the superiority of stature in some men above others. Johnson did not strut or stand on tip-toe; he only did

[2] "Rod . . . duty": from *King Henry* VI, *Part 2*

not stoop. From his earliest years, his superiority was perceived and acknowledged. He was from the beginning, ῎Αναξ ανδρῶν, a king of men. His schoolfellow, Mr. Hector, has obligingly furnished me with many particulars of his boyish days; and assured me that he never knew him corrected at school, but for talking and diverting other boys from their business. He seemed to learn by intuition; for though indolence and procrastination were inherent in his constitution, whenever he made an exertion he did more than any one else. In short, he is a memorable instance of what has been often observed, that the boy is the man in miniature: and that the distinguishing characteristics of each individual are the same, through the whole course of life. His favourites used to receive very liberal assistance from him; and such was the submission and deference with which he was treated, such the desire to obtain his regard, that three of the boys, of whom Mr. Hector was sometimes one, used to come in the morning as his humble attendants, and carry him to school. One in the middle stooped, while he sat upon his back, and one on each side supported him; and thus he was borne triumphant. Such a proof of the early predominance of intellectual vigour is very remarkable, and does honour to human nature.—Talking to me once himself of his being much distinguished at school, he told me, "they never thought to raise me by comparing me to any one; they never said, Johnson is as good a scholar as such a one; but such a one is as good a scholar as Johnson; and this was said but of one, but of Lowe; and I do not think he was as good a scholar."

He discovered a great ambition to excel, which roused him to counteract his indolence. He was uncommonly inquisitive; and his memory was so tenacious, that he never forgot anything that he either heard or read. Mr. Hector remembers having recited to him eighteen verses, which, after a little pause, he repeated *verbatim*, varying only one epithet, by which he improved the line.

He never joined with the other boys in their ordinary diversions: his only amusement was in winter, when he took a pleasure in being drawn upon the ice by a boy barefooted, who pulled him along by a garter fixed around him; no very easy operation, as his size was remarkably large. His defective sight, indeed, prevented him from enjoying the common sports; and he once pleasantly remarked to me, "how wonderfully well he had contrived to be idle without them." Lord Chesterfield, however, has justly observed in one of his letters, when earnestly cautioning a friend against the pernicious effects of idleness, that active sports are not to be reckoned idleness in young people; and that the listless torpor of doing nothing alone deserves that name. Of this dismal inertness of disposition, Johnson had all his life too great a share. Mr. Hector relates, that "he could not oblige him more than by sauntering away the hours of vacation in the fields, during which he was more engaged in talking to himself than to his companion."

Dr. Percy, the Bishop of Dromore, who was long intimately acquainted with him, and has preserved a few anecdotes concerning him, regetting that he was not a more diligent collector, informs me, that "when a boy he was immoderately fond of reading romances of chivalry, and he retained his fondness for them through life; so that (adds his Lordship) spending part of a summer at my parsonage-house in the country, he chose for his regular reading the old Spanish romance of FELIXMARTE OF HIRCANIA, in folio, which he read quite through. Yet I have heard him attribute to these extravagant fictions that unsettled turn of mind which prevented his ever fixing in any profession."

After having resided for some time at the house of his uncle, Cornelius Ford, Johnson was, at the age of fifteen, removed to the school of Stourbridge, in Worcestershire, of which Mr. Wentworth was then master. This step was taken by the advice of his cousin, the Rev. Mr. Ford, a man in whom both talents and good dispositions were disgraced by licentiousness, but who was a very able judge of what was right. At this school he did not receive so much benefit as was expected. It has been said, that he acted in the capacity of an assistant to Mr. Wentworth, in teaching the younger boys. "Mr. Wentworth (he told me) was a very able man, but an idle man, and to me very severe; but I cannot blame him much. I was then a big boy; he saw I did not reverence him; and that he should get no honour by me. I had brought enough with me, to carry me through; and all I should get at his school would be ascribed to my own labour, or to my former master. Yet he taught me a great deal."

He thus discriminated, to Dr. Percy, Bishop of Dromore, his progress at his two grammar-schools. "At one, I learned much in the school, but little from the master; in the other, I learnt much from the master, but little in the school."

The Bishop also informs me, that "Dr. Johnson's father, before he was received at Stourbridge, applied to have him admitted as a scholar and assistant to the Rev. Samuel Lea, M.A., head master of Newport school, in Shropshire; (a very diligent good teacher, at that time in high reputation, under whom Mr. Hollis is said, in the Memoirs of his Life, to have been also educated). This application to Mr. Lea was not successful; but Johnson had afterwards the gratification to hear that the old gentleman, who lived to a very advanced age, mentioned it as one of the most memorable events of his life, that "he was *very near* having that great man for his scholar."

He remained at Stourbridge little more than a year, and then he returned home, where he may be said to have loitered for two years, in a state very unworthy his uncommon abilities. . . .

*   *   *   *   *

1763

This is to me a memorable year; for in it I had the happiness to obtain the acquaintance of that extraordinary man whose memoirs I am now writing; an acquaintance which I shall ever esteem as one of the most fortunate circumstances in my life. Though then but two-and-twenty, I had for several years read his works with delight and instruction, and had the highest reverence for their authour, which had grown up in my fancy into a kind of mysterious veneration, by figuring to myself a state of solemn elevated abstraction, in which I supposed him to live in the immense metropolis of London. Mr. Gentleman, a native of Ireland, who passed some years in Scotland as a player, and as an instructor in the English language, a man whose talents and worth were depressed by misfortunes, had given me a representation of the figure and manner of DICTIONARY JOHNSON! as he was then generally called; and during my first visit to London, which was for three months in 1760, Mr. Derrick the poet, who was Gentleman's friend and countryman, flattered me with hopes that he would introduce me to Johnson, an honour of which I was very ambitious. But he never found an opportunity; which made me doubt that he had promised to do what was not in his power; till Johnson some years afterwards told me, "Derrick, Sir, might very well have introduced you. I had a kindness for Derrick, and am sorry he is dead." . . .

*   *   *   *   *

Mr. Thomas Davies the actor, who then kept a bookseller's shop in Russel-street, Covent-garden, told me that Johnson was very much his friend, and came frequently to his house, where he more than once invited me to meet him: but by some unlucky accident or other he was prevented from coming to us.

Mr. Thomas Davies was a man of good understanding and talents, with the advantage of a liberal education. Though somewhat pompous, he was an entertaining companion; and his literary performances have no inconsiderable share of merit. He was a friendly and very hospitable man. Both he and his wife, (who has been celebrated for her beauty,) though upon the stage for many years, maintained an uniform decency of character; and Johnson esteemed them, and lived in as easy an intimacy with them as with any family which he used to visit. Mr. Davies recollected several of Johnson's remarkable sayings, and was one of the best of the many imitators of his voice and manner, while relating them. He increased my impatience more and more to see the extraordinary man whose works I highly valued, and whose conversation was reported to be so peculiarly excellent.

At last, on Monday the 16th of May, when I was sitting in Mr. Davies's back-parlour, after having drunk tea with him and Mrs. Davies, Johnson unexpectedly came into the shop; and Mr. Davies having perceived him through the glass-door in the room in which we were sitting, advancing towards us,—he announced his awful approach to me, somewhat in the manner of an actor in the part of Horatio, when he addresses Hamlet on the appearance of his father's ghost, "Look, my Lord, it comes." I found that I had a very perfect idea of Johnson's figure, from the portrait of him painted by Sir Joshua Reynolds soon after he had published his Dictionary, in the attitude of sitting in his easy chair in deep meditation; which was the first picture his friend did for him, which Sir Joshua very kindly presented to me, and from which an engraving has been made for this work. Mr. Davies mentioned my name, and respectfully introduced me to him, I was much agitated; and recollecting his prejudice against the Scotch, of which I had heard much, I said to Davies, "Don't tell where I come from."—"From Scotland," cried Davies, roguishly. "Mr. Johnson, (said I) I do indeed come from Scotland, but I cannot help it." I am willing to flatter myself that I meant this as light pleasantry to soothe and conciliate him, and not as an humiliating abasement at the expence of my country. But however that might be, this speech was somewhat unlucky; for with that quickness of wit for which he was so remarkable, he seized the expression "come from Scotland," which I used in the sense of being of that country; and, as if I had said that I had come away from it, or left it, retorted, "That, Sir, I find, is what a very great many of your countrymen cannot help." This stroke stunned me a good deal; and when we had sat down, I felt myself not a little embarrassed, and apprehensive of what might come next. He then addressed himself to Davies: "What do you think of Garrick? He has refused me an order for the play for Miss Williams, because he knows the house will be full, and that an order would be worth three shillings." Eager to take any opening to get into conversation with him, I ventured to say, "O, Sir, I cannot think Mr. Garrick would grudge such a trifle to you." "Sir, (said he, with a stern look,) I have known David Garrick longer than you have done: and I know no right you have to talk to me on the subject." Perhaps I deserved this check; for it was rather presumptuous in me, an entire stranger, to express any doubt of the justice of his animadversion upon his old acquaintance and pupil.[3] I now felt myself much mortified, and began to think, that the hope which I had long indulged of obtaining his acquaintance was blasted. And, in truth, had not my ardour been uncommonly strong, and my resolution uncommonly persevering, so rough a reception might have deterred me for ever from making any further attempts. Fortunately, however, I remained upon the field not wholly discomfited; and was soon rewarded by hearing some of his conversation. . . .

*   *   *   *   *

A few days afterwards I called on Davies, and asked him if he thought I might take the liberty of waiting on Mr. Johnson at his chambers in the Temple. He said I certainly might, and that Mr. Johnson would take it as a compliment. So on Tuesday the 24th of

---

[3] That this was a momentary sally against Garrick there can be no doubt; for at Johnson's desire he had, some years before, given a benefit-night at his theatre to this very person by which she had got two hundred pounds. Johnson, indeed, upon all other occasions, when I was in his company, praised the very liberal charity of Garrick. I once mentioned to him, "It is observed, Sir, that you attack Garrick yourself, but will suffer nobody else to do it." Johnson (smiling): "Why, Sir, that is true."

May, after having been enlivened by the witty sallies of Messieurs Thornton, Wilkes, Churchill, and Lloyd, with whom I had passed the morning, I boldly repaired to Johnson. His chambers were on the first floor of No. 1, Inner-Temple-lane, and I entered them with an impression given me by the Reverend Dr. Blair, of Edinburgh, who had been introduced to him not long before, and described his having "found the Giant in his den"; an expression which, when I came to be pretty well acquainted with Johnson, I repeated to him, and he was diverted at this picturesque account of himself. Dr. Blair had been presented to him by Dr. James Fordyce. At this time the controversy concerning the pieces published by Mr. James Macpherson, as translations of Ossian, was at its height. Johnson had all along denied their authenticity; and, what was still more provoking to their admirers, maintained that they had no merit. The subject having been introduced by Dr. Fordyce, Dr. Blair, relying on the internal evidence of their antiquity, asked Dr. Johnson whether he thought any man of a modern age could have written such poems? Johnson replied, "Yes, Sir, many men, many women, and many children." Johnson at this time, did not know that Dr. Blair had just published a Dissertation, not only defending their authenticity, but seriously ranking them with the poems of Homer and Virgil; and when he was afterwards informed of this circumstance, he expressed some displeasure at Dr. Fordyce's having suggested the topick, and said, "I am not sorry that they got thus much for their pains. Sir, it was like leading one to talk of a book, when the authour is concealed behind the door."

He received me very courteously: but, it must be confessed, that his apartment, and furniture, and morning dress, were sufficiently uncouth. His brown suit of cloaths looked very rusty: he had on a little old shrivelled unpowdered wig, which was too small for his head; his shirt-neck and knees of his breeches were loose; his black worsted stockings ill drawn up; and he had a pair of unbuckled shoes by way of slippers. But all these slovenly particularities were forgotten the moment that he began to talk. Some gentlemen, whom I do not recollect, were sitting with him; and when they went away, I also rose; but he said to me, "Nay, don't go."—"Sir, (said I), I am afraid that I intrude upon you. It is benevolent to allow me to sit and hear you." He seemed pleased with this compliment, which I sincerely paid him, and answered, "Sir, I am obliged to any man who visits me."—I have preserved the following short minute of what passed this day.

"Madness frequently discovers itself merely by unnecessary deviation from the usual modes of the world. My poor friend Smart [4] showed the disturbance of his mind, by falling upon his knees, and saying his prayers in the street, or in any other unusual place. Now although, rationally speaking, it is greater madness not to pray at all, then to pray as Smart did, I am afraid there are so many who do not pray, that their understanding is not called in question."

Concerning this unfortunate poet, Christopher Smart, who was confined in a mad-house, he had, at another time, the following conversation with Dr. Burney.—BURNEY. "How does poor Smart do, Sir; is he likely to recover?" JOHNSON. "It seems as if his mind had ceased to struggle with the disease; for he grows fat upon it." BURNEY. "Perhaps, Sir, that may be from want of exercise." JOHNSON. "No, Sir; he has partly as much exercise as he used to have, for he digs in the garden. Indeed, before his confinement, he used for exercise to walk to the alehouse; but he was *carried* back again. I did not think he ought to be shut up. His infirmities were not noxious to society. He insisted on people praying with him; and I'd as lief pray with Kit Smart as any one else. Another charge was, that he did not love clean linen; and I have no passion for it."

Johnson continued. "Mankind have a great aversion to intellectual labour; but even supposing knowledge to be easily attainable, more people would be content to be ignorant than would take even a little trouble to acquire it.

"The morality of an action depends on the motive from which we act. If I flung half a crown to a beggar with intention to break his head, and he picks it up and buys victuals with it, the physical effect is good; but, with respect to me, the action is very wrong. So, religious exercises, if not performed with an intention to please GOD, avail us nothing. As our Saviour says of those who perform them from other motives, 'Verily they have their reward.' "

"The Christian religion has very strong evidences. It, indeed, appears in some degree strange to reason; but in History we have undoubted facts, against which, in reasoning *à priori*, we have more arguments than we have for them; but then, testimony has great weight, and casts the balance. I would recommend to every man

[4] Smart: Christopher Smart, 18th-century poet, allegedly insane

whose faith is yet unsettled, Grotius,—Dr. Pearson,—and Dr. Clarke."

Talking of Garrick, he said, "He is the first man in the world for sprightly conversation."

When I rose a second time, he again pressed me to stay, which I did.

He told me, that he generally went abroad at four in the afternoon, and seldom came home till two in the morning. I took the liberty to ask if he did not think it wrong to live thus, and not make more us of his great talents. He owned it was a bad habit. On reviewing, at the distance of many years, my journal of this period, I wonder how, at my first visit, I ventured to talk to him so freely, and that he bore it with so much indulgence.

Before we parted, he was so good as to promise to favour me with his company one evening at my lodgings: and, as I took my leave, shook him cordially by the hand. It is almost needless to add, that I felt no little elation at having now so happily established an acquaintance of which I had been so long ambitious. . . .

from *Boswell's London Journal*

MONDAY, 15 NOVEMBER, 1762.

Elated with the thoughts of my journey to London, I got up. I called upon my friend Johnston,[1] but found he was not come from the country, which vexed me a little, as I wished to bid him cordially adieu. However, I excused him to myself, and as Cairnie[2] told me that people never took leave in France, I made the thing sit pretty easy. I had a long serious conversation with my father and mother. They were very kind to me. I felt parental affection was very strong towards me; and I felt a very warm filial regard for them. The scene of being a son setting out from home for the wide world and the idea of being my own master, pleased me much. I parted with my brother Davy, leaving him my best advices to be diligent at his business as a banker and to make rich and be happy.

At ten I got into my chaise,[3] and away I went. As I passed the

---

[1] Johnston: not to be confused with Dr. Johnson
[2] Cairnie: Edinburgh doctor who supported the exiled Stuarts
[3] chaise: type of coach

Cross, the cadies and the chairmen bowed and seemed to say, "GOD prosper long our noble Boswell." I rattled down the High Street in high elevation of spirits, bowed and smiled to acquaintances, and took up my partner at Boyd's Close. He was a Mr. Stewart, eldest son to Ardsheal, who was forfeited [4] in the year 1746. He had made four voyages to the East Indies, and was now going out first mate. I made the chaise stop at the foot of the Canongate; asked pardon of Mr. Stewart for a minute; walked to the Abbey of Holyroodhouse, went round the Piazzas, bowed thrice: once to the Palace itself, once to the crown of Scotland above the gate in front, and once to the venerable old Chapel. I next stood in the court before the Palace, and bowed thrice to Arthur Seat, that lofty romantic mountain on which I have so often strayed in my days of youth, indulged meditation and felt the raptures of a soul filled with ideas of the magnificence of GOD and his creation. Having thus gratified my agreeable whim and superstitious humour, I felt a warm glow of satisfaction. Indeed, I have a strong turn to what the cool part of mankind have named superstition. But this proceeds from my genius for poetry, which ascribes many fanciful properties to everything. This I have great pleasure from; as I have now by experience and reflection gained the command of it so far that I can keep it within just bounds by the power of reason, without losing the agreeable feeling and play to the imagination which it bestows. I am surely much happier in this way than if I just considered Holyroodhouse as so much stone and lime which has been put together in a certain way, and Arthur Seat as so much earth and rock raised above the neighbouring plains.

We then pursued our journey. I found my companion a jolly honest plain fellow. I set out with a determined resolution against *shaving*, that is to say, playing upon people; and therefore I talked sensibly and roughly. We did very well till we passed Old Camus, when one of the wheels of our chaise was so much broke that it was of no use. The driver proposed that we should mount the horses and ride to Berwick. But this I would by no means agree to; and as my partner let me be the principal man and take the direction of our journey, I made the chaise be dragged on to Ayton, where we waited till the driver rode to Berwick and brought us a chaise. Never

[4] who . . . forfeited: whose estate was forfeited by the government because of his action in the Rebellion of 1745

did I pass three hours more unhappily. We were set down in a cold ale-house in a little dirty village. We had a beefsteak ill-dressed and had nothing to drink but thick muddy beer. We were both out of humour so that we could not speak. We tried to sleep but in vain. We only got a drowsy headache. We were scorched by the fire on the one hand and shivering with frost on the other. At last our chaise came, and we got to Berwick about twelve at night. We had a slice of hard dry toast, a bowl of warm negus,[5] and went comfortable to bed.

THURSDAY, 18 NOVEMBER.

The noise, the crowd, the glare of shops and signs agreeably confused me. I was rather more wildly struck than when I first came to London. My companion could not understand my feelings. He considered London just as a place where he was to receive orders from the East India Company. We now parted, with saying that we had agreed well and been happy, and that we should keep up the acquaintance. I then had a bit of dinner, got myself shaved and cleaned, and had my landlord, a civil jolly man, to take a glass of wine with me. I was all in a flutter at having at last got to the place which I was so madly fond of, and being restrained, had formed so many wild schemes to get back to. I had recourse to philosophy, and so rendered myself calm.

I immediately went to my friend Douglas's, surgeon in Pall Mall, a kind-hearted, plain, sensible man, where I was cordially received. His wife is a good-humoured woman, and is that sort of character which is often met with in England: very lively without much wit. Her fault is speaking too much, which often tires people. He was my great adviser as to everything; and in the mean time insisted that I should have a bed in his house till I got a lodging to my mind. I agreed to come there next day. I went to Covent Garden—*Every Man in His Humour*.[6] Woodward played Bobadil finely. He entertained me much. It was fine after the fatigues of my journey to find myself snug in a theatre, my body warm and my mind elegantly amused. I went to my inn, had some negus, and went comfortably to bed.

[5] negus: warmed drink of spiced wine
[6] *Every Man in His Humour*: comedy by Ben Jonson

WEDNESDAY, 15 DECEMBER.

The enemies of the people of England who would have them considered in the worst light represent them as selfish, beef-eaters, and cruel. In this view I resolved today to be a true-born Old Englishman. I went into the City to Dolly's Steak-house in Paternoster Row and swallowed my dinner by myself to fulfill the charge of selfishness; I had a large fat beefsteak to fulfill the charge of beef-eating; and I went at five o'clock to the Royal Cockpit in St. James's Park and saw cock-fighting for about five hours to fulfill the charge of cruelty.

A beefsteak-house is a most excellent place to dine at. You come in there to a warm, comfortable, large room, where a number of people are sitting at table. You take whatever place you find empty; call for what you like, which you get well and cleverly dressed. You may either chat or not as you like. Nobody minds you, and you pay very reasonably. My dinner (beef, bread and beer and waiter) was only a shilling. The waiters make a great deal of money by these pennies. Indeed, I admire the English for attending to small sums, as many smalls make a great, according to the proverb.

At five I filled my pockets with gingerbread and apples (quite the method), put on my old clothes and laced hat, laid by my watch, purse, and pocket-book, and with oaken stick in my hand sallied to the pit. I was too soon there. So I went into a low inn, sat down amongst a parcel of arrant blackguards, and drank some beer. The sentry near the house had been very civil in showing me the way. It was very cold. I bethought myself of the poor fellow, so I carried out a pint of beer myself to him. He was very thankful and drank my health cordially. He told me his name was Hobard, that he was a watch-maker but in distress for debt, and enlisted that his creditors might not touch him.

I then went to the Cockpit, which is a circular room in the middle of which the cocks fight. It is seated round with rows gradually rising. The pit and the seats are all covered with mat. The cocks, nicely cut and dressed and armed with silver heels, are set down and fight with amazing bitterness and resolution. Some of them were quickly dispatched. One pair fought three quarters of an hour. The uproar and noise of betting is prodigious. A great deal of money made a very quick circulation from hand to hand. There was a number of professed gamblers there. An old cunning dog whose face I had seen at Newmarket sat by me a while. I told him I knew nothing of the matter. "Sir," said he, "you have as good a chance as anybody." He thought I would be a good subject for him. I was young-like. But he found himself balked. I was shocked to see the distraction and anxiety of the betters. I was sorry for the poor cocks. I looked round to see if any of the spectators pitied them when mangled and torn in a most cruel manner, but I could not observe the smallest relenting sign in any countenance. I was therefore not ill pleased to see them endure mental torment. Thus did I complete my true English day, and came home pretty much fatigued and pretty much confounded at the strange turn of this people.

For Discussion

"The Life of Samuel Johnson"

1. Boswell records Johnson's interesting reflections on education. What seemed to be Johnson's ideas on punishment in school? How does this differ from our modern idea on this subject?
2. "The memorable year" in Boswell's life was the one in which he met Dr. Johnson. Does Boswell seem too reverent in describing this meeting? What is Boswell's attitude toward Dr. Johnson? How does his attitude affect his biography?
3. What do we learn of Johnson's physical appearance? Was he a neat person? What were Johnson's views on intellectual labor?
4. A good biographer interprets facts so that we can better see and understand his central character. How does Boswell *interpret?*

"Boswell's London Journal"

1. What facts show that Boswell was often sentimental?
2. Details of background and persons give us a good insight into the times in which Boswell wrote. Point out five significant details of clothes, transportation, and food which "date" the *Journal.*
3. Boswell's arrival in London seems to be that of a wide-eyed youth. What details strike him?
4. How does our modern restaurant differ from the steak-house of 1762? What amusements have replaced the cock fights? Why was Boswell "pretty much confounded at the strange turn of this people"?
5. Read "The Case of the Ebony Cabinet" in Richard Altick's *The Scholar Adventurers* for the amazing story of the discovery of Boswell's letters and papers.
6. Compare Pepys' *Diary* with Boswell's *Journal.* Which gives a better insight into the personality of its author? Why?

SAMUEL JOHNSON

(1709–1784)

We know more about Samuel Johnson than about any other writer in English literature. This vast knowledge of Johnson has been preserved and handed down with amazing fidelity through his biography *The Life of Samuel Johnson*. The figure that emerges from Boswell's biography is that of a heavy-set man, with deep voice, rolling gait, and awkward form. Though near-sighted, he saw more than people realized, and his gruff behavior with strangers covered a genuine Christian charity for the poor and helpless. We see him at the Literary Club in his old brown suit with brass buttons and hanging black stockings, his small wig perched on top of his huge head. We hear him constantly expressing his opinions on every topic under the sun, impressing everyone by the sheer force of his character and personality. His great qualities won him the friendship of the most important men of his time, including Joshua Reynolds, David Garrick, Edmund Burke, and Oliver Goldsmith.

Johnson was 28 years old when he came to London to try his fortune, and suffered in these early years from hardships and privations. Finally, a syndicate of booksellers approached him with a proposal for a dictionary of the English language. He accepted their offer and produced a plan of his work addressed to Lord Chesterfield. Lord Chesterfield, however, gave him no encouragement or financial aid, and Johnson started on his great project, *A Dictionary of the English Language*, with little help. During this time, he suffered from great poverty. Eight years later, in 1755, he produced his great work in two volumes, and his reputation was established. Lord Chesterfield now tried to make amends for his earlier neglect. In one of the most famous letters in English literature, Johnson wrote to him, stating that he no longer needed or wanted Lord Chesterfield's help.

The *Dictionary* is notable for its definitions and for the inclusion of quotations for the first time in any dictionary which illustrated the correct uses of the words defined. The selection below represents what Johnson himself called "risible absurdities," and it should not be thought that they are typical of his great achievement.

Johnson's other great work was *The Lives of the English Poets*, a masterly collection of short biographies. His essays on Dryden and Pope have become classics of English criticism. Unfortunately, he made no attempt to separate the poet from his poetry, and if he disliked the author's personality, he often disliked his poetry. This is very marked in his essays on Thomas Gray and John Milton.

Johnson stood for order in Church, State, and Society. Therefore nonconformists, Whigs, American Colonists, and Scots were "out of order" and he inveighed against them. But time has shown that the character and mind of Johnson was greater than any specific opinions he may have held erroneously. He has continued to delight readers with his great personal style and wit and because in him can be seen a genuine, warmhearted man with all the frailties, prejudices, and idiosyncracies that are part of every human nature.

from The Dictionary

dry: desiccative.

dryness: siccity or aridity.

excise: a hateful tax levied upon commodities, and adjudged, not by the common judges of property, but wretches hired by those to whom excise is paid.

Grub Street: the name of a street in London, much inhabited by writers of small histories, *dictionaries*, and temporary poems; whence any mean production is called Grub Street.

hatchet-faced: an ugly face; such, I suppose, as might be hewn out of a block by a hatchet.

lexicographer: a writer of dictionaries, a harmless drudge that busies himself in tracing the original and detailing the significance of words.

network: anything reticulated or decussated at equal distances with interstices between the intersections.

oats: a grain which in England is generally given to horses, but in Scotland supports the people.

patriotism: the last refuge of a scoundrel.

patron: one who countenances, supports, or protects. Commonly a wretch who supports with insolence, and is paid with flattery.

pension: an allowance made to anyone without an equivalent. In England it is generally understood to mean pay given to a state hireling for treason to his country.

pensioner: a slave of state, hired by a stipend to obey his master.

politician: a man of artifice; one deep of contrivance.

Redcoat: a name of contempt for a soldier.

thunder: a most bright flame rising on a sudden, moving with great violence, and with a very rapid velocity, through the air, according to any determination, and commonly ending with a loud noise or rattling.

Tory: one who adheres to the ancient constitution of the state, and the apostolical hierarchy of the Church of England, opposed to a Whig.

transpire: to escape from secrecy to notice, a sense lately innovated from France without necessity.

Whig: the name of a faction.

willow: a tree worn by forlorn lovers.

Letter to Lord Chesterfield

To the Right Honorable the Earl of Chesterfield,

February 7, 1755.

My Lord: I have lately been informed by the proprietor of *The World*,[1] that two papers, in which my *Dictionary* is recommended to the public, were written by your lordship. To be so distinguished is an honor which, being very little accustomed to favors from the great, I know not well how to receive, or in what terms to acknowledge.

When, upon some slight encouragement, I first visited your lordship, I was overpowered, like the rest of mankind, by the enchantment of your address; and I could not forbear to wish that I might boast myself *"Le vainqueur du vainqueur de la terre"*;[2] that I might obtain that regard for which I saw the world contending; but I found my attendance so little encouraged, that neither pride nor modesty would suffer me to continue it. When I had once addressed your lordship in public, I had exhausted all the art of pleasing which a retired and uncourtly scholar can possess. I had done all that I could; and no man is well pleased to have his all neglected, be it ever so little.

[1] proprietor . . . *World:* Edward Moore, an old friend of Johnson's
[2] *Le vainqueur . . . terre:* conqueror of the conqueror of the earth

Seven years, my lord, have now passed, since I waited in your outward rooms, or was repulsed from your door; during which time I have been pushing on my work through difficulties, of which it is useless to complain, and have brought it at last to the verge of publication, without one act of assistance, one word of encouragement, or one smile of favor. Such treatment I did not expect, for I never had a patron before.

The shepherd [3] in Virgil grew at last acquainted with Love, and found him a native of the rocks.

Is not a patron, my lord, one who looks with unconcern on a man struggling for life in the water, and, when he has reached ground, encumbers him with help? The notice which you have been pleased to take of my labors, had it been early, had been kind; but it has been delayed till I am indifferent, and cannot enjoy it; till I am solitary, and cannot impart it; till I am known, and do not want it. I hope it is no very cynical asperity not to confess obligations where no benefit has been received, or to be unwilling that the public should consider me as owing that to a patron, which Providence has enabled me to do for myself.

Having carried on my work thus far with so little obligation to any favorer of learning, I shall not be disappointed though I should conclude it, if less be possible, with less; for I have been long wakened from that dream of hope, in which I once boasted myself with so much exaltation,

My Lord,
    Your Lordship's most humble,
        Most obedient servant,

SAM. JOHNSON.

[3] **shepherd:** the shepherd in the *Eclogues* of Virgil

from The Lives of the English Poets

DRYDEN

Dryden may be properly considered as the father of English criticism, as the writer who first taught us to determine upon principles the merit of composition. Of our former poets, the greatest dramatist [1] wrote without rules, conducted through life and nature by a

[1] **greatest dramatist:** Shakespeare

genius that rarely misled, and rarely deserted him. Of the rest, those who knew the laws of propriety had neglected to teach them.

Two *Arts of English Poetry* were written in the days of Elizabeth by Webb and Puttenham,[2] from which something might be learned, and a few hints had been given by Jonson and Cowley; but Dryden's *Essay on Dramatic Poetry* was the first regular and valuable treatise on the art of writing.

He who, having formed his opinions in the present age of English literature, turns back to peruse this dialogue will not perhaps find much increase of knowledge, or much novelty of instruction; but he is to remember that critical principles were then in the hands of a few, who had gathered them partly from the ancients and partly from the Italians and French. The structure of dramatic poems was then not generally understood. Audiences applauded by instinct, and poets perhaps often pleased by chance.

A writer who obtains his full purpose loses himself in his own luster. Of an opinion which is no longer doubted, the evidence ceases to be examined. Of an art universally practiced, the first teacher is forgotten. Learning once made popular is no longer learning; it has the appearance of something which we have bestowed upon ourselves, as the dew appears to rise from the field which it refreshes.

To judge rightly of an author, we must transport ourselves to his time, and examine what were the wants of his contemporaries, and what were his means of supplying them. That which is easy at one time was difficult at another. Dryden at least imported his science and gave his country what it wanted before; or rather, he imported only the materials and manufactured them by his own skill.

The dialogue on the drama was one of his first essays [3] of criticism, written when he was yet a timorous candidate for reputation, and therefore labored with that diligence which he might allow himself somewhat to remit when his name gave sanction to his positions, and his awe of the public was abated, partly by custom, and partly by success. It will not be easy to find, in all the opulence of our language, a treatise so artfully variegated with successive representations of opposite probabilities, so enlivened with imagery, so brightened with illustrations. His portraits of the English dramatists are wrought with great spirit and diligence. The account of Shakespeare may

[2] **Webb and Puttenham:** two writers of the 16th century
[3] **essays:** attempts

stand as a perpetual model of encomiastic [4] criticism; exact without minuteness, and lofty without exaggeration. The praise lavished by Longinus [5] on the attestation of the heroes of Marathon,[6] by Demosthenes,[7] fades away before it. In a few lines is exhibited a character so extensive in its comprehension, and so curious in its limitations, that nothing can be added, diminished, or reformed; nor can the editors and admirers of Shakespeare, in all their emulation of reverence, boast of much more than of having diffused and paraphrased this epitome of excellence, of having changed Dryden's gold for baser metal, of lower value though of greater bulk.

In this, and in all his other essays on the same subject, the criticism of Dryden is the criticism of a poet; not a dull collection of theorems, nor a rude detection of faults, which perhaps the censor was not able to have committed; but a gay and vigorous dissertation, where delight is mingled with instruction, and where the author proves his right of judgment, by his power of performance.

The different manner and effect with which critical knowledge may be conveyed was perhaps never more clearly exemplified than in the performances of Rymer [8] and Dryden. It was said of a dispute between two mathematicians, "*malim cum Scaligero* [9] *errare, quam cum Clavio recte sapere,*" that *it was more eligible to go wrong with one than right with the other.* A tendency of the same kind every mind must feel at the perusal of Dryden's prefaces and Rymer's discourses. With Dryden we are wandering in quest of Truth, whom we find, if we find her at all, dressed in the graces of elegance, and if we miss her, the labor of the pursuit rewards itself; we are led only through fragrance and flowers. Rymer, without taking a nearer, takes a rougher way; every step is to be made through thorns and brambles, and Truth, if we meet her, appears repulsive by her mien and ungraceful by her habit. Dryden's criticism has the majesty of a queen; Rymer's has the ferocity of a tyrant.

As he had studied with great diligence the art of poetry, and enlarged or rectified his notions, by experience perpetually increasing, he had his mind stored with principles and observations; he poured

---

[4] encomiastic: praising
[5] Longinus: Greek philosopher of the third century
[6] Marathon: site of a famous battle between the Greeks and Persians, 490 B.C.
[7] Demosthenes: celebrated Greek orator of the fourth century B.C.
[8] Rymer: critic of the 17th century whose criticism was unfriendly to Shakespeare
[9] Scaligero: Joseph Scaliger, leading mathematician and philosopher of the Renaissance

out his knowledge with little labor; for of labor, notwithstanding the multiplicity of his productions, there is sufficient reason to suspect that he was not a lover. To write *con amore*, with fondness for the employment, with perpetual touches and retouches, with unwillingness to take leave of his own idea, and an unwearied pursuit of unattainable perfection, was, I think, no part of his character.

His criticism may be considered as general or occasional. In his general precepts, which depend upon the nature of things and the structure of the human mind, he may doubtless be safely recommended to the confidence of the reader; but his occasional and particular positions were sometimes interested, sometimes negligent, and sometimes capricious. . . .

He is therefore by no means constant to himself. His defense and desertion of dramatic rime is generally known. Spence,[10] in his remarks on Pope's *Odyssey*, produces what he thinks an unconquerable quotation from Dryden's preface to the *Aeneid*, in favor of translating an epic poem into blank verse; but he forgets that when his author attempted the *Iliad*, some years afterwards,[11] he departed from his own decision, and translated into rime.

When he has any objection to obviate, or any license to defend, he is not very scrupulous about what he asserts, nor very cautious, if the present purpose be served, not to entangle himself in his own sophistries. But when all arts are exhausted, like other hunted animals, he sometimes stands at bay; when he cannot disown the grossness of one of his plays, he declares that he knows not any law that prescribes morality to a comic poet.

His remarks on ancient or modern writers are not always to be trusted. His parallel of the versification of Ovid [12] with that of Claudian [13] has been very justly censured by Sewell.[14] His comparison of the first line of Virgil with the first of Statius [15] is not happier. Virgil, he says, is soft and gentle, and would have thought Statius mad if he had heard him thundering out

Quae superimposito moles geminata colosso.[16]

[10] **Spence:** English critic of the 18th century
[11] **some . . . afterwards:** Johnson is mistaken; Pope wrote the *Iliad* several years before he wrote the *Odyssey*
[12] **Ovid:** famous Roman poet
[13] **Claudian:** Latin poet of the fourth century
[14] **Sewell:** George Sewell, critic of the time of Pope
[15] **Statius:** Roman poet of the first century
[16] **Quae . . . colosso:** "With a colossus on top there is a double weight."

Statius perhaps heats himself, as he proceeds, to exaggerations somewhat hyperbolical; but undoubtedly Virgil would have been too hasty if he had condemned him to straw for one sounding line. Dryden wanted an instance, and the first that occurred was impressed into the service.

What he wishes to say, he says at hazard; he cited *Gorbuduc*,[17] which he had never seen; gives a false account of Chapman's [18] versification; and discovers,[19] in the preface to his Fables, that he translated the first book of the *Iliad* without knowing what was in the second.

It will be difficult to prove that Dryden ever made any great advances in literature. As having distinguished himself at Westminster under the tuition of Busby,[20] who advanced his scholars to a height of knowledge very rarely attained in grammar schools, he resided afterwards at Cambridge, it is not to be supposed that his skill in the ancient languages was deficient, compared with that of common students; but his scholastic acquisitions seem not proportionate to his opportunities and abilities. He could not, like Milton or Cowley, have made his name illustrious merely by his learning. He mentions but few books, and those such as lie in the beaten track of regular study; from which if ever he departs, he is in danger of losing himself in unknown regions.

In his dialogue on the drama, he pronounces with great confidence that the Latin tragedy of *Medea* [21] is not Ovid's, because it is not sufficiently interesting and pathetic. He might have determined the question upon surer evidence; for it is quoted by Quintilian [22] as the work of Seneca; and the only line which remains of Ovid's play, for one line is left us, is not there to be found. There was therefore no need of the gravity of conjecture, or the discussion of plot or sentiment, to find what was already known upon higher authority than such discussions can ever reach.

His literature, though not always free from ostentation, will be commonly found either obvious, and made his own by the art of dressing it; or superficial, which, by what he gives, shows what

[17] *Gorbuduc*: generally considered to be the first of the English tragedies, written by Norton and Sackville
[18] Chapman: George Chapman, poet and dramatist who translated Homer
[19] discovers: reveals
[20] Busby: Richard Busby, headmaster of Westminster
[21] *Medea:* probably Seneca's version
[22] Quintilian: famed Roman orator of the first century

he wanted; or erroneous, hastily collected, and negligently scattered.

Yet it cannot be said that his genius is ever unprovided of matter, or that his fancy languishes in penury of ideas. His works abound with knowledge, and sparkle with illustrations. There is scarcely any science or faculty that does not supply him with occasional images and lucky similitudes; every page discovers a mind very widely acquainted both with art and nature, and in full possession of great stores of intellectual wealth. Of him that knows much, it is natural to suppose that he has read with diligence; yet I rather believe that the knowledge of Dryden was gleaned from accidental intelligence and various conversation, by a quick apprehension, a judicious selection, and a happy memory, a keen appetite of knowledge, and a powerful digestion; by vigilance that permitted nothing to pass without notice, and a habit of reflection that suffered nothing useful to be lost. A mind like Dryden's, always curious, always active, to which every understanding was proud to be associated, and of which everyone solicited the regard, by an ambitious display of himself, had a more pleasant, perhaps a nearer way to knowledge than by the silent progress of solitary reading. I do not suppose that he despised books, or intentionally neglected them; but that he was carried out, by the impetuosity of his genius, to more vivid and speedy instructors; and that his studies were rather desultory and fortuitous than constant and systematical.

It must be confessed that he scarcely ever appears to want book-learning but when he mentions books; and to him may be transferred the praise which he gives his master Charles.[23]

His conversation, wit, and parts,
His knowledge in the noblest useful arts,
    Were such, dead authors could not give,
    But habitudes of those that live;
Who, lighting him, did greater lights receive,
    He drained from all, and all they knew,
    His apprehension quick, his judgment true;
    That the most learned with shame confess
His knowledge more, his reading only less.

Of all this, however, if the proof be demanded, I will not under-

[23] Charles: King Charles II

take to give it; the atoms of probability, of which my opinion has been formed, lie scattered over all his works; and by him who thinks the question worth his notice, his works must be perused with very close attention.

Criticism, either didactic [24] or defensive, occupies almost all his prose, except those pages which he has devoted to his patrons; but none of his prefaces were ever thought tedious. They have not the formality of a settled style, in which the first half of a sentence betrays the other. The clauses are never balanced, nor the periods modeled; every word seems to drop by chance, though it falls into its proper place. Nothing is cold or languid; the whole is airy, animated, and vigorous: what is little, is gay; what is great, is splendid. He may be thought to mention himself too frequently; but while he forces himself upon our esteem, we cannot refuse him to stand high in his own. Everything is excused by the play of images and the sprightliness of expression. Though all is easy, nothing is feeble; though all seems careless, there is nothing harsh; and though since his earlier works more than a century has passed, they have nothing yet uncouth or obsolete.

He who writes much will not easily escape a manner, such a recurrence of particular modes as may be easily noted. Dryden is always "another and the same"; he does not exhibit a second time the same elegances in the same form, nor appears to have any art other than that of expressing with clearness what he thinks with vigor. His style could not easily be imitated, either seriously or ludicrously; for, being always equable and always varied, it has no prominent or discriminative characters. The beauty who is totally free from disproportion of parts and features, cannot be ridiculed by an overcharged resemblance.

From his prose, however, Dryden derives only his accidental and secondary praise; the veneration with which his name is pronounced by every cultivator of English literature is paid to him as he refined the language, improved the sentiments, and tuned the numbers [25] of English Poetry.

After about half a century of forced thoughts and rugged meter, some advances towards nature and harmony had been already made by Waller and Denham; they had shown that long discourses in rime

[24] **didactic:** of an instructive nature
[25] **tuned the numbers:** refined the meter

grew more pleasing when they were broken into couplets, and that verse consisted not only in the number but the arrangement of syllables.

But though they did much, who can deny that they left much to do? Their works were not many, nor were their minds of very ample comprehension. More examples of more modes of composition were necessary for the establishment of regularity, and the introduction of propriety in word and thought.

Every language of a learned nation necessarily divides itself into diction scholastic and popular, grave and familiar, elegant and gross; and from a nice distinction of these different parts arises a great part of the beauty of style. But if we except a few minds, the favorites of nature, to whom their own original rectitude was in the place of rules, this delicacy of selection was little known to our authors. Our speech lay before them in a heap of confusion, and every man took for every purpose what chance might offer him.

There was therefore before the time of Dryden no poetical diction, no system of words at once refined from the grossness of domestic use, and free from the harshness of terms appropriated to particular arts. Words too familiar, or too remote, defeat the purpose of a poet. From those sounds which we hear on small or on coarse occasions, we do not easily receive strong impressions, or delightful images; and words to which we are nearly strangers, whenever they occur, draw that attention on themselves which they should transmit to things.

Those happy combinations of words which distinguish poetry from prose had been rarely attempted; we had few elegances or flowers of speech; the roses had not yet been plucked from the bramble, or different colors had not yet been joined to enliven one another.

It may be doubted whether Waller and Denham could have overborne the prejudices which had long prevailed, and which even then were sheltered by the protection of Cowley. The new versification, as it was called, may be considered as owing its establishment to Dryden; from whose time it is apparent that English poetry has had no tendency to relapse to its former savageness. . . . Perhaps no nation ever produced a writer that enriched his language with such variety of models. To him we owe the improvement, perhaps the completion of our meter, the refinement of our language, and much of the correctness of our sentiments. . . .

POPE

. . . [Pope] professed to have learned his poetry from Dryden, whom, whenever an opportunity was presented, he praised through his whole life with unvaried liberality; and perhaps his character may receive some illustration if he be compared with his master.

Integrity of understanding and nicety of discernment were not allotted in a less proportion to Dryden than to Pope. The rectitude of Dryden's mind was sufficiently shown by the dismission [1] of his poetical prejudices, and the rejection of unnatural thoughts and rugged numbers. But Dryden never desired to apply all the judgment that he had. He wrote, and professed to write, merely for the people; and when he pleased others, he contented himself. He spent no time in struggles to rouse latent powers; he never attempted to make that better which was already good, nor often to mend what he must have known to be faulty. He wrote, as he tells us, with very little consideration; when occasion or necessity called upon him, he poured out what the present moment happened to supply, and, when once it had passed the press, ejected it from his mind; for when he had no pecuniary interest, he had no further solicitude.

Pope was not content to satisfy; he desired to excel, and therefore always endeavored to do his best: he did not court the candor, but dared the judgment of his reader, and, expecting no indulgence from others, he showed none to himself. He examined lines and words with minute and punctilious observation, and retouched every part with indefatigable diligence, till he had left nothing to be forgiven.

For this reason he kept his pieces very long in his hands, while he considered and reconsidered them. The only poems which can be supposed to have been written with such regard to the times as might hasten their publication were the two satires of *Thirty-eight*,[2] of which Dodsley [3] told me that they were brought to him by the author, that they might be fairly copied. "Almost every line," he said, "was then written twice over; I gave him a clean transcript, which he sent some time afterwards to me for the press, with almost every line written twice over a second time."

His declaration that his care for his works ceased at their publication was not strictly true. His parental attention never abandoned

[1] dismission: putting aside
[2] satires of *Thirty-eight*: dialogues written in 1738
[3] Dodsley: poet and dramatist of the 18th century

them; what he found amiss in the first edition, he silently corrected in those that followed. He appears to have revised the *Iliad,* and freed it from some of its imperfections; and the *Essay on Criticism* received many improvements after its first appearance. It will seldom be found that he altered without adding clearness, elegance, or vigor. Pope had perhaps the judgment of Dryden; but Dryden certainly wanted the diligence of Pope.

In acquired knowledge, the superiority must be allowed to Dryden, whose education was more scholastic, and who before he became an author had been allowed more time for study, with better means of information. His mind has a larger range, and he collects his images and illustrations from a more extensive circumference of science. Dryden knew more of man in his general nature, and Pope in his local manners. The notions of Dryden were formed by comprehensive speculation, and those of Pope by minute attention. There is more dignity in the knowledge of Dryden, and more certainty in that of Pope.

Poetry was not the sole praise of either; for both excelled likewise in prose; but Pope did not borrow his prose from his predecessor. The style of Dryden is capricious and varied; that of Pope is cautious and uniform. Dryden obeys the motions of his own mind; Pope constrains his mind to his own rules of composition. Dryden is sometimes vehement and rapid; Pope is always smooth, uniform, and gentle. Dryden's page is a natural field, rising into inequalities, and diversified by the varied exuberance of abundant vegetation; Pope's is a velvet lawn, shaven by the scythe, and leveled by the roller.

Of genius, that power which constitutes a poet; that quality without which judgment is cold, and knowledge is inert; that energy which collects, combines, amplifies, and animates; the superiority must, with some hesitation, be allowed to Dryden. It is not to be inferred that of this poetical vigor Pope had only a little, because Dryden had more; for every other writer since Milton must give place to Pope; and even of Dryden it must be said, that, if he has brighter paragraphs, he has not better poems. Dryden's performances were always hasty, either excited by some external occasion, or extorted by domestic necessity; he composed without consideration, and published without correction. What his mind could supply at call, or gather in one excursion, was all that he sought, and all that he gave. The dilatory caution of Pope enabled him to condense his sentiments, to multiply his images, and to accumulate all that study might produce or chance might supply. If the flights of Dryden therefore are higher, Pope continues longer on the wing. If of Dryden's fire the blaze is brighter, of Pope's the heat is more regular and constant. Dryden often surpasses expectation, and Pope never falls below it. Dryden is read with frequent astonishment, and Pope with perpetual delight.

This parallel will, I hope, when it is well considered, be found just; and if the reader should suspect me, as I suspect myself, of some partial fondness for the memory of Dryden, let him not too hastily condemn me; for meditation and inquiry may, perhaps, show him the reasonableness of my determination. . . .

For Discussion

"The Dictionary"

Some of Johnson's definitions are humorous because they show his prejudices; others because they are ponderous and unclear. Select three examples of each type. Find the proper definitions for these words in a good modern dictionary and point out Johnson's "risible absurdities."

"Letter to Lord Chesterfield"

1. What is the spirit of Johnson's letter to Lord Chesterfield? What had hurt Johnson most?
2. Who was Lord Chesterfield and what was he famous for?

"Dryden"

1. What is Johnson's estimate of Dryden? What general critical principle does Johnson enunciate for judging writers of the past? According to Johnson, which of Dryden's essays is his best? What general faults does he find in Dryden's critical works?
2. What does Johnson think of Dryden's prose style? Reread Dryden's essay on Shakespeare (p. 194) and find examples of his refined style.

"Pope"

1. In what way did Pope differ from Dryden? In what particular fields did each excel? Which of the two authors does Johnson prefer? Why?
2. Johnson possessed many of the qualities which he admired in Dryden and Pope. Name three such qualities. What was Johnson's attitude toward the personalities of Dryden and Pope?
3. From what we know of Johnson through Boswell's *Life*, we see that he had definite preferences for styles of literature. Would he prefer Neo-Classical literature to Elizabethan literature? Why?

OLIVER GOLDSMITH

(1728–1774)

When Oliver Goldsmith died in his mid-forties, he had written an outstanding work in each of the major fields of literature: the novel, drama, and poetry. His early life, however, gave no hint of such achievements. Born in Ireland, he grew up in a family with little money. He tried to study law and medicine with little success, and for a time wandered penniless on the Continent. When he came to London, he worked as a druggist, proof-reader, author, quack doctor, and teacher. Although he was an extremely likable person, he was irresponsible with money and was constantly poor. In 1761 Samuel Johnson met him, and Goldsmith began his emergence into the literary world. He became a member of the Literary Club, thanks to Johnson, who saw his potential literary genius and helped him express himself in a clear and effective style.

In 1766, Goldsmith published *The Vicar of Wakefield*. After an initial indifferent reception, this novel was widely acclaimed. His next great work was *The Deserted Village* in which he expressed his great pain at being separated from his beloved countryside. The poem is somewhat autobiographical, recalling Goldsmith's early days in Ireland. But the real meaning of the poem concerns the contemporary social conditions in England, where the Enclosure Acts and the Industrial Revolution were destroying a way of life that had been in existence as long as England could remember. In his dedication to Sir Joshua Reynolds, the famous painter, Goldsmith says "in regretting the depopulation of the country, I inveigh against the increase of luxuries . . . and continue to think those luxuries prejudicial to states, by which so many vices are introduced, and so many kingdoms undone."

In 1772 he occupied his time trying "to do something to make people laugh." The result was his comedy *She Stoops to Conquer*. None of his major successes, however, earned him much money, and he had to write constantly to meet his many financial debts. After fifteen years, the strain left him exhausted and discouraged. Following a series of illnesses, he died quite suddenly. He was buried in Westminster Abbey in the Poets' Corner, and Johnson wrote a fine Latin epitaph for his tomb that was designed by Joshua Reynolds.

ELEGY ON THE DEATH OF A MAD DOG

Good people all, of every sort,
  Give ear unto my song;
And if you find it wondrous short,
  It cannot hold you long.

In Islington there was a man   5
  Of whom the world might say
That still a godly race he ran,
  Whene'er he went to pray.

A kind and gentle heart he had,
  To comfort friend and foes;   10
The naked every day he clad,
  When he put on his clothes.

And in that town a dog was found,
  As many dogs there be,
Both mongrel, puppy, whelp, and hound   15
  And cur of low degree.

This dog and man at first were friends;
  But when a pique ¹ began,
The dog to gain his private ends,
  Went mad and bit the man.   20

Around from all the neighboring streets
  The wondering people ran,
And swore the dog had lost his wits,
  To bite so good a man.

The wound it seemed both sore and sad   25
  To every Christian eye;
And while they swore the dog was mad,
  They swore the man would die.

pique: resentment, offense

But soon a wonder came to light,
    That showed the rogues they lied;   30
The man recovered of the bite;
    The dog it was that died.

THE DESERTED VILLAGE

Sweet Auburn! [1] loveliest village of the plain,
Where health and plenty cheered the laboring swain,[2]
Where smiling spring its earliest visit paid,
And parting summer's lingering blooms delayed:
Dear lovely bowers of innocence and ease,   5
Seats of my youth, when every sport could please:
How often have I loitered o'er thy green,
Where humble happiness endeared each scene!
How often have I paused on every charm,
The sheltered cot,[3] the cultivated farm,   10
The never failing brook, the busy mill,
The decent church that topt the neighboring hill,
The hawthorn bush, with seats beneath the shade,
For talking age and whispering lovers made!
How often have I blest the coming day,   15
When toil remitting lent its turn to play,
And all the village train, from labor free,
Led up their sports beneath the spreading tree;
While many a pastime circled in the shade,
The young contending as the old surveyed;   20
And many a gambol frolicked o'er the ground,
And sleights of art and feats of strength went round.
And still, as each repeated pleasure tired,
Succeeding sports the mirthful band inspired;
The dancing pair that simply sought renown,   25
By holding out to tire each other down;
The swain, mistrustless of his smutted face,
While secret laughter tittered round the place;

[1] Auburn: a poetical name which suggests Goldsmith's childhood home of Lissoy, Ireland
[2] swain: young farmer, a rustic
[3] cot: cottage

The bashful virgin's sidelong looks of love,
The matron's glance that would those looks reprove.   30
These were thy charms, sweet village! sports like these,
With sweet succession taught even toil to please;
These round thy bowers their cheerful influence shed,
These were thy charms—but all these charms are fled.
    Sweet smiling village, loveliest of the lawn,[4]   35
Thy sports are fled, and all thy charms withdrawn;
Amidst thy bowers the tyrant's hand is seen,
And desolation saddens all thy green:
One only master grasps the whole domain,
And half a tillage stints thy smiling plain;   40
No more thy glassy brook reflects the day,
But choked with sedges works its weedy way;
Along thy glades, a solitary guest,
The hollow-sounding bittern [5] guards its nest;
Amidst thy desert walks the lapwing flies,   45
And tires their echoes with unvaried cries.
Sunk are thy bowers in shapeless ruin all,
And the long grass o'ertops the mouldering wall;
And, trembling, shrinking from the spoiler's hand,
Far, far away thy children leave the land.   50
    Ill fares the land, to hastening ills a prey,
Where wealth accumulates, and men decay;
Princes and lords may flourish, or may fade;
A breath can make them, as a breath has made:
But a bold peasantry, their country's pride,   55
When once destroyed, can never be supplied.
    A time there was, ere England's griefs began,
When every rood of ground maintained its man;
For him light labor spread her wholesome store,
Just gave what life required, but gave no more: 60
His best companions, innocence and health,
And his best riches, ignorance of wealth.
    But times are altered; trade's unfeeling train
Usurp the land, and dispossess the swain;
Along the lawn, where scattered hamlets rose,   65

[4] lawn: countryside
[5] bittern: small heron

Unwieldy wealth, and cumbrous pomp repose;
And every want to opulence allied,
And every pang that folly pays to pride.
Those gentle hours that plenty bade to bloom,
Those calm desires that asked but little room,   70
Those healthful sports that graced the peaceful scene,
Lived in each look, and brightened all the green;
These, far departing, seek a kinder shore,
And rural mirth and manners are no more.

Sweet AUBURN! parent of the blissful hour,   75
Thy glades forlorn confess the tyrant's power.
Here, as I take my solitary rounds,
Amidst thy tangling walks and ruined grounds,
And, many a year elapsed, return to view
Where once the cottage stood, the hawthorn grew,   80
Remembrance wakes with all her busy train,
Swells at my breast, and turns the past to pain.

. . . . .

Beside yon straggling fence that skirts the way
With blossomed furze,[6] unprofitably gay,
There, in his noisy mansion, skilled to rule,   85
The village master taught his little school:
A man severe he was, and stern to view,
I knew him well, and every truant knew;
Well had the boding tremblers learned to trace
The day's disasters in his morning face;   90
Full well they laughed with counterfeited glee
At all his jokes, for many a joke had he;
Full well the busy whisper, circling round,
Conveyed the dismal tidings when he frowned;
Yet he was kind, or if severe in aught,   95
The love he bore to learning was in fault;
The village all declared how much he knew,
'Twas certain he could write, and cipher too;
Lands he could measure, terms and tides presage,[7]
And even the story ran that he could gauge.[8]   100

[6] furze: sharp-pointed evergreen shrub
[7] presage: foretell
[8] gauge: judge

In arguing too, the parson owned his skill,
For even though vanquished, he could argue still;
While words of learned length and thundering sound
Amazed the gazing rustics ranged around;
And still they gazed, and still the wonder grew   105
That one small head could carry all he knew.
    But past is all his fame. The very spot,
Where many a time he triumphed, is forgot.
Near yonder thorn, that lifts its head on high,
Where once the sign-post caught the passing eye,   110
Low lies that house where nut-brown draughts inspired,
Where gray-beard mirth and smiling toil retired,
Where village statesmen talked with looks profound,
And news much older than their ale went round.
Imagination fondly stoops to trace   115
The parlor splendors of that festive place;
The whitewashed wall, the nicely sanded floor,
The varnished clock that clicked behind the door:
The chest contrived a double debt to pay,
A bed by night, a chest of drawers by day;   120
The pictures placed for ornament and use,
The twelve good rules,[9] the royal game of goose;[10]
The hearth, except when winter chilled the day,
With aspen boughs, and flowers, and fennel gay;
While broken teacups, wisely kept for show,   125
Ranged o'er the chimney, glistened in a row.
    Vain transitory splendors! could not all
Reprieve the tottering mansion from its fall?
Obscure it sinks, nor shall it more impart
An hour's importance to the poor man's heart;   130
Thither no more the peasant shall repair
To sweet oblivion of his daily care;
No more the farmer's news, the barber's tale,
No more the woodman's ballad shall prevail;
No more the smith his dusky brow shall clear,   135
Relax his ponderous strength, and lean to hear;
The host himself no longer shall be found

[9] twelve good rules: Charles I supposedly drew up twelve rules of conduct.
[10] royal . . . goose: game resembling parchesi

Careful to see the mantling bliss go round;
Nor the coy maid, half willing to be prest,
Shall kiss the cup to pass it to the rest.   140
    Yes! let the rich deride, the proud disdain,
These simple blessings of the lowly train;
To me more dear, congenial to my heart,
One native charm, than all the gloss of art;
Spontaneous joys, where Nature has its play,   145
The soul adopts, and owns their first-born sway;
Lightly they frolic o'er the vacant mind,
Unenvied, unmolested, unconfined.
But the long pomp, the midnight masquerade,
With all the freaks of wanton wealth arrayed,   150
In these, ere triflers half their wish obtain,
The toiling pleasure sickens into pain;
And, even while fashion's brightest arts decoy,
The heart distrusting asks, if this be joy?
    Ye friends to truth, ye statesmen, who survey   155
The rich man's joys increase, the poor's decay,
'Tis yours to judge how wide the limits stand
Between a splendid and a happy land.
Proud swells the tide with loads of freighted ore,
And shouting Folly hails them from her shore;   160
Hoards e'en beyond the miser's wish abound,
And rich men flock from all the world around.
Yet count our gains. This wealth is but a name,
That leaves our useful products still the same.
Not so the loss. The man of wealth and pride   165
Takes up a space that many poor supplied;
Space for his lake, his park's extended bounds,
Space for his horses, equipage,[11] and hounds;
The robe that wraps his limbs in silken sloth
Has robbed the neighboring fields of half their growth;   170
His seat, where solitary sports are seen,
Indignant spurns [12] the cottage from the green;
Around the world each needful product flies,
For all the luxuries the world supplies;

[11] equipage: carriage
[12] spurns: pushes aside

While thus the land, adorned for pleasure all,   175
In barren splendor feebly waits the fall,
  As some fair female, unadorned and plain,
Secure to please while youth confirms her reign,
Slights every borrowed charm that dress supplies,
Nor shares with art the triumph of her eyes;   180
But when those charms are past, for charms are frail,
When time advances, and when lovers fail,
She then shines forth, solicitous to bless,
In all the glaring impotence of dress:
Thus fares the land, by luxury betrayed,   185
In nature's simplest charms at first arrayed:
But verging to decline, its splendors rise,
Its vistas strike, its palaces surprise;
While, scourged by famine, from the smiling land,
The mournful peasant leads his humble band;   190
And while he sinks, without one arm to save,
The country blooms—a garden and a grave
  Where then, ah! where shall poverty reside,
To 'scape the pressure of contiguous pride?
If to some common's [13] fenceless limits strayed,   195
He drives his flock to pick the scanty blade,
Those fenceless fields the sons of wealth divide,
And even the bare-worn common is denied.
  If to the city sped—What waits him there?
To see profusion that he must not share;   200
To see ten thousand baneful arts combined
To pamper luxury, and thin mankind:
To see those joys the sons of pleasure know,
Extorted from his fellow-creatures' woe.
Here, while the courtier glitters in brocade,   205
There the pale artist [14] plies the sickly trade;
Here, while the proud their long-drawn pomp display,
There the black gibbet [15] glooms beside the way;
The dome where Pleasure holds her midnight reign,
Here, richly decked, admits the gorgeous train;   210

[13] common's: tract of public land used freely by all the inhabitants of a place
[14] artist: artisan, workman
[15] gibbet: gallows

Tumultuous grandeur crowds the blazing square,
The rattling chariots clash, the torches glare.
Sure scenes like these no troubles e'er annoy!
Sure these denote one universal joy!
Are these thy serious thoughts?—Ah, turn thine eyes   215
Where the poor houseless shivering female lies:
She once, perhaps, in village plenty blest,
Has wept at tales of innocence distrest;
Her modest looks the cottage might adorn,
Sweet as the primrose peeps beneath the thorn;   220
Now lost to all; her friends, her virtue fled,
Near her betrayer's door she lays her head,
And, pinched with cold, and shrinking from the shower,
With heavy heart, deplores that luckless hour,
When idly first, ambitious of the town,   225
She left her wheel and robes of country brown.
      Do thine, sweet AUBURN, thine, the loveliest train,
Do thy fair tribes participate her pain?
Even now, perhaps, by cold and hunger led,
At proud men's doors they ask a little bread!   230
      Ah, no. To distant climes, a dreary scene,
Where half the convex world intrudes between,
Through torrid tracts with fainting steps they go,
Where wild Altama [16] murmurs to their woe.
Far different there from all that charmed before,   235
The various terrors of that horrid shore;
Those blazing suns that dart a downward ray,
And fiercely shed intolerable day;
Those matted woods where birds forget to sing,
But silent bats in drowsy clusters cling;   240
Those poisonous fields with rank luxuriance crowned,
Where the dark scorpion gathers death around:
Where at each step the stranger fears to wake
The rattling terrors of the vengeful snake;
Where crouching tigers wait their hapless prey,   245
And savage men more murderous still than they:
While oft in whirls the mad tornado flies,
Mingling the ravaged landscape with the skies.
Far different these from every former scene,

[16] **Altama:** river in Georgia

The cooling brook, the grassy vested green,   250
The breezy covert of the warbling grove,
That only sheltered thefts of harmless love.
   Good Heaven! what sorrows gloomed that parting day,
That called them from their native walks away;
When the poor exiles, every pleasure past,   255
Hung round the bowers, and fondly looked their last,
And took a long farewell, and wished in vain
For seats like these beyond the western main;
And, shuddering still to face the distant deep,
Returned and wept, and still returned to weep.   260
The good old sire the first prepared to go,
To new-found worlds, and wept for others' woe;
But for himself, in conscious virtue brave,
He only wished for worlds beyond the grave.
His lovely daughter, lovelier in her tears,   265
The fond companion of his helpless years,
Silent went next, neglectful of her charms,
And left a lover's for a father's arms.
With louder plaints the mother spoke her woes,
And blest the cot where every pleasure rose: 270
And kissed her thoughtless babes with many a tear,
And clasped them close, in sorrow doubly dear;
Whilst her fond husband strove to lend relief
In all the silent manliness of grief.
   O Luxury! thou curst by Heaven's decree,   275
How ill exchanged are things like these for thee!
How do thy potions, with insidious joy,
Diffuse their pleasures only to destroy!
Kingdoms by thee, to sickly greatness grown,
Boast of a florid vigor not their own: 280
At every draught more large and large they grow,
A bloated mass of rank unwieldy woe;
Till sapped their strength, and every part unsound,
Down, down they sink, and spread a ruin round.
   Even now the devastation is begun,   285
And half the business of destruction done;
Even now, methinks, as pondering here I stand,
I see the rural Virtues leave the land.
Down where yon anchoring vessel spreads the sail,

That idly waiting flaps with every gale,   290
Downward they move, a melancholy band,
Pass from the shore, and darken all the strand.
Contented toil, and hospitable care,
And kind connubial tenderness are there;
And piety with wishes placed above,   295
And steady loyalty, and faithful love.
And thou, sweet Poetry, thou loveliest maid,
Still first to fly where sensual joys invade;
Unfit in these degenerate times of shame,
To catch the heart, or strike for honest fame;   300
Dear charming nymph, neglected and decried,
My shame in crowds, my solitary pride;
Thou source of all my bliss, and all my woe,
That found'st me poor at first, and keep'st me so;
Thou guide, by which the nobler arts excell,   305
Thou nurse of every virtue, fare thee well;
Farewell! and O! where'er thy voice be tried,
On Torno's [17] cliffs, or Pambamarca's [18] side,
Whether where equinoctial fervors glow,
Or winter wraps the polar world in snow,   310
Still let thy voice, prevailing over time,
Redress the rigors of the inclement clime;
Aid slighted truth with thy persuasive strain;
Teach erring man to spurn the rage of gain;
Teach him, that states of native strength possest,   315
Though very poor, may still be very blest;
That trade's proud empire hastes to swift decay,
As ocean sweeps the labored mole away;
While self-dependent power can time defy,
As rocks resist the billows and the sky.   320

[17] Torno's: Torno, river in Sweden
[18] Pambamarca: mountain in Ecuador

For Discussion

"Elegy on the Death of a Mad Dog"

1. What is the tone of this poem? Does the title give a hint of the tone?
2. Does the meter and rhythm give an indication of the poet's attitude? Explain your answer.

"The Deserted Village"

1. What is Goldsmith's attitude toward the country and its people? Is his portrayal idealistic or realistic? Explain. What is the change in emotion beginning with line 34? What is the poet referring to in lines 35–56?
2. What was old England like before the social changes detailed in the poem? Luxury has brought about a terrible change. What does the author mean by "luxury"?
3. What is the emotion in the poem? Does this indicate that the poem different from the typical Neo-Classical poetry of the age? Explain. Is this poem "sentimental"? Discuss.
4. Did Goldsmith intend his remarks only for England? Explain.
5. Compare this poem with Thomas Gray's "Elegy Written in a Country Churchyard." What features in both poems are similar? What features are different? Discuss.
6. Show how literature of this kind can have a more lasting effect than many speeches and tracts written on the reformation of social conditions. What other literature criticized the same conditions?